THE
NEWSPAPER
DESIGNER'S
HANDBOOK

THE
NEWSPAPER
DESIGNER'S
HANDBOOK

SECOND EDITION

Written & designed
by
TIM HARROWER

 Wm. C. Brown Publishers

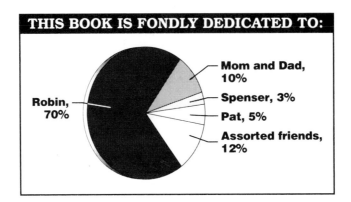

THIS BOOK IS FONDLY DEDICATED TO:

- Mom and Dad, 10%
- Spenser, 3%
- Pat, 5%
- Assorted friends, 12%
- Robin, 70%

Cover illustration by Fred Ingram

Copyright © 1989 by Oregonian Publishing Company

Copyright © 1991, 1992 by Wm. C. Brown Publishers. All rights reserved

Library of Congress Catalog Card Number: 91–71788

ISBN 0–697–13382–6

Printed in the United States of America by Wm. C. Brown Publishers, 2460 Kerper Boulevard, Dubuque, IA 52001

10   9   8   7   6   5   4

CONTENTS

INTRODUCTION

2 Foreword
4 Some quick history
6 Current trends

FUNDAMENTALS

10 What it's called
12 Tools of the trade
13 The four basic elements
14 Headlines
18 Text
20 Photos
22 Cutlines
24 A sample dummy
25 The dummy

STORY DESIGN

30 Stories without art
32 Mug shots
35 Text shapes
36 One horizontal photo
39 One vertical photo
42 The dominant photo
44 Big vertical, small horizontal
46 Big horizontal, small vertical
48 Two verticals
50 Two horizontals
52 Adding mug shots
53 Exercises

PAGE DESIGN

56 Broadsheet formats
57 Tabloid formats
58 Pages without art
64 Pages with art
66 Modules and modular design
68 Page One design
69 Flow chart: Page One design

70 Making stories fit
72 Inside pages
74 Double trucks
76 Bad juxtapositions
77 Rules of thumb
78 Exercises

PHOTOS & ART

82 General guidelines
83 Good photos
88 Bad photos
90 Cropping photos
92 The proportion wheel
93 Halftones & line shots
94 Stand-alone photos
95 Photo spreads
98 Photo spread guidelines
100 Studio shots
101 Photo illustrations
102 Illustrations
104 A feature art checklist
106 Risky business
107 Exercises

PACKAGING

110 Flags
111 Standing heads
112 Logos & sigs
114 Liftout quotes
116 Decks
117 Breaking up text
118 Bylines
119 Credit lines
120 Spacing
121 Rules & boxes
122 Refers & teasers
123 Jumps

SPECIAL EFFECTS

126 Stretching the limits
127 The Cosby variations
132 Wraparounds & skews
134 Photo cutouts
135 Mortises & insets
136 Screens & reverses
138 Display headlines
140 How to build a mechanical
141 Color
148 Risky business

INFOGRAPHICS

150 Current trends
151 Computers & graphics
152 General guidelines
153 Sidebars
154 Fact boxes
155 Tables
156 Charts & graphs
158 Maps
160 Diagrams
162 Graphics packages

APPENDIX

164 Exercise answers: story design
167 Exercise answers: page design
169 Exercise answers: photos & art
173 Glossary
178 Index
180 Acknowledgments

For a more detailed breakdown of chapter contents, consult the pages that begin each chapter.

New York American

BUSINESS PROPERTY

J. J. ASTOR LOST ON TITANIC
1,500 TO 1,800 DEAD

John Jacob Astor was among the passengers who went down with the ship, according to a wireless dispatch received by Bradstreets last night from the liner Olympic. Mrs. Astor was saved and is being brought to shore by the Carpathia.

The Wireless Operator at Cape Race, Newfoundland, Flashes: "Eighteen Hundred Lives Have Been Lost in the Wreck of the Titanic."

JFK ASSASSINATED

The Oregonian

Death Comes Within Hour After Attack

Death Shocks Nation

U.S. Numb As Reports Affirmed

LYNDON B. JOHNSON — Death of President Kennedy puts Johnson in office. — JOHN F. KENNEDY

Aide Denies LBJ 'Attack'

Beginning Of Fateful Ride

Firemen Probe Blast, Blaze

Mayor Feels Deep Shock

Salary Donated To Charities

The Weather

THE HOUSTON POST
MOON SPECIAL

NEIL WALKS THE MOON!

'A Great Moment of Our Time'

U.S. Flag Is Planted Near Ship

TELECAST FROM SPACECRAFT EAGLE, TRANQUILITY BASE, THE MOON
Apollo 11 Commander Neil Armstrong, Left, and Lunar Module Pilot Edwin Aldrin, on Lunar Surface

Nixon Counts Seconds on TV

Eagle Crew All Calm as History Made

Old Man Moon Not The Same

Best Words Of Descent: Eagle Lands

INTRODUCTION

FOREWORD

A long, long time ago, people actually *enjoyed* reading newspapers. Imagine.

They'd flip a nickel to the newsboy, grab a paper from the stack, slap it open and gawk at headlines shouting things like:

SOLONS MULL LEVY HIKE BID

Then they'd gaze down those long, gray columns of type that looked like this —

— and they'd say: *"Wow!* What a lot of news!"

Today, people have changed. They've got color TVs. Home computers. Portable stereos. Glitzy magazines. They collect data in a dizzying array of ways. They don't need long, gray columns of type anymore. They won't *read* long, gray columns of type anymore.

In fact, when they look at newspapers and see those long, gray columns of type, they say: *"Yuck!* What a waste of time!"

Today's readers want something different. Something snappy. Something easy to grasp, instantly inviting, instantly informative.

And that's where you come in.

If you can design a newspaper that's inviting, informative and easy to read, you can — for a few minutes each day — successfully compete with all those TVs, radios, computers and magazines. You can keep a noble old American institution — the newspaper — alive for another day.

Because let's face it: To many people, newspapers are dinosaurs. They're big, clumsy and slow. And though they've endured for eons, it may be only a matter of time before newspapers either:

■ become extinct (this has already happened to other famous forms of communication — remember smoke signals? The telegraph?). Or else they'll:

■ evolve into a new, different species (imagine a combination video newspaper/TV shopping catalog that lets you tune into sports highlights, scan some comics, then view the hottest fashions on sale at your local TechnoMall).

FOREWORD

Those days are still a ways off. For now, we need to do our best with what we have: Black ink. White paper. Lots of lines, dots, letters and numbers. A good designer can put all those things together quickly and smoothly, so that today's news feels both familiar and . . . *new.*

But where do newspaper designers come from, anyway? Face it: You never hear children saying, "When I grow up, I'm gonna *lay out the business section.*" You never hear college students saying, "I've got a major in English Lit and a minor in *sports infographics.*"

No, most journalists stumble into newspaper design. Usually it's by accident. Without warning.

Maybe you're a reporter on a small weekly, and one day your editor says, "Congratulations! I'm promoting you to assistant editor. You'll start Monday. Oh, and . . . you know how to lay out pages, don't you?"

Or maybe you're just starting out at a student newspaper. You want to be a reporter, a movie critic, a sports columnist. So you write your first story. When you turn it in, the adviser says to you, "Uh, we're a little short-handed in production right now. You could really help us out if you'd lay out that page your story's on. OK?"

Now, journalism textbooks usually discuss design in the broadest of terms. They ponder vague concepts like *balance* and *harmony* and *rhythm.* They show award-winning pages from The New York Times or USA Today.

"Interesting pages," you think. But meanwhile, you're in a hurry. And you're still confused: "How do I connect *this picture* to *this headline?*"

That's where this book comes in.

This book assumes you need to learn the rules of good page design as quickly as you can. It assumes you've been reading a newspaper for a while, but you've never really paid attention to things like headline sizes. Or liftout quotes, like the one above. Or whether pages use five columns of text instead of six.

> **"*I* am not the editor of a newspaper and shall always try to do right and be good, so that God will not make me one."**
>
> **— MARK TWAIN**

This book will guide you through the fundamental building blocks of newspaper design: headlines, text, photos, cutlines. We'll show you how to shape them into a story. Then we'll show you how to shape stories into pages.

After that, we'll look at the small stuff — logos, teasers, charts and graphs, type trickery — that makes more complicated pages work. We'll even show you a few reader-grabbing gimmicks, like subheads, to break up gray columns of type:

HEY! CHECK OUT THIS ATTENTION-GRABBING SUBHEAD

And bullets, to make short lists "pop" off the page:
- This is a bullet item.
- And so is this.
- Ditto here.

And, of course, there are liftout quotes, which let you lift a quote from some famous person — say, Mark Twain — then play it up big to catch your reader's eye.

Yes, some designers will do *anything* to get you to read their forewords.

SOME QUICK HISTORY

THE SIMPLE BEGINNINGS

America's first newspaper, Publick Occurrences, made its debut 300 years ago. But like most colonial newspapers, it looked more like a pamphlet or newsletter, and was printed on paper smaller than the pages in this book.

Most colonial weeklies ran their news items one after another in deep, wide columns of text. There were no headlines and very little art (though it was young Ben Franklin who printed America's first newspaper cartoon in 1754).

After the Revolutionary War, dailies first appeared and began looking more like *real* newspapers: thinner columns, primitive headlines (one-line labels like PROCLAMATION) and — this will come as no surprise — a growing number of ads.

Colonial printing presses couldn't handle large sheets of paper, so when Publick Occurrences appeared in Boston on Sept. 25, 1690, it was only 7 inches wide, with two 17-pica columns of text. The 4-page paper had 3 pages of news (the last page was blank), including mention of a "newly appointed" day of Thanksgiving in Plimouth. (*Plimouth? Publick?* Where were all the copy editors in those days?)

THE 19TH CENTURY

Throughout the 19th century, all newspapers looked pretty much the same. Text was hung like wallpaper, in long, thin rows, with vertical rules separating each column. Maps or engravings were occasionally used as art.

During the Civil War, papers began devoting more space to headline display. They began piling headlines in layers (called *deckers* or decks), using a dizzying variety of typefaces. For instance, The Chicago Tribune used 15 different decks to trumpet its report on the great fire of 1871.

The first newspaper photograph was printed in 1880, but news photos didn't become common until the early 1900s.

This 1865 edition of The Philadelphia Inquirer announces the assassination of President Lincoln with 15 headline decks. Like most newspapers of its era, it uses a very vertical text format: When a story hits the bottom of one column, it leaps to the top of the next column to continue.

MORE QUICK HISTORY

THE EARLY 20TH CENTURY

By about 1900, newspapers began looking more modern. Headlines became bigger, bolder and wider. Those deeply stacked decks were eventually dropped to save space. Page designs grew more flexible. News was departmentalized ("Crime," "Sports," "Foreign," etc.).

The '20s saw the rise of tabloids — those small, half-sheet papers packed with photos and sensational sledgehammer headlines.

As the years went by, papers kept increasing the traffic on each page, using ever more photos, stories and ads.

This 1898 edition of the New York Journal tries its best to stir up readers with sensational allegations about the destruction of the battleship Maine. Notice how loud the type is and how horizontal the page's design elements are: The headline, the illustration and even the text run the full width of the page in a very symmetrical layout.

THE NOT-TOO DISTANT PAST

By today's standards, even the handsomest papers from 20 years ago look clumsy and old-fashioned. Others, like the page at right, look downright *ugly*.

Still, most of the current trends in page design were in place by the late '60s:

■ more and bigger photos;

■ quieter, more refined headline type (except for special feature stories and front-page banners);

■ a move from 8- and 9-column pages to a standardized 6-column page;

■ white gutters between columns instead of rules.

As printing technology advanced, presses continued to improve, allowing full-color photos to become common in the early '80s — thus ushering in a new era of newspaper design.

This 1966 Sports page from The Oregon Journal is astoundingly bad — but to be fair, it's a typical example of mid-'60s design. The bizarre shapes of its photos and stories collide in a disorganized jumble. After printing pages like these for years, editors finally realized that taking page design seriously might not be such a bad idea.

CURRENT TRENDS

Compared to the newspapers of yesteryear, today's news pages look clean, sharp and sophisticated. That's partly due to technological advances. But today's editors also realize that readers are inundated by slickly designed media, from movies to billboards to TV commercials. Sad to say, most modern consumers judge a product by the package it comes in. And they simply won't respect a product — or a newspaper — that looks amateurish.

To look modern, newspapers now use:

■ **Color,** which can be applied both decoratively (in ads and illustrations) and functionally (in charts and graphs, and in headers that organize pages and guide readers).

■ **Digests and briefs**, which round up related stories and boil them down so they're easy to find and quick to read.

■ **Graphic devices** — charts, maps, liftout quotes, quick-read sidebars — which catch the reader's eye and make information easier to grasp.

■ **Modular layout.** We'll explore this later. In a nutshell, it simply means all stories are neatly stacked in rectangular shapes.

Virtually all modern newspapers come in one of two sizes: *broadsheet* (large, full-sized papers like USA Today) or *tabloid* (half-sized papers like The National Enquirer — OK, maybe that's a bad example — or, say, The Christian Science Monitor).

Below, we'll show you some examples of modern American newspaper design. Like most examples in this book, these are broadsheet pages. But whatever your paper's format, the same basic design principles apply .

PAGE ONE

At many papers, Page One is a curious mix of traditional reporting and modern marketing that tries to answer the question: *What sells?*

Do readers want splashy colors? Loud headlines? Large photos? News briefs and summaries? Promotional gimmicks? Juicy stories?

Since it's hard to pinpoint precisely what readers want, most papers include some or all of these elements on Page One. Many papers now use the front page as a menu — one that serves up lots of short, appetizing images to guide readers through the best of the day's entrees.

And since more and more readers have less and less time to spend with their newspapers, shrewd editors are finding ways to increase both the *volume* and *variety* on Page One.

In 1990, The News (in Boca Raton, Florida) made a splash with this trendy new design. The front page combines briefs, a short opinion column, several news stories (which aren't allowed to jump to other pages) — and a bold pink box promoting news and features inside. It's a busy mix with a modern look.

CURRENT TRENDS

SPORTS SECTIONS

Television seems to be the perfect medium for covering sports. It's immediate. Visual. Colorful. Yet in many cities, more readers buy newspapers for sporting news than for any other single reason. Why?

A good sports section combines strong photos, lively writing, snappy headlines and shrewd analysis into a package with a personality all its own. And sports pages often include features you won't find on TV:

■ **Statistics:** team standings, players' records, schedules, etc. These are often packaged on one special page.

■ **Columnists:** opinionated writers whom sports fans can relate to — or hate.

■ **Local news:** scores, stories and profiles that simply aren't available anywhere else.

■ **News briefs and gossip.**

USA Today has capitalized on America's love of sports with an enormously popular sports section. It caters to hardcore fans by packing each page with roundups, stats, trivia and post-game analyses, all packaged with reader-friendly graphics.

FEATURE PAGES

As time goes by, the feature section of the newspaper gets more and more popular — and its range gets broader and broader. Most modern feature sections offer a mix of:

■ **Lifestyle stories:** trend stories, how-to's, coverage of personalities and social issues.

■ **Entertainment:** music, movies, books, art, TV listings.

■ **Food:** recipes, nutrition advice, new kitchen products.

■ **Fashion, health, travel,** and so on — along with columnists, comics, crossword puzzles and horoscopes.

Feature sections usually produce the most lively, ambitious page designs in the paper. Though many feature sections load up their front pages with a wide array of stories, most use a "poster page" display to dress up one prominent feature.

Good feature designs find ways to stretch the rules. This color page from The Washington Times combines photo cutouts, text wraparounds and special headline treatments to lure readers into three celebrity-oriented features. Most daily feature sections give one story big play like this; others use an approach like USA Today (above), emphasizing volume and variety.

CURRENT TRENDS

EDITORIAL & OPINION PAGES

One of longest-standing traditions in American newspapers is the editorial page. And the format for most editorial pages is nearly universal, consisting of:

■ **Editorial cartoons**;

■ **Opinion columns** by the paper's editors, local writers or syndicated columnists;

■ **Letters from readers**; and

■ **The masthead**, which lists the paper's top brass (editors, publishers, etc.).

In addition — because editorial pages are often so rigidly formatted — many papers run a separate opinion page, like the one at right. These pages explore current issues in depth. And more importantly, they set themselves apart from ordinary news pages by incorporating more aggressive, feature-style design techniques.

Opinion pages often run provocative cartoons to satirize public issues. On this Commentary page from The Washington Times, the lead story focuses on efforts to "carve up" then-House Speaker Jim Wright of Texas; the huge caricature shows Wright being roasted on a barbecue grill. The smaller stories on this page use more straightforward art.

SPECIAL SECTIONS

Most newspapers repeat the same standard formats every day. But opportunities often arise for designing special pages or sections with formats all their own. These include:

■ **Special enterprise packages** on a hot current topic or trend (AIDS, The Homeless).

■ **Special reports** on news events, either printed in advance (Summer Olympics Preview, Baseball '91) or as a wrap-up (The Crash of Flight 116, The Pope's Visit).

■ **Special-interest packages** — often printed regularly — that focus on a single theme (a kids' page, a restaurant guide, a monthly section for senior citizens). In the future, newspapers will focus upon an increasingly wide range of topics to appeal to their readers' specialized interests.

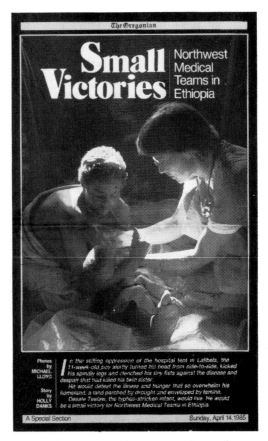

Most newspapers try, at least several times a year, to give their readers special reports on topical issues. These reports are printed either as a daily series or as a special section — such as the one shown here. This 12-page package that ran in The Oregonian documented the efforts of a local medical team treating famine victims in Ethiopia.

A s we said in the Foreword (you *did* read the Foreword, didn't you? It's not nearly as dull as it looks), you're probably in a hurry to start learning the Mysteries of Page Design. But before you begin banging out prize-winning pages, there are a few fundamentals you'll need to know.

You'll need to know some vocabulary. You'll need to know the tools of the trade. But most importantly, you'll need to know the basic components of page design: headlines, text, photos and cutlines.

This book is designed so you can skip this chapter if you're in a hurry. Or you can just skim through it and catch the highlights. So don't feel as if you need to learn everything immediately. But the better you understand these basics now, the easier you'll be able to manipulate them later on.

To make this book as handy as possible, we've repeated the chapter contents in detail at the bottom of each chapter's introductory page.

And each section *within* this book is cross-referenced, too, with those small "MORE ON" boxes in the upper-right corner of the page. As you study each topic, feel free to bounce back and forth throughout the book to expand upon what you're learning.

CHAPTER CONTENTS

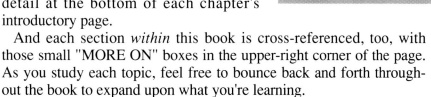

■ **What it's called:** A look at design components on two typical pages.................................. **10-11**

■ **Tools of the trade:** An introduction to basic design aids (pica poles, pencils, knives, the proportion wheel)................................. **12**

■ **The basic elements:** The four components (headlines, text, photos, cutlines) used to build most pages...................................... **13**

■ **Headlines:** Tips for writing good headlines; types of headlines; guides for sizing and measuring; weights and fonts; determining number of lines........ **14-17**

■ **Text:** An overview of different types of type (roman, italic, boldface), and how it can be shaped into legs of text.................... **18-19**

■ **Photos:** The three shapes of newspaper photographs (vertical, horizontal and square).........**20-21**

■ **Cutlines:** Common typographic treatments, and options for placing them on the page (below, beside or between photos... **22-23**

■ **Sample dummy:** A page dummy to use with this book's design exercises....................... **24**

■ **The dummy:** How it works and why it's important; how to draw a dummy; elements you must include to make dummies effective **25-28**

WHAT IT'S CALLED

To survive in the design world, you need to know the jargon. In a typical newsroom, for instance, you'll find *slugs, bugs, bastards, dummies,* maybe even a *widow* in the *gutter* (and if our mothers knew we talked like this, they'd never let us become journalists).

Not all newspapers use the same jargon, but there's plenty of agreement on most terms. Here's a look at some common elements found on Page One:

TEASERS
These promote other stories inside the paper (also called *promos* or *skyboxes*)

HEADLINE
The story's title or summary, in large type above or beside the text

BYLINE
The writer's name, often followed by some credentials

DISPLAY HEAD
A jazzed-up headline adding graphic emphasis to special stories

INITIAL CAP
A big capital letter set into the opening paragraph of a special feature (also called a *drop cap*)

HEADER
A label used for packaging special items (graphics, teasers, briefs, columns, etc.)

INDEX
A guide to contents

LOGO
A small, boxed title (with art) used for labeling a special story or series

FLAG
The newspaper's name (also called the *nameplate*)

REVERSE HEAD
A white headline set against a dark background

INFOGRAPHIC
A diagram, chart or map conveying information pictorially

DECK
A smaller headline added below the main headline (shown here is a *summary deck,* which summarizes news stories)

MUG SHOT
A small photograph (usually just the face) of someone in the story

REFER
A brief reference to a related story elsewhere in the paper

CUTLINE
Information about a photo or piece of art (also called a *caption*)

JUMP LINE
A line telling the reader what page this story continues on

TRAVEL
Just Maui-ed
Romantic sunsets draw newlyweds to Hawaii/ **Page T1**

LIVELY ARTS
Tan lines
A beach-blanket list of summertime reading/ **Page B2**

SPORTS
One 'O' will go
Battle of the unbeatens pits Tyson, Spinks for title/ **Page F1**

The Sunday Oregonian

NORTHWEST EDITION · PORTLAND, OREGON, JUNE 26, 1988 · 262 PAGES · $1.00

Linking drugs to crime

By KATHIE DURBIN
of The Oregonian staff

☐ A sampling of men and women arrested in Portland showed one of the nation's highest rates of narcotics use, according to a study

A national study of illegal drug use among criminal suspects confirms strong links between narcotics and crime and pinpoints a particularly high rate of drug use among suspects in Portland.

The results are part of a two-year study, called Drug Use Forecasting, begun in June 1987, by the National Institute of Justice. Twelve cities, including Portland, have participated in the study, and 13 additional cities are expected to be added during the next year.

Test samples, involving men and women arrested for a variety of crimes, have been taken quarterly since the study began. Detailed analysis from the most recent sampling in April are not available. Results, however, from the second round of tests conducted this winter show:

● Portland tied for third place with Chicago among 10 cities, behind only New York and San Diego, for the highest rate of drug use among men arrested.

● When marijuana was excluded from the results, Portland's ranking among the test cities dropped to seventh.

● Portland was second highest for use of marijuana and amphetamines among men.

● Portland was one of seven cities in which the rate of heroin use was 10 percent or more, ranking it with such cities as New York, Washington and Detroit where heroin use is "a continuing and significant problem," according to the institute.

● Three out of four men tested positive for one or more illicit drugs.

● Seventy-nine percent of the men charged with property crimes tested positive for one or more illegal drugs; 72 percent charged with person-to-person crimes, such as assault and armed robbery, tested positive.

● Women tested higher than men for every drug except marijuana and claimed substantially greater dependence on cocaine and heroin.

Proving drug-crime link

"This reconfirms the close and striking relationship between drug use and criminal behavior," said Oregon Attorney General Dave Frohnmayer.

Analysts caution that the results don't prove a cause-and-effect relationship between narcotics use and the criminal acts those tested are accused of committing.

"It doesn't say that the person either committed the crime to get drugs or was under

Please turn to
DRUGS, Page C2

CITY-BY-CITY RANKINGS

Positive drug-test rates for males arrested in 10 cities, based on urinalysis results from volunteers tested between November 1987 and March 1988.

Portland tied with Chicago for the third-highest rate of drug use, with 75 percent of the volunteers testing positive for one or more illicit drugs. Only New York and San Diego had higher positive test rates.

When marijuana was excluded from the results, Portland's ranking dropped to seventh.

(Comparative data were available for only 10 of the 12 cities.)

New York	
San Diego	
Portland	75%
Chicago	75%
Fort Lauderdale	
Detroit	
New York	
Phoenix	
Houston	
New Orleans	

Source: National Institute of Justice
The Oregonian

OREGON'S Little Mexico

HOME AWAY FROM HOME

By NANCY McCARTHY
of The Oregonian staff

☐ Migrants naturally gravitate to a hospitable community that has a large population speaking their own language

CORNELIUS — The lunch-time crowd at the Sunrise Cafe is like one big family.

Four men at a corner table, dusty from outdoor work, joke with a young mother and father trying to feed french fries to their 2-year-old. Across the room, a woman passes pictures of her new baby from table to table for admiring compliments. The waitress, dressed casually in a blouse and jeans, sits down to chat with customers.

During this lunch hour, all the customers are "Anglos," as they are called by the town's Hispanic residents. Usually, migrant workers also patronize the cafe, but the strawberry harvest is in full swing, and they are working in the fields surrounding the city.

For the migrants who hitch-hiked to Oregon or paid $400 to the contractors for bringing them here, Cornelius has been the focus of their lives for several months. It is where they received free food and clothing from social service agencies, where they turned to religious leaders for personal help and where they went for medical attention.

Called "Little Mexico" by some of the town's residents, Cornelius, a pause in the highway between the bigger cities of Forest Grove and Hillsboro, has for decades played host to

thousands of migrants, desperately poor in their native countries of Mexico and Guatemala, moved into the county earlier than ever, lured by labor contractors who tantalized them with stories about the money they could get from the fields.

When the harvest is done, some of the migrants who are seeking legal status to stay in the United States will settle in Cornelius, as migrants have been doing for the past 25 years.

Their experience may be easier than those who are picking in the fields near Silverton. The Silverton City Council, concerned about potential criminal activity, voted June 7 to direct city staff members to work with federal officials to reduce the population of illegal migrants in the Marion County community.

However, the Oregon office of the U.S. Immi-

Gilbert Martinez, a clerk at Hank's Thriftway in Cornelius, counts money from Agustin Guerrero (left), while his daughter, Ana Maria Negrete, 10, and his wife, Irene Guerrero Negrete look on. Cornelius is a center for migrant workers in Washington County.

gration and Naturalization Service will not remove illegal migrants working in agriculture until Dec. 1, said Dave Beebe, INS district director in Portland. The policy was made to allow farmers time to get their fields picked this year and to plan how they will get legal workers next year, when new INS regulations mandating heavy fines for using illegal migrants become effective.

In Cornelius, where about 20 percent of the 5,130 permanent residents are Hispanic, the relationship of non-Hispanics and Hispanics is, on the surface, an easy one. Few residents admit wishing the Hispanics lived elsewhere, and few Hispanics will say they have trouble

Please turn to
MIGRANTS, Page A22

Aquino paves way for Marcos' return, newspapers report

☐ The Philippines president finally agrees to allow the return of the deposed leader to face trial, although no times have been set

The Associated Press

MANILA, Philippines — President Corazon Aquino has agreed to allow exiled former President Ferdinand Marcos to return to the Philippines to face trial, two Manila newspapers reported Saturday.

The Manila Bulletin and The Manila Chronicle quoted Aquino's press secretary, Teodoro Benigno, as saying that Aquino made the assurance to two Swiss lawyers before she visited Switzerland earlier in June.

But the reports did not say when criminal charges against Marcos will be filed and when Aquino will allow him to return.

Aquino consistently has refused to allow Marcos to return to the country for security reasons although she has said he will eventually be allowed to come home.

The president had said she would allow Marcos to return now only if he and his family swore allegiance to her government and returned the money he allegedly stole during his 20-year rule. She said later she would abide by any court decision if

MARCOS

Marcos' lawyers in the Philippines raised the matter of his return to the courts.

Benigno was quoted as saying that Aquino "has to accept the possibility of Marcos returning home."

The Swiss lawyers are helping the Philippine government trace money Marcos and his family allegedly placed in Swiss bank accounts.

Marcos has been living in Hawaii since he was toppled by the civilian-military revolt that swept Aquino to power in 1986.

assets of Marcos in Switzerland but has not received information on them to the Philippine government because of legal challenges posed by Marcos' lawyers and Swiss banks.

The unidentified Swiss lawyers said the information will not be turned over "unless and until there is an assurance that formal charges will be filed against him," Benigno was quoted as saying.

Swiss law allows the lifting of banking secrecy laws only in case of criminal prosecution.

Aquino's government repeatedly has said it will file criminal charges against Marcos.

■ ELECTION CONCERNS: President Aquino requests backup from government troops as Manila gears up for Tuesday's elections. **Page A5**

Long-term nursing aid poses dilemma

By ROBERT ...
...ence Monitor

☐ The much-evaded issue surrounding the elderly looms for the next administration

ST. PETERSBURG, Fla. — Several elderly couples stroll the banks of Mirror Lake, enjoying the warmth of a welcome spring sun. Across the street, the shuffleboard courts are packed. And a game is in progress at the nearby lawn bowling club.

Everywhere, it seems, the elderly are in motion.

But while these active oldsters don't seem to have a care in the world, appearances can be deceiving. Many have at least one major concern — that someday they might need long-term care.

"Everybody I know is thinking about it," insisted a retired Pinellas County, Fla., volunteer who preferred not to give her name.

Every day an average of 1.5 million Americans, nearly 90 percent of them elderly, are being cared for in nursing homes. Many are receiving long-term assistance. Perhaps three times that number get similar aid at home.

Quality and cost vary widely, but nursing home care is expensive. Experts project that by the year 2000 several times the current number of elderly will need financial assistance, and that Americans will be paying $129 billion a year to nursing homes by then.

Yet long-term care is a subject that many older Americans seem to want to discuss only in the abstract. When asked about their own concerns, they quickly change the sub-

THE COST OF CARE
1st of 5 parts

ject. But they are more willing to talk about what they are doing to help others — which is, in fact, how

Mrs. Herb Edmonds, 76, of St. Petersburg, Fla., pictured with her husband, is a volunteer worker at the Sunshine center for the elderly.

Christian Science Monitor

Please turn to
CARE, Page A14

INSIDE

SECTION A		SECTION E	
Foreign	4-13	Forum	1-4
Nation	2, 14-23	Classified	5
Teleword	13	Editorials	2
		Metro/Northwest	5
SECTION B		Obituary	5
Lively arts	1-8		
Books	2	**SECTION F**	
		Sports	1-18
SECTION C			
Metro/Northwest	1-6	**SECTION H**	
Local news	5	Homes	1, 2, 4
		Residential real estate	
SECTION D			
Business	1-9	**SECTION ...**	
Classified	10-50	Living	1-10
Real estate	6		
Stocks	8	**SECTION T**	
		...avel	1-8

WEATHER

ALSO INSIDE
Northwest magazine
Parade magazine
TV Click
Color comics

15 sections

Classified advertising ... 224-4511
Circulation hot line 221-8240

Copyright © 1988, Oregonian Publishing Co.
Vol. 137 — No. 46,814

Cool, cloudy;
high 76, low 60 **Page A2**

WHAT IT'S CALLED

As you can see, Page One is often loaded with devices designed to entice and entrap prospective readers. Inside the paper, however, graphic elements become more subdued, less decorative. They're there to inform and guide readers, not sell papers.

Here are some typical design elements used on inside pages:

MORE ON:

■ Terms: A complete glossary of newspaper design jargon.................173

Labels (left side)

FOLIO
A line showing the page number, date, paper's name, etc.

JUMP LINE
A line showing the page number this story continues from

LIFTOUT QUOTE
A quote taken from the story and given graphic emphasis (also called a *pull quote*, *popout quote* or *breakout*)

SUBHEAD
A boldface line of type used to organize the story and break up gray text

GUTTER
The white space running vertically between elements on a page

BASTARD MEASURE
Type set in a different width than the standard column measure

SIG
A special label set into stories giving typographic emphasis to the topic, title, writer's name, etc. (also called a *bug* or *logo*)

Labels (right side)

HEADER
A label used for packaging special stories or features

JUMP HEAD
A headline treatment reserved for stories jumping from another page (styles vary from paper to paper)

PHOTO CREDIT
A line giving the photographer's name (often adding the paper or wire service he or she works for)

TEXT
Type in a standard size and font, set in columns (or legs)

SIDEBAR
A related story, often boxed, that accompanies the main story

CUTOFF RULE
A line used to separate elements on a page

CUTOUT
A photo (or part of a photo) where the background has been cut away (also called a *silhouette*)

Newspaper page (center)

F12   ■   THE SUNDAY OREGONIAN, JUNE 12, 1988

A BIG YEN FOR BASEBALL

Japan: Clubs hope when money talks, U.S. players listen

■ Continued from Page F1

Times, said the sky could be the limit for future offers.

"I think that if a guy were available in the George Bell, Andre Dawson, Don Mattingly class, a team here would pay $5 million or $6 million per year," Graczyk said. "I think there'll be a lot more big-money offers, mainly because of the dollar-yen exchange rate."

"After all," Nagino said, "$5 million can only buy a small condominium in the Tokyo area. . . . It seem like much money"

"$5 million can only buy a small condominium in the Tokyo area, so it doesn't seem like much money to us."
Masaaki Nagino,
Central League planner

A nondescript player in the U.S. major leagues, Randy Bass became a superstar with the Hanshin Tigers.
Associated Press

WARREN CROMARTIE
Ex-Expo now a Japanese veteran

BILL MADLOCK
Worth more than $1 million

BILL GULLICKSON
Packing 'em in in Tokyo

Not everyone likes Japan's best-loved team

By MICHIO YOSHIDA
The Associated Press

Is expansion in the works?

Drysdale's streak was highlight of 1968 — season of the pitcher

By LARRY BORTSTEIN
Knight-Ridder News Service

FOR THE RECORD

Don Drysdale (left) and Bob Gibson, shown during a joint appearance at a baseball camp, dominated National League pitching in 1968. Drysdale pitched 58 consecutive scoreless innings, a major league record.
Associated Press

TOOLS OF THE TRADE

As a page designer, you'll spend a lot of time drawing boxes (to show where photos go). And drawing lines (to show where text goes). And drawing more boxes (for graphics and sidebars and corrections). And drawing more lines (to keep those boxes from bumping into each other).

As you'd expect, the tools of the trade are pretty straightforward: Pencils (for drawing lines). Rulers (for measuring lines). Calculators (for estimating the lengths of those lines and boxes). And a proportion wheel (to calculate the exact dimensions of boxes as they grow larger or smaller).

Before you begin, then, get familiar with these tools and terms:

MORE ON:

■ **The proportion wheel:** A guide to how it works........ **92**

■ **Terms:** A complete glossary of newspaper design jargon................**173**

This is your basic pencil (with eraser). It's used for drawing page dummies. Designers who draw page dummies with pens are just showing off.

Grease pencils are used for making crop marks and notes on photos. Afterwards, these markings can easily be rubbed off with cloth.

In art departments and composing rooms, X-ACTO knives are used for trimming photos, cutting stories and moving items around during paste-up.

You'll need a calculator for sizing photos and for computing line lengths in a hurry (unless you're a whiz with fractions).
For example: If you have an 18-inch story, and if it's divided into 5 columns (or legs), and if there's a map in the second leg that's 3 inches deep — how deep are each of the legs?

This is a pica pole, the ruler used in newsrooms. It has inches down one side and picas down the other. You can see, for instance, that 6 picas equal one inch; you can also see that it's about 45 picas to the bottom of this page.

HOW NEWSPAPERS MEASURE THINGS

If you're trying to measure something very short or very thin, inches are too clumsy and imprecise. So printers devised *picas* and *points* for precise calibrations. There are 12 points in one pica, 6 picas in one inch — or, in all, 72 points in one inch.

This is a 1-point line (or *rule*); 72 of these would be one inch thick.

This is a 12-point rule. It is 1 pica thick; 6 of these would be 1 inch thick.

Points, picas and inches are used in different places. Here's a quick summary of what's measured with what:

POINTS
■ Thickness of rules
■ Sizes of type (headlines, text, cutlines, etc.)
■ All measurements smaller than a pica

PICAS
■ Lengths of rules
■ Widths of text, photos, cutlines, gutters, etc.

INCHES
■ Lengths of stories
■ Depths of photos and ads (though some papers use picas for photo depths)

This circular object is called a proportion wheel. It's a quick and easy-to-use gizmo for calculating proportions. For instance, if a photo is 5 inches wide and 7 inches deep, how deep will it be if you enlarge it to 8 inches wide? A proportion wheel can tell you instantly.

THE FOUR BASIC ELEMENTS

Newspaper pages are like puzzles — puzzles that can fit together in a number of different ways.

And though pages may look complicated at first, you'll find there are really only four basic elements — four kinds of puzzle pieces — that are essential. These four elements get used over and over again and occupy 90% of all editorial turf. Once you've mastered these four basic building blocks, you've mastered page design. (Well, that's not *exactly* true — but it makes it sound easy, doesn't it?)

The four elements are:

- **Headlines** — the oversized type that labels each story;
- **Text** — the story itself;
- **Photos** — the pictures that accompany stories; and
- **Cutlines** — the type that accompanies photographs.

MORE ON:

- **Headlines:** Sizes, types and writing tips......... 14
- **Text:** Some basic typographic terms...................18
- **Photos:** The three shapes (vertical, horizontal and square).............. 20
- **And** a complete chapter on photos and photo spreads begins on 81
- **Cutlines:** Types and treatments... 22

This is how the page actually printed . . .

. . . and this is how we'll represent that page — and the four basic design elements — in this book:

PHOTO

CUTLINE

HEADLINE

TEXT

PHOTO

CUTLINE

HEADLINE

TEXT

In the pages ahead, we'll examine each of these elements in quick detail. If you're interested only in page design, feel free to browse through this material and come back to it when you need it.

HEADLINES

When you study a page like the one at right — which probably happens every time you stand in the checkout line at the grocery store — there's one thing that leaps out, that grabs you, that sucks you in and forces you to dig down into your pocket, yank out some change and *buy* the thing:

The headlines.

Headlines can be mighty powerful. In fact, they're often the strongest weapon in your design arsenal. Stories can be beautifully written, photos can be wild and colorful — but neither is noticeable from 10 feet away the way headlines are.

You probably won't ever write heads as strange and tacky as these tabloid heads are (though to give credit where it's due, note how cleverly crafted they are). If you stick strictly to design, you may never even write heads at all (since most headlines are written by copy editors). But you still need to know what headlines are, where they go, and what styles, shapes and sizes are available.

WARNING: This style of page design has little to do with "serious" journalists like us (though it's appealing in a cheesy way).

WRITING GOOD HEADLINES

Because this is a book on design, not copy editing, we won't rehash all the rules of good headline-writing. But we'll hit the highlights, which are:

■ **Keep them conversational.** Be reader-friendly. Write the way people speak. Avoid pretentious jargon, odd verbs, omitted words (*Solons said bid mulled*). As the stylebook for The St. Petersburg Times warns, "Headlines should not read like a telegram."

■ **Write in present tense, active voice.** Like this: *President vetoes tax bill.* Not *President vetoed tax bill* or *Tax bill vetoed by President.*

■ **Avoid bad splits.** Old-time copy-deskers were fanatical about this. And though things are looser these days, you should still try to avoid any dangling verbs, adjectives or prepositions at the end of a line.

Instead of this:

**Sox catch
up with
Yankees**

Try this:

**Sox catch
Yankees
in AL East**

Above all else, headlines should be accurate and instantly understandable. If you can get a better headline by writing it a little short or by changing the size a bit — do it. Readability always comes first.

Remember, headlines serve three functions on a newspaper page:

1. They *summarize* the content of the story.
2. They *entice* the reader into reading the story.
3. They *anchor* the story design to help visually organize the page.

HEADLINES

TYPES OF HEADLINES

This headline is from The Sun (New York City) of April 13, 1861. Papers often wrote a dozen decks like this before finally reaching the start of the story. Why no wide horizontal heads in those days? Because the old type-revolving presses used metal type locked into blocks to print each page. Type set too wide tended to come loose and fly off the cylinder as the presses spun around.

A century ago, newspaper headlines looked like the one at left. Those old-fashioned heads:

- Mixed typefaces at random.
- Combined all caps and lower case.
- Were centered horizontally.
- Stacked layers and layers of decks atop one another, with rules between each deck.

Today's headlines, by comparison:

- Are generally written downstyle (that is, using normal rules of capitalization).
- Run flush left.
- Use decks optionally, as in this example:

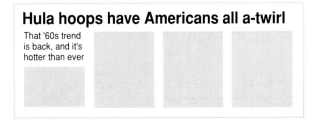

That's the standard way to treat a news headline (it's called a *banner* headline). But it's not the only way. Below are examples of alternative head styles — styles that go in and out of fashion as time goes by:

Kickers

Kickers use a short lead-in phrase to catch your eye — usually underlined, half the size of the main head, and in a contrasting font or weight. Many papers now regard kickers as clumsy and old-fashioned.

Hammers

Hammer heads are the flip side of kickers. They use a big, bold phrase to catch your eye, then add a wordy deck below. They're effective and appealing, but are usually reserved for special stories or features.

Slammers

Who knows where these crazy names came from? This two-part head uses a boldface word or phrase to lead into a contrasting main headline. Some papers limit its use to special features or jump headlines.

Tripods

This head comes in three parts: a bold word or phrase (often all caps) and two smaller lines of deck squaring off alongside. Like most gimmicky heads, it generally works better for features than for hard news.

Raw wraps

Most headlines cover all the text below; this treatment lets the text wrap alongside. It's a risky idea — but later on, we'll see instances where this headline style comes in handy. (It's also known as a Dutch wrap.)

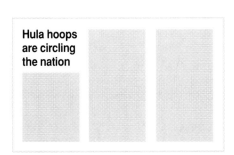

Sidesaddle heads

This style lets you park the head beside, rather than above, the story. It's best for squeezing a story — preferably, one that's boxed — into a shallow horizontal space. Can be flush left, flush right or centered.

HEADLINES

Headlines are measured in points. And traditionally, they were restricted to these point sizes: 14, 18, 24, 30, 36, 42, 48, 54, 60, 72 and 84. Nowadays, computers can create headlines in any size, but in keeping with tradition, most editors generally stick to those sizes listed above.

The biggest head you're likely to see looks like this —

A 72-pt. headline

— and it's usually reserved for blockbuster stories on Page One.

Most stories, of course, don't need headlines that loud. Yet if the head's too small, the story gets lost. This, then, is about as small as headlines get:

This 18-pt. headline is a lot smaller than that huge one up above

That 18-point headline is *one-fourth* as big as the 72-point headline. To find a headline's size, you measure only its height — from the bottom of the *descenders* to the top of the *ascenders*. Here's a closer look at a few components of type (and these terms apply to both headline and text type):

■ *SERIFS:* Those decorative strokes at the tips of letters.
■ *BASELINE:* The invisible grid line the letters sit on.
■ *X-HEIGHT:* The height of a typical lower-case letter (in particular, the "x").

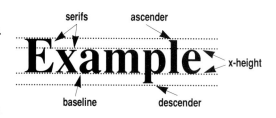

serifs   ascender

x-height

baseline   descender

SIZING TYPE:
To find the point size, measure from the bottom of the descender "p" to the top of the ascender "l". Here, it measures 36 points (a half-inch). So it's 36-pt. type.

It's hard to generalize about sizing headlines. Some papers like them big; others prefer them small and bold. And heads in tabloids are almost always smaller than heads in broadsheets. Still, this much is certain: Headlines should get smaller as you move down the page, as shown below:

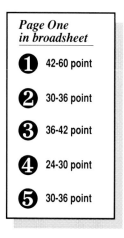

Page One in broadsheet

❶ 42-60 point

❷ 30-36 point

❸ 36-42 point

❹ 24-30 point

❺ 30-36 point

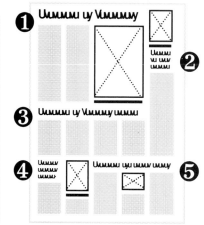

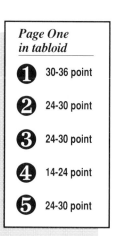

Page One in tabloid

❶ 30-36 point

❷ 24-30 point

❸ 24-30 point

❹ 14-24 point

❺ 24-30 point

HEADLINES

TYPEFACES & WEIGHTS

There are hundreds of typefaces available today, with names like:

Helvetica   Times Roman   Optima   Bookman

As you can see, each typeface has a distinct personality. So for consistency, a newspaper will choose just one or two *families* of type for all news headlines. Otherwise, too many typefaces noodle around like alphabet soup, readers get distracted, and pages look like circus posters.

Within each type family, a variety of weights and styles are available:

SERIF type has tiny strokes at the tips of each letter. The typefaces at right are all Bookman.

Light
This headline is 14 points

Bold
This headline is 14 points

Italic
This headline is 14 points

SANS SERIF type ("sans" means "without" in French) have no serifs. The typefaces at right are all Helvetica.

Light
This headline is 14 points

Bold
This headline is 14 points

Italic
This headline is 14 points

A newspaper may, within one type family, use different styles in different places: say, a medium-weight face for standard headlines, a heavy boldface for special stories or sidebars, a light italic for decks or features.

Just as you can show a story's importance by the size of its headline (bigger stories getting bigger heads), you can boost or soften its impact by changing faces and weights.

MORE ON:

■ Butting headlines: When it's permissible and how it works................... 59

■ Standing heads: How they differ from headlines........... 111

■ Fancy headlines: Treatments that add variety and graphic pizzazz to feature headlines........... 138

NUMBER OF LINES

Most newspapers use a traditional coding format for headlines that lists: 1) *the column width*, 2) *the point size* and 3) *the number of lines*. That means a 3-30-1 headline would be a 3-column, 30-pt. headline that runs on 1 line, like this:

Rock 'n' roll causes acne, doctor says

(Not shown actual size)

Headlines for news stories usually run *on top* of the text. That means a wide story needs a wide headline; a narrow story needs a narrow one. So in a narrow layout, that headline above could be rewritten as a 1-30-3 (1 column, 30-pt., 3 lines deep):

Rock 'n' roll causes acne, doctor says

Since 5-10 words are optimum for most headlines, narrow stories may need 3-4 lines of headline to make sense; wide headlines can work in a line or two.

The chart below will give you an idea of how many lines usually work best:

HOW MANY LINES FOR HEADLINES?					
If headline is this wide (in columns):	1	2	3	4	5	6
Then make it this deep (in lines):	3-5*	2-3*	1-2*	1	1	1

* For headlines 24-point and smaller, subtract one line.

TEXT

COMPONENTS OF TYPE

Text is the essential building block of any page. Without it, there's no news.

Most readers take text type for granted. Most page designers do, too. But you really ought to acquaint yourself with the components that give text its personality and legibility. Briefly, these are:

■ **The typeface.** Some type is easier on the eyes than others. Studies show that sans serif type, for instance, is more tiring to read in large doses than serif type. (The text you're now reading uses Times, a serif typeface.)

■ **Point size.** Text type has been getting bigger in recent years. A century ago, newspapers used 8-point type; today, 10-point is increasingly common. (This text uses 11.5 point, a comfortable size for these wide columns.)

■ **Letter spacing** and **word spacing.** Readers get tired and stories get long if there's too much air in your type (like this, for instance). To speed the read, you can tighten the gaps between letters (called *kerning*) or between words. But if letters start colliding, you've kerned too much (like this, for instance).

■ **Character width.** Today's computers let you condense or expand fonts to suit your taste. Some newspapers sneakily condense their type 5-10% to squeeze more characters in. (The cutlines below are set at 80% of their standard width — which lets us pack more information into a tighter space.)

■ **Leading.** *Leading* refers to the vertical space between lines. Too much (or too little) subconsciously slows the reader down. (This text uses 12.4 points of leading; that means it's 12.4 points from line to line. And notice how we add 2 points of extra leading between paragraphs to space them apart.)

Put all these components together and you get this typical text block:

This 2-inch text excerpt uses 9-point Nimrod type (a serif face) with 10 points of leading. It's 12.2 picas wide, a fairly standard width for modern newspaper columns. (Six of these columns side by side would fill a typical broadsheet page.) Plain type like this is called roman or regular type (as opposed to italic or boldface, below).

As "Big Top Pee-wee" begins, life is perfect. Pee-wee rises from bed, even though his bunky Vance the Talking Pig doesn't, and does his chores: feeding his barnyard menagerie and himself. They make their own beds in the barn while he whomps up breakfast.

The rest of the day he and Vance spend in the lab, devising ways to multiply vegetables prodigiously and cultivate a hot dog tree.

At lunch with schoolteacher Winnie, however, he playfully jumps

Note how this excerpt has straight margins on both the right and left sides. That's known as *justified* type. Type that's unjustified is called *ragged* type. This cutline, for instance, is ragged right, since the right margin is unjustified. The cutline at far left is ragged left. Cutlines are often ragged, but text is almost always justified.

OTHER TYPES OF TYPE

Newspapers will often use certain types of type for certain types of material. For instance, classified ads and sports stats are printed in *agate,* a tiny (5-7 point) sans serif typeface. There are other options, as well:

Ghostbusters 2
★★★

Starring: Bill Murray, Dan Aykroyd, Sigourney Weaver
Director: Ivan Reitman
Rating: PG for language, slime

Boldface type is excellent for highlighting key words or phrases. Many papers use boldface for cutlines (like the one you're reading right now). Boldface is hard to read in large doses, however.

Have a consumer question? Action gets answers. Send a letter with your full name, address, daytime telephone number and copies of supporting documents to Action, The Oregonian, 1320 S.W. Broadway, Portland 97201-3499.

Italics are used for editor's notes, literary excerpts, foreign phrases, or titles of books, movies, songs, etc. Italics can also be used within stories to give words *emphasis* — but should be used sparingly.

⑫ **Movie** ★★★ "Condorman" (1981) Michael Crawford. A cartoonist acting as a CIA courier becomes his comic-strip hero, Condorman, to help a KGB agent named Natalia defect.

Many papers with serif text use a sans-serif font in all maps, charts, promos, listings, etc. This is a good way to help readers distinguish between standard text and non-standard, special features.

TEXT

Newspapers measure stories in inches. A short filler item might be only 2 inches long; a major investigative piece might be 200. But since one inch of type set in a *wide* leg is bigger than one inch of type in a *narrow* leg, editors avoid confusion by assuming all stories will be one standard width — and that's usually around 12 picas. (See the example on the facing page.)

You can design an attractive newspaper without ever varying the width of your text. Sometimes, though, you may decide to stretch or shrink the width of a column; those non-standard column widths are called *bastard* measures.

Generally speaking, text becomes hard to follow if it's set in legs narrower than 10 picas. It's tough to read, too, if it's set wider than 20 picas.

The ideal depth for text is between 2 and 10 inches per leg. Shorter than that, legs look shallow and weak; longer than that, they become dull, gray stacks. (We'll fine-tune these guidelines in the pages ahead.)

MORE ON:

■ **Story designs** using only text.... 30

■ **Text shapes:** How to choose the best configurations when dummying stories................ 35

■ **Page designs** using only text.... 58

SHAPING TEXT

Text is very flexible. It can be shaped into all kinds of vertical and horizontal configurations, as these examples show:

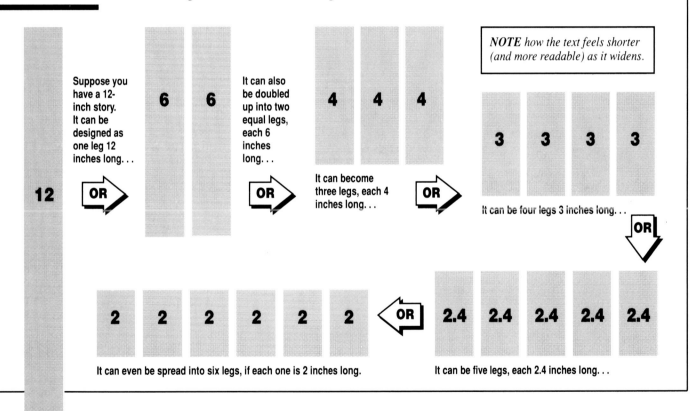

Suppose you have a 12-inch story. It can be designed as one leg 12 inches long...

It can also be doubled up into two equal legs, each 6 inches long...

It can become three legs, each 4 inches long...

NOTE how the text feels shorter (and more readable) as it widens.

It can be four legs 3 inches long...

It can be five legs, each 2.4 inches long...

It can even be spread into six legs, if each one is 2 inches long.

There's a lot of math involved in page design, especially when you calculate story lengths. To succeed, you need a good sense of geometry — an understanding of how changing one element in a story's design will affect every other element.

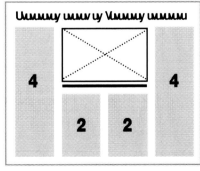

Here's that same 12-inch story. But now it wraps around a photograph. Can you see how, if the photo became deeper, each leg of text would need to get deeper, too?

PHOTOS

There's nothing like a photograph to give a page motion and emotion. As you can see in these classic images from pages of the past, photojournalism lies at the very heart of newspaper design:

Clockwise from top: Babe Ruth says farewell to baseball; Harry Truman displays a famous headline; a captured Viet Cong officer is shot in Saigon; the space shuttle Challenger explodes after launch; Buzz Aldrin walks on the moon; Jack Ruby shoots accused Kennedy assassin Lee Harvey Oswald.

PHOTOS

Every picture tells a story — and every story deserves a picture. Today's readers are so spoiled by TV and magazines that they now expect photos — *color* photos, yet — to accompany every story they read.

Now, you may not have the space for that many photos. You may not have enough photographers to *shoot* that many photos. And printing color may be downright impossible.

But try anyway. Add photos every chance you get. Without them, you simply can't create an appealing newspaper.

MORE ON:

■ **Horizontals:** Tips on sizing and dummying........... **36**

■ **Verticals:** Tips on sizing and dummying................. **39**

■ **The dominant photo:** What it is and how to use it effectively............ **42**

■ **PLUS:** A complete chapter on photos................ **81**

THE THREE BASIC SHAPES

It sounds obvious, but news photos come in three basic shapes. Each of those three shapes has its strengths and weaknesses. And each is best suited to certain design configurations.

The three shapes are *rectangular:* horizontal, vertical and square.

Horizontal

This is the most common shape for newspaper photos. We see the world horizontally through our own eyes, and when you pick up a camera, this is the shape you instantly see. Horizontals can get static and dull after a while, and some subjects — like basketball players and space shuttle launches — demand a different composition.

Vertical

Vertical shapes are often considered more dramatic and dynamic than either squares or horizontals. But verticals can be a bit trickier to design than squares or horizontals. Because they're so deep, they often look related to any stories parked alongside — even if they're not.

Square

Squares are considered the dullest of the three shapes. In fact, some page designers and photographers avoid squares altogether. Remember, however, that the content of a photo is more important than its shape. Accept each photo on its own terms, and design it onto the page so it's as strong as possible — whatever its shape.

CUTLINES

You're browsing through the newspaper. Suddenly, without warning, you confront a photo that looks like this:

You look at the pig. You look at the men. You look at the bulldozer. You look back at the pig. *What,* you wonder, is going on? Is it funny? Cruel? Tragic? Is this pig doomed?

Fortunately, there's a cutline below the photo. The cutline says this:

Highway workers use a loader to lift Mama, a 600-pound sow, onto a truck Monday on Interstate 84 near Lloyd Center. The pig fell from the back of the truck on the way to the slaughterhouse. It took the men two hours to oust the ornery oinker.

Now the photo makes sense.

Sure, every picture tells a story. But it's the cutline's job to tell the story behind every picture: *who*'s involved, *what*'s happening, *when* and *where* the event took place. A well-written cutline makes the photo instantly understandable and tells the reader *why* the photo — and the story — are important.

TYPOGRAPHY

Cutlines are quite different from text. And to make sure that difference is obvious to readers, most newspapers run their cutlines in a different typeface. Some use boldface. Some use italic. Some use sans serifs. (This book, for example, uses a smaller, bolder sans serif font for its cutlines.)

Boldface, justified

President Quayle welcomes Mikhail Gorbachev to the White House Friday as the two leaders begin a new round of high-level summit talks.

Italic, ragged right

President Quayle welcomes Mikhail Gorbachev to the White House Friday as the two leaders begin a new round of high-level summit talks.

Sans serif with boldface lead-in

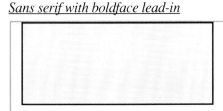

SUMMIT STARTING — President Quayle welcomes Mikhail Gorbachev to the White House Friday as the two leaders begin a new round of talks.

CUTLINES

How long should cutlines be? Long enough to describe — briefly — all significant details in the photo. Some photos are fairly obvious and don't deserve much explanation. Others (old historical photos, works of art, photos that run without stories) may require wordier descriptions.

And what about photos of clubs or teams? Should every face — all 19 of them — be identified? Most newspapers set guidelines for such occasions, so it's hard to generalize. But remember that readers expect cutlines to offer quick hits of information. So don't overdo it.

Where do you dummy cutlines? On news pages, they should generally run *below* each photo. But for variety, especially on feature pages, cutlines can also run *beside* and *between* photos, as shown below:

MORE ON:

■ **Mug shots:**
They've got their own style of cutlines................... 32

■ **Photo spreads:**
Cutline treatments and placement.... 99

BELOW

The Bugle-Beacon/PAT MINNIEAR

Cutlines below photos should align along both edges of the photo. They should *never* extend beyond either edge. If a photo is more than 30 picas wide, long cutlines should be set in two legs, side by side, since wide type — such as the type in this cutline — is difficult to read. And be sure the last line extends at least halfway across the column. (This line just barely makes it.)

BESIDE

This ragged left cutline is set *flush right* along the edge of the photo. (Notice how ragged left type is somewhat annoying to read.) When you dummy cutlines like this, put them on the *outside* of the page design. That way, the cutline won't butt up against any text type, confusing your readers and uglifying your page.

This ragged right cutline is *flush left* against the photo and flush to the *bottom.* And it's thin — perhaps too thin. Cutlines should always be at least 6 picas wide. If they're narrow, they shouldn't be very deep.

BETWEEN

Ideally, every photo should get its own cutline. But photos can also share a joint cutline, as these two do. Just be sure you make it clear which photo (at left or at right) you're discussing. And be sure the cutline squares off at either the top or bottom. Don't just let it float. (Note how this cutline is justified on both sides.)

A SAMPLE DUMMY

This is a typical page dummy for a 6-column broadsheet newspaper. Most broadsheets use a 6-column format like this; most tabloids use a 5-column format (and they're not this deep).

HOW DUMMIES WORK:

■ The numbers along the left margin show you inches measured *down* from the top of the page. The entire page, as you can see, is 21.5 inches deep.

■ The numbers along the right margin show you inches measured *up* from the bottom of the page. (This is useful for dummying ads.)

■ Each vertical line represents one column. A 6-column photo, for instance, would be as wide as the entire page.

■ Each horizontal line represents an inch of depth. A leg of text that's 1 inch deep would take up just one of those sections.

NEED A DUMMY?
In the pages ahead, you'll need lots of blank page dummies like this one in order to do the exercises at the end of each chapter. Feel free to duplicate this sample dummy as often as you like if no other dummies are available for you to practice on.

THE DUMMY

How do you show where stories go on each page? Or what size the headlines should be? Or how big the photo halftones will run?

By drawing a dummy.

Now, some editors try to wing it, improvising in the composing room as they patch together pages on deadline. But that's a dangerous waste of time. It's smarter to plan ahead by drawing a detailed page diagram — a dummy — and fine-tuning each element in advance, *before* you begin assembling the real thing.

Dummies are usually about half the size of actual pages, but proportioned precisely. (If your design calls for a thin vertical photo, it shouldn't look square on the dummy.) For complicated pages, designers often draw full-sized dummies using the grid sheets that pages are pasted up on. But for most pages, a dummy like the one below is sufficient.

And absolutely necessary.

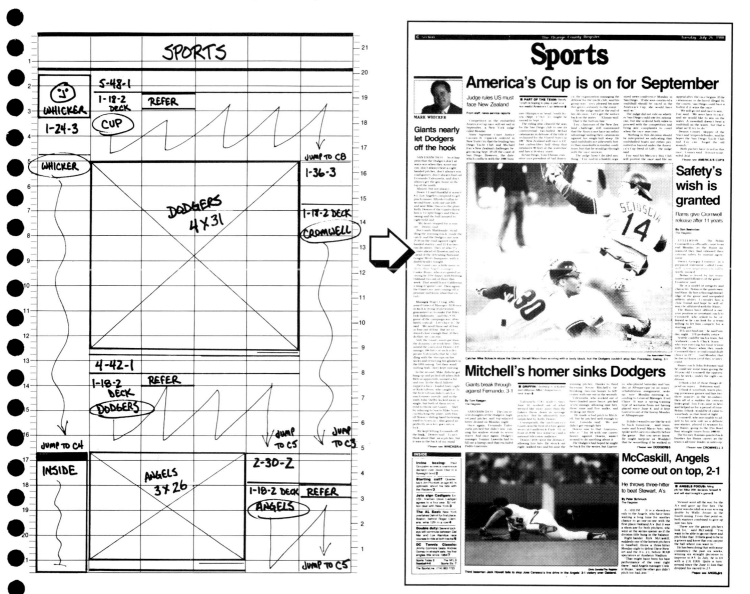

This is how most pages begin. An editor or designer draws (in pencil) a series of lines and boxes to indicate where photos, cutlines, headlines and text will go. This page is actually quite simple: not too many stories or graphic extras.

And here is how that dummy was translated into print. Note how every story jumps (continues on a later page). That made the page easier to build; stories were pasted into place, then cut according to the layout on the dummy.

THE DUMMY

Drawing up a page dummy isn't an exact science. Stories don't always fit the way you'd like. And even when you're sure you've measured everything perfectly, you'll inevitably find yourself fudging here and there, once you start pasting things up.

So relax. When it's time to fine-tune a page, you can always trim a photo. Plug in a liftout quote, a deck, a filler item. Write a bigger headline. Shuffle ads around. Add extra air between paragraphs. Cut an inch or two from the story. Or (worst of all) start over.

To give you an idea of how dummying works, let's build a page *backwards* — that is, we'll take a finished story and build a dummy from it. That way, you can see how the parts of a dummy work together to create a finished product.

EXAMPLE

The Oregonian / KRAIG SCATTARELLA

Highway workers use a loader to lift Mama, a 600-pound sow, onto a truck Monday on Interstate 84 near Lloyd Center. The pig had fallen off the truck on the way to slaughter.

Freeway closed for two hours as ornery oinker hogs traffic

Westbound traffic on Interstate 84 near the Lloyd Center exit was backed up for nearly two miles early Monday when a 600-pound hog on the way to slaughter fell from the back of a truck.

For nearly two hours, the sow refused to budge.

Fred Mickelson told police that he was taking six sows and a boar from his farm in Lyle, Wash., to a slaughterhouse in Carlton when Mama escaped.

"I heard the tailgate fall off, and I looked back and saw her standing in the road," Mickelson said with a sigh. "I thought: 'Oh, no. We've got some real trouble now.'"

Mickelson said Mama was "pretty lively" when she hit the ground, lumbering between cars and causing havoc on a foggy day. There were no automobile accidents, however.

After about an hour of chasing the pig with the help of police, Mickelson began mulling over his options, which included having a veterinarian tranquilize the hog.

About 10 a.m., a crew of highway workers arrived and decided to use a front-end loader to pick up the sow and load her back into the truck.

THE DUMMY

1 Measure all the elements in the example on page 26, and you'll find:

■ **Text** — The text is in two legs. Each leg is a bit wider than 12 picas, or roughly 12.2 (often written *1202*). We said earlier that 12 picas is a standard column width for text, so this is a typical example of a typical 2-column story. Each leg is 2 inches deep. The whole story, then, is 4 inches long.

■ **Headline** — Measure from the top of an ascender to the bottom of a descender, and you'll find it's a 24-point headline. There are two lines, with a 6-point space *between* lines. So the whole headline is 54 points deep, or — if you do a little math — three-quarters of an inch.

■ **Photo** — Photos measure their widths in picas or columns. (This one is roughly 25.4 picas, or 2 columns wide.) And though some papers measure photo depths in inches, it's easier to use picas. (This photo is 18 picas deep.)

■ **Cutline** — Note the spacing above and below this cutline. From the bottom of the photo to the top of the headline is roughly half an inch.

MORE ON:

■ **Headlines:** How they're measured and how to code them.................... **16**

2 Suppose we want to design this story into the top left corner of the page. Grab a page dummy. Find the two left-hand columns. Move up to the top, and we'll begin drawing in the elements.

At the top of the page, draw a box to represent the photo. Make it two columns wide; count down 3 inches for the depth. Run a big "X" into the corners. (The "X" is a traditional way to indicate that it's a photo, not an ad or a box for another story.)

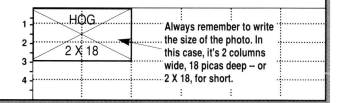

Always remember to write the size of the photo. In this case, it's 2 columns wide, 18 picas deep -- or 2 X 18, for short.

3 Next comes the cutline. There are different ways to indicate cutlines on dummies, but what we'll do is this:

Calculate how many lines of cutline there'll be (in this case, two). Allowing a little air under the photo, draw a line where the bottom of the cutline will be. In this case, it's about a half-inch below the photo.

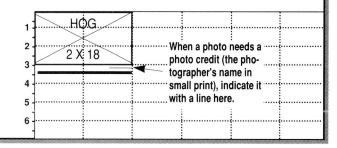

When a photo needs a photo credit (the photographer's name in small print), indicate it with a line here.

4 Now we'll dummy the headline. Most designers just draw a horizontal line and jot down the headline code — and that's quick and easy.

But for now, you might want to imitate the *feel* of the headline by drawing either a row of X's or a squiggly horizontal wave to represent each line of headline. Then write the headline code on that line somewhere.

Allow a little space below the cutline. Like this:

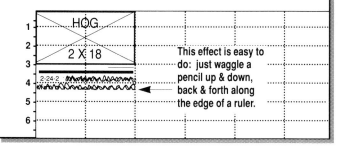

This effect is easy to do: just waggle a pencil up & down, back & forth along the edge of a ruler.

5 Finally, indicate where the text goes. There are many ways to do this: straight lines, wavy lines, arrows — some papers even use blank space.

For now, let's use a directional line. Write the name (or *slug*) of the story where the text begins; under it, draw a line down the center of the leg. When you reach the bottom of the leg, jog the line up (the way your eye moves) to the top of the next leg. This will trace the path of the text, like so:

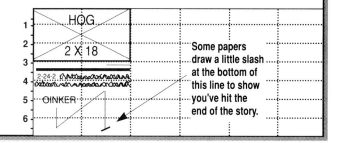

Some papers draw a little slash at the bottom of this line to show you've hit the end of the story.

THE DUMMY

WHAT EVERY GOOD DUMMY SHOULD SHOW

Every newspaper has its own system for drawing up dummies. Some, for instance, size photos in picas; others use inches, or a combination of picas and inches. Some papers use different colored pens for each different element (boxes, photos, text). Some use wavy lines to indicate text, while others use arrows — or nothing at all.

Whatever the system, remember: *Make your dummies as complete and legible as possible.* Be sure that every finished dummy contains:

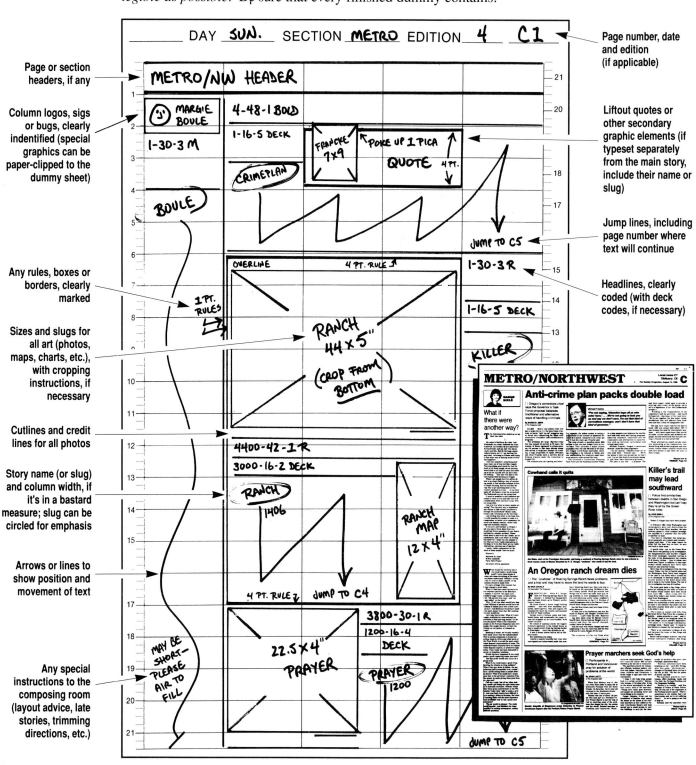

Page or section headers, if any

Column logos, sigs or bugs, clearly indentified (special graphics can be paper-clipped to the dummy sheet)

Any rules, boxes or borders, clearly marked

Sizes and slugs for all art (photos, maps, charts, etc.), with cropping instructions, if necessary

Cutlines and credit lines for all photos

Story name (or slug) and column width, if it's in a bastard measure; slug can be circled for emphasis

Arrows or lines to show position and movement of text

Any special instructions to the composing room (layout advice, late stories, trimming directions, etc.)

Page number, date and edition (if applicable)

Liftout quotes or other secondary graphic elements (if typeset separately from the main story, include their name or slug)

Jump lines, including page number where text will continue

Headlines, clearly coded (with deck codes, if necessary)

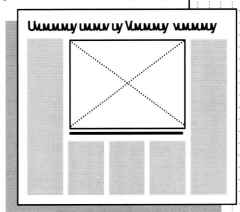

Headlines, text, photos, cutlines. Those are the basic building blocks of design — like the pieces of a puzzle. Over the years, page designers have tried assembling their puzzles in every conceivable way. Some solutions worked; others didn't.

In the pages ahead, we'll show you what works, what doesn't, and what comes close. You may think there are thousands of possible combinations for every story and every page, but there are really only a few basic design formats you can count on. And those formats are well worth knowing.

In this chapter, we'll show you the different shapes a story can take, whether it's:

- a story without art;
- a story with a mug shot;
- a story with a large photograph; or
- a story with two photographs.

Later on, we'll show you how to combine stories to make a page. But first things first.

There's a lot of information in the pages ahead. Don't try to absorb it all at once. Consider the examples to be swipeable formats; the next time you're laying out pages, look through the section that applies, explore your options, and choose a format that will fit the bill. You'll soon understand why some things work and others don't.

STORY DESIGN

CHAPTER CONTENTS

■ **Stories without art:** Design options for stories that consist only of headlines and text... **30-31**

■ **Mug shots:** Design options for stories that add a mug shot to the text.................................. **32-34**

■ **Text shapes:** A look at the different configurations text blocks can and should take................ **35**

■ **One horizontal photo:** Design options for stories that use horizontal art **36-38**

■ **One vertical photo:** Design options for stories that use vertical art................................. **39-41**

■ **The dominant photo:** How to select lead art for multi-element stories **42-43**

■ **Big vertical, small horizontal:** Design options for two-photo stories................................ **44-45**

■ **Big horizontal, small vertical:** More design options for two-photo stories....................... **46-47**

■ **Two verticals:** Still more design options for two-photo stories................................... **48-49**

■ **Two horizontals:** Even more design options for two-photo stories................................... **50-51**

■ **Adding mug shots:** Tips for adding mugs to stories with a dominant photo......................... **52**

■ **Exercises**........................ **53-54**

STORIES WITHOUT ART

In a typical issue of either The New York Times or USA Today, 70% of the stories run without any art, 25% use just one piece of art (a photo, chart or map), and only 5% use two or more pieces of art.

MORE ON:

■ **Designing pages without art:** Tips and techniques for creating attractive pages when photos aren't available.... 58

On this day's Page One, The New York Times ran six stories. One used a mug shot; one used a horizontal photo; one used a vertical photo. The rest of the page was taken up by stories without art, by refers and promos, and by the index.

On its Page One (for the same day as The New York Times at left), USA Today ran seven stories, though only one used a photo. The rest of the page was taken up by promos, briefs, the index, and other graphic elements locked into a standard format.

So relax. Most of the stories you'll dummy will consist of just headlines and text — and those are the easiest kind to design. Since there are only a few ways to design stories without art, it's fairly hard to goof them up.

Basically, when you dummy stories, they tend to run either *vertically* or *horizontally* along the page:

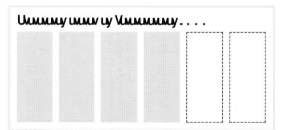

This story runs vertically. The headline is on top, and the text drops straight down below it. And that's that until the story reaches the end.

This story, on the other hand, runs horizontally. Instead of just one leg, it uses several stacked side by side. You can keep adding new legs — and extending the headline — until you run out of room at the right edge of the page.

THE RULE ABOUT RECTANGLES

Perhaps the single most important page design guideline is this one:

Whether they're vertical, horizontal or square, *stories should always be shaped like rectangles.*

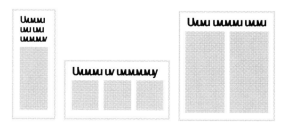

STORIES WITHOUT ART

VERTICAL DESIGN OPTIONS

Years ago, stories were *all* dummied vertically. Printers would simply lay in strips of text below the headline. When they reached the bottom of the page, they'd either end the story or jump the text up into the next column.

Try that today and they'll laugh you out of the newsroom. In fact, you should avoid dummying legs more than 12 inches deep, since long legs look gray and dull. In other words, the longer the story, the more it needs to go horizontal.

In news stories (right), the headline usually sits atop the text. In features, as you'll soon see, that rule is frequently broken.

Vertical stories are clean and attractive. They're the easiest shape to follow (just start at the headline and read straight down). Vertical design *does* have drawbacks, however:
- Long vertical legs like these can be very tiring to read.
- Headlines are harder to write when they're this narrow.
- Pages full of these long, skinny legs look awfully dull.

HORIZONTAL DESIGN OPTIONS

Horizontal shapes are modern, pleasing to the eye, and create the illusion that stories are shorter than they really are.

Again, avoid dummying legs deeper than 12 inches. But avoid short, squat legs, too. For most stories, legs should generally be at least 2 inches deep — never shorter than 1 inch.

Horizontal layouts flow left to right, the way readers naturally read. You'll create the most attractive designs by keeping legs between 2 and 10 inches deep. Again, note how the headline covers the story, and how it touches the start of the text.

TWO ODD OPTIONS TO PONDER

Probably 99% of all stories look like those above: basically vertical or horizontal, with the headline running above the text, covering the entire story like an umbrella.

Life is full of exceptions, however, and here are two more: the raw wrap and the sidesaddle head (below). They both break the rule about headlines running above all the text. And they're both potentially dangerous. (See how those right-hand legs of text could collide with any text set above them?)

But on certain occasions, they're very handy. For now, view them with suspicion — but stay tuned.

RAW WRAP: The headline is indented into 1, 2 or 3 left-hand legs, and the text wraps up alongside, squaring off with the top of the headline.

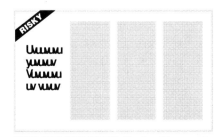

SIDESADDLE HEADLINE: The headline runs in the left-hand column (either flush left, flush right or centered). The story runs alongside.

MUG SHOTS

Yes, you can design stories without art. But from a designer's perspective, that gets awfully gray. And from a reader's perspective, it's downright dull.

Most stories are about people: people winning, losing, getting arrested, getting elected. Readers want to know what those people *look* like. So show them.

Remember, mug shots attract readers. And attracting readers is your job.

■ **Size:** Mugs usually run the full width of a column, 3 to 4 inches deep.

■ **Cropping:** Most mug shots fill the frame with a little air on each side. Crop comfortably close, but avoid slicing into ears, foreheads or chins.

■ **Cutline:** Every mug needs a cutline. Mug cutlines often use a two-line format: The first line is the person's name; the second is a description, title, position, etc.

CLAY FROST
Claims a UFO melted his dog

VERTICAL DESIGN OPTIONS

In vertical designs, mug shots go at the very top of the story. In descending order, then, arrange story elements like this: *photo, cutline, headline, text.* Any other sequence may get you into trouble.

PHOTO ——→
CUTLINE ——→
HEADLINE ——→
TEXT ——→

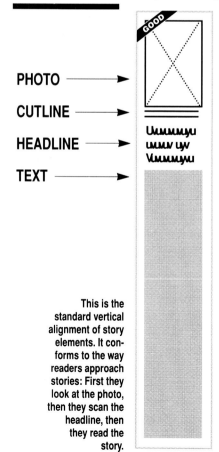

This is the standard vertical alignment of story elements. It conforms to the way readers approach stories: First they look at the photo, then they scan the headline, then they read the story.

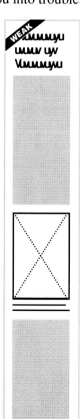

This layout is weak because it violates a basic principle of story design: Never interrupt any leg of text with an art element. Readers might think the story has ended and that a new one begins below the photo.

Designers will sometimes park a photo here, at the bottom of a column, to keep it from butting against another photo higher up on the page. A good idea, but a weak design. Avoid placing art at the *bottom* of a leg of type. Readers will assume either that it's an ad or that the photo belongs to another story.

MUG SHOTS

Because mug shots are usually one column wide, it's easy to attach them to a horizontal story. You simply square them off beside the headline and text.

And this is where a little math comes in. Assume the mug is 3 inches deep. Assume the cutline is roughly a half-inch deep. That adds up to a total depth of 3½ inches.

For short stories like this, headlines are small: roughly a half-inch to an inch deep. So that makes every leg of text in this design approximately 3 inches deep.

Here's a typical layout for a 6-inch story:

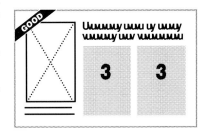

To keep the story cleanly rectangular, the headline aligns with the top of the photo, and the bottom of each leg squares off with the bottom of the cutline.

If each leg of type in this design is roughly 3 inches deep, that means you can keep adding on legs to make a 9-, 12- or 15-inch story:

Note how, as the headline gets wider, it goes from two lines (above) to one (left). But since bigger stories use bigger headlines, the depths of the legs will stay roughly the same.

You can dummy mugs at either end of the story, too. Since the mugee generally stares straight ahead, one side's just as good as the other:

Note how the headline covers only the text — not the photo. Sometimes, though, extending the headline above the mug will help the layout fit better.

Longer stories need more depth, so they'll wrap *under* the mug. **Note:** Since the text has just grown one column wider, the headline must now extend one more column, too:

The mug can now go in any leg except the first; many designers would choose one of the middle legs. Allow at least 1 pica of air between the bottom of the cutline and the text. And always dummy *at least* 1 inch of text under any photo.

In longer stories, a mug can run in any leg (except the first leg — nothing should come between the headline and the start of the text). Or you can park several mugs side by side:

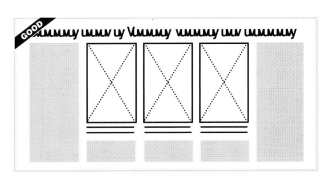

Note how these three mugs are evenly aligned. Two reasons for that: 1) It's ordered, balanced and pleasing to the eye; 2) It gives each mug equal weight, instead of emphasizing one person more prominently.

MUG SHOTS

Don't think that layouts *must* be either vertical or horizontal. We've simply made those distinctions to help you develop a feel for story shapes. You'll soon see that, as stories get more complex, they tend to expand both vertically and horizontally — and that's where you may need to begin bending the rules. For example:

MORE ON:

■ **Adding mugs to story designs** that already use a larger photo..................52

■ **Raw wraps:** How they help keep headlines from butting................ 62

■ **Wraparounds and skews:** Tips on special text treatments............... 132

■ **Liftout quotes:** Formats and guidelines................ 114

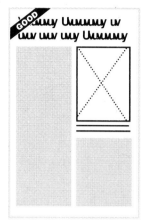

Here's a layout that isn't purely vertical, since it uses not one but two legs side by side. And it's not purely horizontal, since it's more deep than wide. But it's a good design solution when you need to fit a short story into a square-shaped hole. And it could easily be deepened to accommodate a longer story.

Note the rules we've observed in dummying this story:
■ The headline covers all the text.
■ All elements of the design align neatly with each other.
■ There's at least an inch of text below the photo.
■ The whole story is shaped like a rectangle.

We've now examined all the basic configurations for stories with mugs. You'll find that the preceding examples also work well for nearly any story where you add a small graphic (a one-column map, chart, sidebar, etc.).

Below, however, are several interesting variations. Beware of the first two; they'll show you what happens when the headline fails to cover all the text:

Remember the raw wrap? Here it is again, this time with a mug atop the second leg. This design can look clumsy, but works well in a 2-column layout, to keep headlines from butting when two stories are parked side by side.

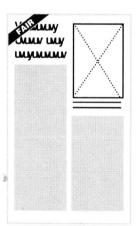

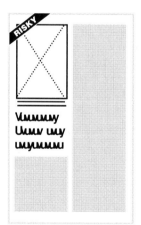

This is a variation of the raw wrap, but only a few papers use it. It's basically a vertical design cut in half, with the bottom half parked alongside the top. The question is: What happens if there's a story above this one?

Half-column mugs (sometimes called *pork-chops)* let you add a mug without wasting much space. These work best in wide bastard legs; the text should be at least 6 picas wide where it wraps around the mug, or it'll be too thin to read.

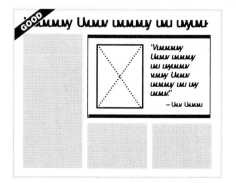

This popular format combines a mug with a liftout quote from the mugee. It's more attractive and more informative than just a mug shot by itself.

TEXT SHAPES

As we've learned, stories should always be shaped into rectangles. That means all four edges of the story should align — or "grid off" — with each other, as in this example:

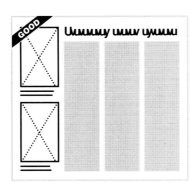

This story is designed into a square-shaped rectangle. The legs are all even lengths, and all outside edges of the story align with each other. It's a clean, well-ordered story design.

This page, by the way, shows you another solution for adding two mugs to a story: putting one atop the other. It's a well-balanced treatment that gives both mugs equal weight.

Beginning designers often find themselves wrenching the text into bizarre shapes as they try to make stories fit. Or they'll choose risky, offbeat designs — like raw wraps — when simpler designs would be better.

One way to keep things clean and controlled is to *watch the shape of your text block.* Some text shapes, as you'll see below, are better than others:

TEXT SHAPES: THE GOOD, THE BAD & THE UGLY

Ranked in descending order, these are the most common text shapes you'll encounter. Arrows trace the reader's eye movement through the text.

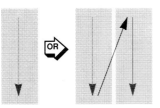

❶ This is the safest shape of all: a rectangle. Whether it's one leg or many, it's very clean: no odd jogs, leaps, wraps or bends.

❷ L-shaped text results when text wraps under a photo. It's still a neat and readable shape.

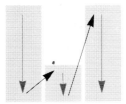

❸ U-shapes break up boring stacks of text, but beware of giant leaps to the top of that far right leg.

❹ These shapes (called *doglegs)* are often inevitable when you dummy around ads. Try to avoid them otherwise, since art placed below text is often mistaken for an ad.

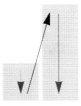

❺ This backward "L" is a risky shape. Readers may think the second leg is where the story starts; besides, that second leg will butt into any leg above it. Be careful.

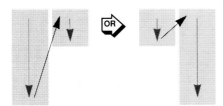

Try to avoid forcing your readers to jump blindly across art, whether it's in the middle of one leg or sandwiched between two legs. It's risky. It's confusing. Beware.

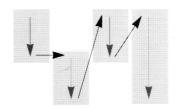

❼ An ugly shape. Anytime your text starts snaking around like this, it means your art is badly scattered. Back up and rearrange things before you lose your readers.

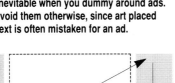

ONE HORIZONTAL PHOTO

The principles of story design are logical and consistent. In fact, if you're careful, you can dummy photos onto pages without ever actually *seeing* the photos. Just stack all the pieces in a clean, pleasing way, and there you are.

That's possible. But it's not recommended. Every photo is unique; every photo needs special consideration before you size it and stick it in a convenient slot. Here, for instance, is a typical photo, along with some typical considerations a designer should make before doing any dummying:

> **MORE ON:**
>
> ■ **Photos:** A complete chapter on cropping, photo spreads, etc....... 81

A FEW FACTS ABOUT THIS PHOTO

❶ In July 1985, photographer Lois Bernstein of The Virginian-Pilot happened upon three bloodied youngsters huddled by the side of the road. The girl, 16, and her two twin 12-year-old brothers had just left the wreckage of their car after smashing into a tree.

The photo caused a stir when it ran in the paper the next day. "Three of my children were still in hospital beds," said the children's father. "I was hurt. I was upset." The family's friends and neighbors accused the paper of using a personal tragedy to sell papers.

Yet the photo is honest and powerful. It later won numerous awards. Would you have chosen to run this photo if you had been in the newsroom that day?

❷ How big should this photo be played? An image this dramatic has maximum impact if it's run 3 or 4 columns wide — in other words, quite a bit bigger than the size shown here. Run larger than that, the photo's grisly content would probably offend some readers; run smaller, the photo's drama and emotion would probably be lost.

❸ For some stories, you need several photos to show readers what happened. Here, for instance, the photographer may also have shot the wrecked car, the tree it collided with, the police at work, and so on. But would additional photos have robbed this shot of its impact? Would they have been necessary — or just padding?

❹ Notice the cropping on this photo. Along the right edge, you can see a hint of a car's bumper; along the bottom, the shoulder of the road. When this photo first ran in the paper, Bernstein cropped it as you see it here. But she now prefers a crop that focuses more tightly on the arms and faces of the children. Which do you prefer?

❺ Many photos are directional — that is, the action in the photo moves strongly left or right and requires that you design the story so the photo faces the text. Here, the children are facing slightly right. But that's not directional enough to matter; the text could be dummied effectively along either side of the photo.

❻ Many design gurus insist that you crop photos into a rectangular shape known as the *golden mean.* This shape — basically 3 X 5, a little shallower than the photo shown here — was discovered by the ancient Greeks, and is often thought to be the most harmonious proportion known to man. Unfortunately, not too many ancient Greeks design newspapers these days. So don't worry too much about golden rectangles — just use the shape that best suits the photo image.

Unlike mug shots — which come in one standard shape and size and are generally interchangeable — full-sized photos require thoughtful analysis. Before you begin designing a story, you must consider each photo's:

■ **Size.** How big must the photo run? (If it's too small, faces and places become undecipherable; too big, and you hog space.) Does the photo gain impact if it's larger? Is there room on the page for jumbo art?

■ **Direction.** Does the action in the photo flow strongly in one direction (someone diving, pointing, throwing a ball)? If so, it's best to design the story so the photo *faces* the text. Photos that seem to move into the wrong story — or off the page — may misdirect your readers.

■ **Effectiveness.** Is one photo enough to tell the story? Is the package more informative with two or more? Or is the photo obvious and expendable — something that could make room for another story?

ONE HORIZONTAL PHOTO

VERTICAL DESIGN OPTIONS

As we've previously seen with stories using mug shots, this vertical layout conforms to the way most readers scan stories. They're attracted by the photo; they read down, through the cutline, into the headline; then, if they're still interested, they read the text.

The main dangers in this design are: 1) keeping elements in the proper order; 2) avoiding long, gray legs of text; and 3) avoiding confusion if you park another story beside the photo (we'll explore this in the next chapter).

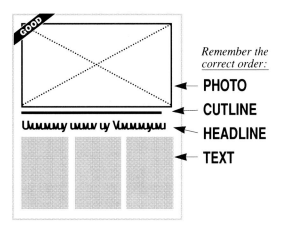

Remember the correct order:

← **PHOTO**
← **CUTLINE**
← **HEADLINE**
← **TEXT**

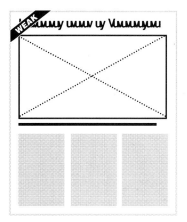

This reliable design will work with nearly any horizontal photo, no matter how deep, wide, or directional it is — as long as all four elements are stacked in the correct order.

When you foul up the sequence of elements — in this case, putting the headline above the photo — you risk confusion. In news stories, the headline should touch the start of the story.

HORIZONTAL DESIGN OPTIONS

As we saw on page 35, the safest shape for text blocks is a rectangle (as opposed to L-shapes, U-shapes, doglegs, etc.) So that makes the examples on this page — both vertical and horizontal — safe, simple solutions.

Whenever you try to square off text beside a photo, you'll probably need to wrestle with photo shapes and story lengths to make the math work out. But remember: Every story is (be careful here) *cuttable*.

IF THE PHOTO FACES RIGHT: Then this is the better solution, since the action of the photo will seem to flow into the text. To anchor this design, however, both the photo and the text block need ample width; the photo should be *at least* two columns wide.

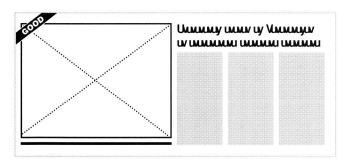

IF THE PHOTO FACES LEFT: Then simply flop the elements so the text is parked on the left. Remember that all elements *must* square off at both the top and the bottom; this design won't work if the text comes up too short.

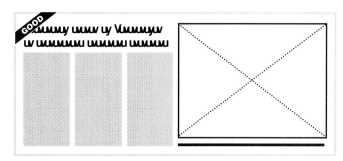

In these two examples, note how the headline runs *beside* the photo, covering only the text. That's the cleanest way to dummy a headline in this format. But you have an alternative design option: running the headline all the way across both the text *and* the photo. The advantages of doing that?

■ It connects the photo to the text more tightly. On busy pages, that's helpful.

■ One long, loud banner headline often gives the story more punch.

■ Since a wide 1-line headline isn't as deep as a 2-line headline, you can squeeze in extra text. That's handy if the story's an inch or two too long.

ONE HORIZONTAL PHOTO

OTHER DESIGN OPTIONS

To a designer's eye, the previous examples are appealing because they're so neatly aligned, so cleanly balanced. Yet these two designs directly below are more common, and perhaps more effective.

The reason? Notice how effectively the headline and text surround the photo to create a self-contained package. There's no way a reader can mistake which story the photo belongs to.

MORE ON:

■ **Raw wraps:** How they help keep headlines from butting................ 62

■ **Feature page designs:** A chapter on special heads and layouts....... 125

This design uses an L-shaped text block to wrap below the photo. If you wanted to play the photo bigger, you could run it 3 columns wide. For longer stories, you could deepen each leg of type — or you could wrap another leg of type along the right side of the photo and extend the headline further.

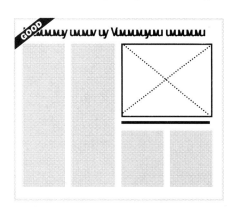

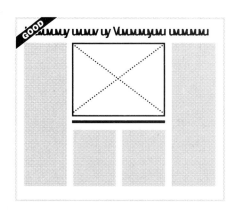

Here, the text wraps around three sides of the photo. Some editors prefer this layout to the one at left because 1) it's symmetrical, and 2) it breaks up those long, gray legs of text more effectively.

Other design options are risky or downright clumsy. Here are several examples to consider — or to avoid altogether:

This, you'll recall, is a raw wrap — where instead of covering the entire story, the headline is parked in a left-hand leg or two. It's not necessarily a *bad* solution. But it's best reserved for times when you're dummying two stories side by side, and you need a way to keep headlines from butting. With a raw wrap, the photo helps you accomplish that.

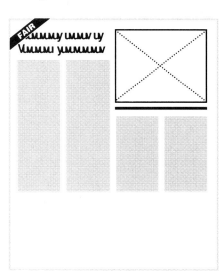

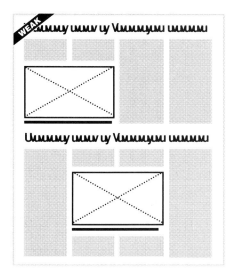

Avoid running photos *below* text. There's too great a danger readers will think the photo's an ad — or that it belongs to a story below. Wrap text *around,* not above, art.

Wrap text *around* art, did we say? Dropping art into the middle of a story destroys the logical flow of text, as readers fumble to figure out which leg goes where. *Never* interrupt a leg of text with a photo.

SWIPEABLE FEATURE FORMATS

These designs are intended for special feature stories. Some of them will need fancy headlines, long decks or text wraps to work effectively.

Very symmetrical. A graceful U-shape centers the headline and deck. A rule below the deck is optional.

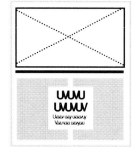

More symmetry. This time, the text wraps around the headline (which could also be enclosed in a box).

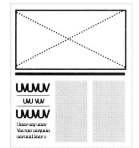

This sidesaddle headline treatment uses short words and a long deck. The text squares off alongside.

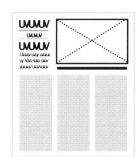

Another sidesaddle headline in a narrow stack. This one squares off beside the photo; the text runs below.

ONE VERTICAL PHOTO

If you understand the design options for horizontal photos, you'll have no problem with verticals. If anything, verticals offer fewer design options than horizontals. They're more dramatic, shape-wise, but it's often difficult to get them to mesh smoothly with their accompanying text.

MORE ON:

■ **Photos:** A complete chapter on cropping, photo spreads, etc....... 81

A FEW FACTS ABOUT THIS PHOTO

❶ This photo of pop songstress Cyndi Lauper was shot in 1987 during a concert in Portland, Ore. Getting a high-quality concert shot of pop superstars is usually a difficult, demanding task. The lighting is poor. Photographers are often forced to stand far away, using telephoto lenses and high-speed, grainy film. And photos are usually allowed only during a few selected songs. No wonder, then, that most concert photos fall a bit flat.

❷ Designers should avoid dictating in advance what photographers should shoot. But here, you know before the concert even starts that you'll want a shot of Cyndi (not the band). Since she's a singer, you'll probably want a dramatic close-up of her while she's singing. And since she doesn't play piano or guitar, you can assume the photo will be vertical. This shot, then, is exactly what the designer — and the readers — would expect.

❸ When the review of this concert ran in The Oregonian, it was the lead element on the Living page, and the photo ran 3 columns wide — a bit wider than shown here. At that size, it had plenty of punch and appeal, and it let the reader study close-up details (such as the mermaid patch on Cyndi's jacket). If space were tight, the photo could have been cropped into a 1-column mug shot.

❹ This photo is slightly directional: Cyndi is belting out her tune toward the right side of the page. Ideally, then, the text would run to the right or underneath the photo.

❺ A photo this dramatic will easily carry the story by itself. For some performers, however, additional photos can enhance the story's appeal by showing other musicians, wild sets, crazily attired crowd members or onstage action (dancing, guitar-bashing, fire-breathing, etc.). Bigger stars deserve bigger spreads.

■ *A word about square photos:* On previous pages, we explored design options using horizontal photos. In the pages ahead, we'll explore options for vertical photos. So what about squares?

Squares, you'll recall, have a reputation for being dull. Many page designers avoid them, though that's overdoing it. But because squares can adapt to all the design options we're showing you, there's no need to give them separate, special treatment. Just modify the principles you've already learned, and you can dummy squares easily and painlessly.

ONE VERTICAL PHOTO

VERTICAL DESIGN OPTIONS

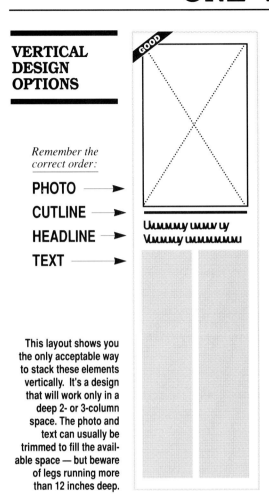

Remember the correct order:

PHOTO ➝

CUTLINE ➝

HEADLINE ➝

TEXT ➝

This layout shows you the only acceptable way to stack these elements vertically. It's a design that will work only in a deep 2- or 3-column space. The photo and text can usually be trimmed to fill the available space — but beware of legs running more than 12 inches deep.

Since vertical photos usually run either 2 or 3 columns wide, that makes them pretty deep — anywhere from 5 to 15 inches deep. Stick a headline and a story below that, and you've got a sleek, dynamic design (if you have enough room for a layout that deep). The only drawback is that it's so far from the top of the photo to the bottom of the story: Will readers get tired — or lost?

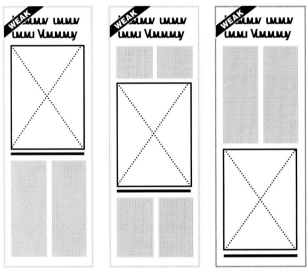

When elements are stacked incorrectly, problems result. Here, we see three basic guidelines ignored. From left to right: 1) The headline should always touch the start of the story. 2) Avoid interrupting any leg of text with an art element. 3) Avoid running art below text.

HORIZONTAL DESIGN OPTIONS

Stacking photos and stories side by side requires careful measurement but creates a graceful design. Note how, in the examples below, the headline covers only the text. (Running a wide headline atop both the photo and the text is a secondary option — see page 37.)

Note, too, how both examples use 2-column photos. A 3-column vertical photo would be extremely deep (8-15 inches). And that could make those legs of text dangerously deep and gray.

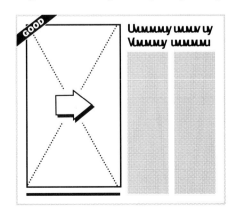

FOR DIRECTIONAL PHOTOS: Try to position the photo on the proper side — whichever side forces the action in the photo to move toward the text . . .

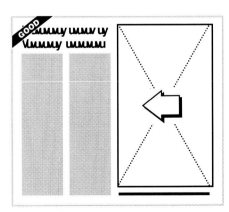

. . . but remember, too, that non-directional photos work well on either side. Your decision should be based on how the overall page fits together.

ONE VERTICAL PHOTO

OTHER DESIGN OPTIONS

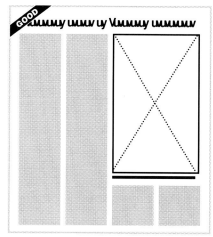

In this L-shaped wrap, all the elements work well together. But consider how deep those left-hand legs could be, especially with a 3-column photo. To break up the gray, designers often dummy a liftout quote into the second leg. That's an easy way to provide graphic relief.

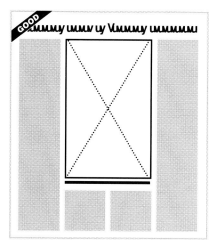

This U-shaped wrap keeps those two long legs of text from merging into one long, gray slab. But beware of two dangers: 1) Those two legs under the photo will look flimsy if they're not deep enough; and 2) It's a long trip from the bottom of the third leg to the top of the fourth.

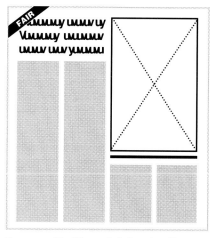

Raw wraps like this one help keep headlines from butting when stories are dummied side by side. But this layout is less graceful than those above. The headline must be huge to keep from being overpowered by the photo and text. If you can, choose a design that holds together better.

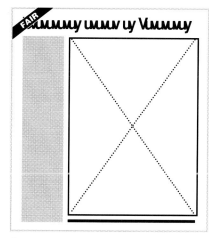

As a rule, news headlines should run above all text — and *only* text. But there are times, especially on Page One, when you need a big photo *and* a big headline to go with it. Running a 1-column head over the text on the left would give you a cleaner design — but a lot less oomph.

SWIPEABLE FEATURE FORMATS

These designs are intended for special feature stories. Some of them need fancy headlines, long decks or liftout quotes to work effectively.

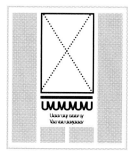

This symmetrical U-shape centers the headline and deck. Box this design if any other stories run nearby.

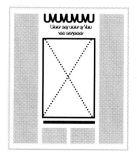

Here, the headline runs *above* the photo. Again, should be boxed to ensure legs won't butt other stories.

A very airy design, and one that can look awkward if all the proportions aren't right. Watch headline, photo size.

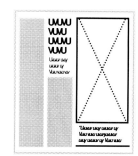

A somewhat risky L-shape, with the headline between the text and photo. A liftout quote could go below the art.

THE DOMINANT PHOTO

Generally speaking, editors and page designers try hard to be fair. That's admirable, right? But as you'll soon discover, some news is more important than others. Some stories are more interesting than others. And some photographs, for one reason or another, are simply *better* than others.

Readers expect their newspapers to make decisions for them: to decide which stories are the biggest, which photos are the best. Readers want editors to *edit* — not just shovel everything onto the page in evenly sized heaps.

Equality, in other words, can be boring. Take a look:

Here you can see what happens when you give every photo equal weight. For one thing, you lose all sense of priority. Who figures prominently in this story? Which characters are most interesting?

But secondly, see how the design suffers? The page is static. Boxy. Tedious. There's no sense of movement because the design isn't guiding your eye anywhere.

This same effect will result anytime you park two or more similarly sized photos anywhere near each other.

Here's a page that plays up certain photos and plays down others. And you can sense the difference immediately: This page has motion. Variety. Impact. We see that some photos are more interesting than others; some of these characters, we assume, are more interesting than others, too.

This principle applies whether there are 2 or 10 photos on the page: *Always make one photo **dominant** — that is, substantially bigger than any competing photo.*

THE DOMINANT PHOTO

CHOOSING A DOMINANT PHOTO

A strong photograph will anchor a story — or a page. Two evenly sized photos side by side, however, will work against each other. They'll compete. They'll clash. Or worse, they'll just sit there in two big, boring lumps.

There are times when photos *may* work better if they're equally sized (a before-and-after comparison, a series of mugs, some frames of time-elapsed events). But usually, you *must* make one photo dominant.

When you evaluate photos to decide which gets bigger play, ask yourself:

■ **Do I *really* need two photos?** Are they that different from each other? Does the story require this extra graphic information? If so, keep asking:

■ **Does one have better content?** Does it capture a key moment of drama? Does it show motion and/or emotion? Does it enhance and explain the story?

■ **Does one have higher readability?** Does it need to be BIG to show faces, details or events? Or will it pack some punch in a smaller space?

■ **Does one have better quality?** Better focus? Exposure? Composition?

■ **Does one have a better shape?** Would I prefer a vertical? A horizontal? A square? Will one shape create a stronger overall design for the story?

Below are four photos from a light news feature we'll call "Hog Farm Holiday." In the pages ahead, we'll pair the photos in different ways to create different story designs. But which makes the best *lead* (dominant) photo?

MORE ON:

■ **Dominant photos:** Using art to visually anchor a page design.........**65**

■ **Photos:** A complete chapter on cropping, photo spreads, etc........ **81**

It's not every day you see a girl riding a pig (left). That's a memorable image, one that's bound to arouse readers' curiosity. It's probably the stronger of the two verticals, since it also shows more of the barnyard than any other photo. The baby pigs (below) are cute, and provide our only look at animals minus the humans. It doesn't read as well as the other photos when it's run small, however.

This image of a man nuzzling a pig (above) is an attention-getter with immediate impact. It's certainly stronger than the other horizontal (far right, bottom), though it shows us less of the barnyard than the other shots do. The photo of the farmer (right) is his only appearance in these four shots. And though this photo's not as engaging as the other vertical, it would be a good choice for a secondary photo if the farmer plays an important role in the story.

BIG VERTICAL, SMALL HORIZONTAL

Suppose you choose to use these two photos to accompany your story. The girl riding the pig will be your dominant (or lead) photo; the guy nuzzling the pig is secondary. Since neither is strongly directional, you have some flexibility in placement.

In the examples below, we'll show you the most common designs for news pages (as well as swipeable feature layouts). We can't show you every possible solution, so feel free to explore other options.

DESIGN OPTIONS

Here's what you get when you stack the photos vertically:

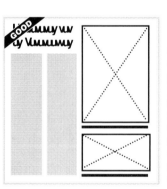

Putting the lead photo directly above the secondary photo (left) is a good, clean solution — provided the story is long enough. Putting the smaller photo on top (right) is OK when it's a before-and-after sequence: the setup, then the punchline. But it's usually best to lead with your strongest image.

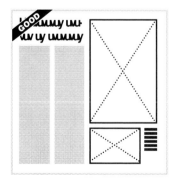

Here, the photos share a cutline, and the shapes become less blocky, less tightly packed than the example above. Note that the cutline goes to the *outside* of the story. For longer stories, the text wraps below the photos, and the headline then extends...

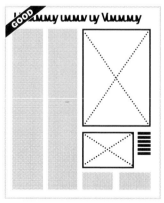

...across the additional two columns. The danger here, however, is that those two left-hand legs of text are getting awfully deep. A liftout quote in the second leg would help...

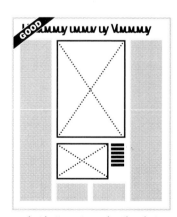

...but better yet, moving the photos into the middle two legs creates a U-shaped text block that's not nearly as gray-looking. The question remains: Is it too high a jump to that last leg?

BIG VERTICAL, SMALL HORIZONTAL

MORE ON:

■ **Feature page designs:** A chapter on special heads and layouts........**125**

MORE DESIGN OPTIONS

*Here's what you get when you stack the photos **horizontally**:*

The biggest problem with those preceding examples was *space* — having enough depth on the page to stack the photos on top of each other, and having enough text to square off alongside.

The examples below extend horizontally and are a bit more flexible:

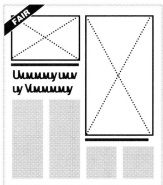

This layout works only with text short enough to square off along the bottom edge of the lead photo. If that horizontal photo were narrower, a joint cutline could go *between* the two photos.

Stack the photos side by side *this* way and what do you get? A raw wrap. Not bad — the whole package seems to hold together pretty well. Still, look for better options before using this one.

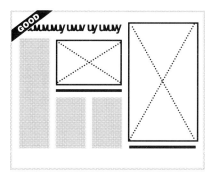

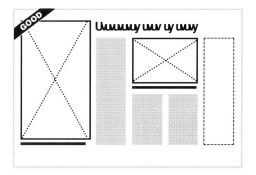

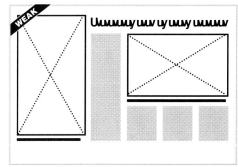

This is probably the most common design option for a big vertical, small horizontal (as long as the lead photo isn't too directional to the right). The text is L-shaped; everything is dummied to the left of the dominant photo. . .

. . . or, for longer stories (or if the lead photo is strongly directional to the right), the whole design can be flopped. The text is still L-shaped. If needed, you can add an additional leg to the text and extend the headline one more column, as well.

Remember: You *must* keep the sizes of the two photos properly balanced. Here, the secondary photo is played too big and starts to compete with the lead photo. Note, too, that this sort of L-shaped text — one tall leg, several squat ones — isn't always graceful.

SWIPEABLE FEATURE FORMATS

These designs are intended for special feature stories. Some of them will need fancy headlines, long decks or text wraps to work effectively.

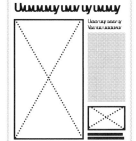

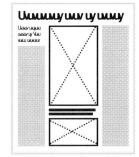

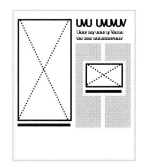

A 1-column photo is OK if the leg is set wide like this one. And if the story's boxed or at the bottom of the page, the photo can go below the text.

We've previously warned you not to let art separate legs of text. But if the story is boxed and the design is symmetrical, this sometimes works.

Centering the small photo above the lead creates room on the left side for a joint cutline and room on the right for a headline/deck combination.

This wraparound text treatment lets you run the smaller photo a column-and-a-half wide. You'll need extra time to make this come together.

BIG HORIZONTAL, SMALL VERTICAL

With a different pair of photos — the pig-smooching close-up as lead art, the pig-riding shot as secondary art — you create an appealing package focusing more on the people than the barnyard. And since neither photo is strongly directional, you'll have plenty of freedom in positioning the art.

As on previous pages, the designs below represent some common solutions for pairing these two photos. Studying them will give you sense of how some design principles work — and why others *don't*.

DESIGN OPTIONS

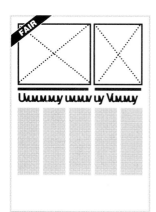

If you have enough width, you can stack the photos horizontally. Note that the photos are exactly 3 and 2 columns wide here, squaring off with the text legs below. This looks OK, but it's a bit blocky, and the cutlines butt.

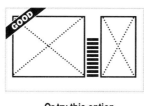

Or try this option instead: Keep the photo heights the same, but crop them so they share one thin cutline between them (it should be at least 6 picas wide).

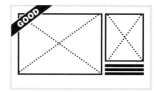

Or here, the depths of the photos vary, and the cutline runs below the shallower photo. Ideally, the bottom of the cutline should square off with the bottom of the lead photo.

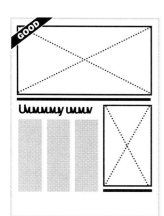

A clean, common layout. All the elements square off neatly. And note that the smaller photo could go on *either* side of the page.

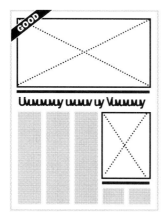

For longer stories, the text can wrap below the smaller photo, with a wider headline. That photo could go in the middle legs, if you prefer.

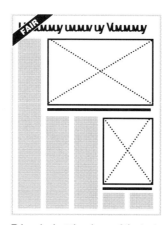

Take a look at the shape of the text: a stairstep, with a mile-high first leg. For a long story, this layout would work in a 5-column format. . .

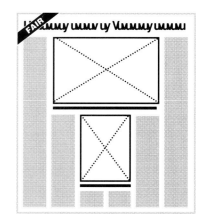

. . . and in a 6-column format, you could try this version, which is symmetrical and almost elegant. But the outside legs are awfully steep, and the text shape is odd.

BIG HORIZONTAL, SMALL VERTICAL

RAW WRAPS

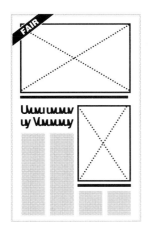

Compare these two designs with the two middle patterns at the bottom of page 46. Which seem cleanest-looking? The only difference is that these use raw-wrap headlines. If you wanted to use a display headline — or if you needed to avoid a long horizontal head — then these are preferable. Otherwise, beware the awkward text wrap.

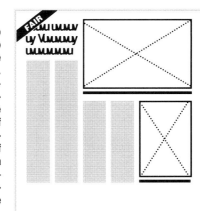

MORE ON:

■ **Raw-wrap head-lines:** Using them to keep headlines from butting..............62

■ **Mortises and insets:** Guidelines for overlapping photos.............. 135

ONE-COLUMN VERTICAL PHOTOS

As a rule, mug shots are the only photos that consistently work in a one-column size. And horizontals almost *never* "read" (i.e., show details clearly) when they're that small. But on occasion — when space is tight, or you just want to squeeze in a bit more art — you can run a vertical photo one column wide instead of two. Just make sure the photo *reads:*

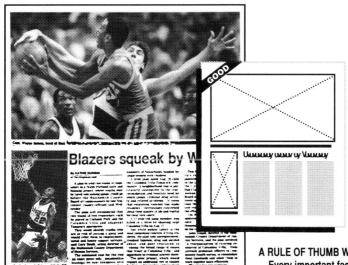

Blazers squeak by W

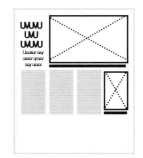

In this layout, the lead photo from the basketball game runs 4 columns wide. A small detail shot, extremely vertical, runs in 1 column. That's awfully small, but in a tight space it lets you squeeze in an extra photo — as long as that photo contains a clean, uncluttered image.

A RULE OF THUMB WORTH REMEMBERING: Every important face in every photo should be *at least* the size of a dime.

SWIPEABLE FEATURE FORMATS

These designs are intended for special feature stories. Some of them will need fancy headlines, long decks or text wraps to work effectively.

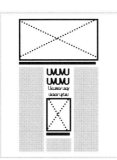

A very vertical, symmetrical design. A narrow head and deck are centered in 3 wide bastard legs. This layout...

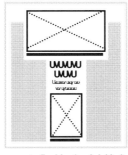

... gets flashier (and riskier) if you wrap text around the top photo and create a blind jump over the center leg.

A sidesaddle headline (with deck) creates a neat, logical design. But box this layout or keep other stories away.

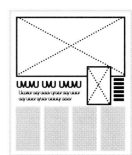

A new twist: mortising the small photo on top of the dominant photo. The head then fills in alongside.

TWO VERTICALS

Always try to vary both the sizes and *shapes* of the photos you use. Though there's nothing wrong with dummying two verticals together, you'll see in the layouts below that your options are limited — and less than ideal.

DESIGN OPTIONS

Stacking vertical photos vertically is a problem. Whether the dominant photo's on top or not, you end up with an extremely deep design that hogs space, makes the text legs too deep and creates too much dead space below the cutline. As we saw earlier, 3-column vertical photos are tricky to deal with.

Stacking the two photos side by side is an appealing solution: tight, attractive, cleanly rectangular. Two slight problems: 1) It's difficult to size the photos *and* the headline so that they all square off cleanly; and 2) Note that the headline is an odd new variation: though not exactly a raw wrap, it doesn't extend across the full text width.

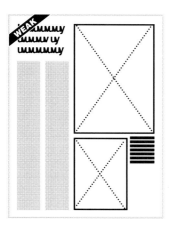 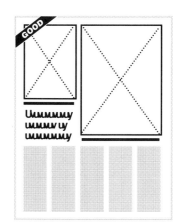 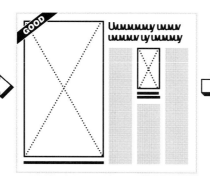 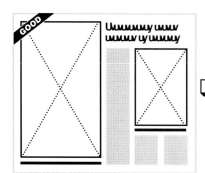 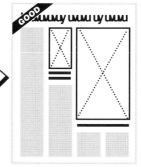 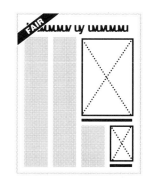

A versatile and common solution, provided the text squares off evenly. You could also flop this layout and dummy the lead photo to the right of the smaller photo. Or. . .

. . . that secondary photo could be reduced to 1-column size — but only if it reads well that small. At that size, it could be dummied into either of the two right-hand legs. . .

. . . or the two photos could trade places. Note that here, we've run the lead photo 2 columns wide instead of 3.

Using a 1-column secondary photo, you could stack them vertically, like this — though the text legs are a bit long.

TWO VERTICALS

MORE ON:

■ **Boxed stories:**
How they work and
when to use
them....................60

■ **Bad juxtaposi-
tions:** How they
happen and how to
avoid them...........76

■ **Mortises and
insets:** Guidelines
for overlapping
photos.............. 135

BOXING STORIES

Designing stories into rectangular shapes (also called *modular* design, since pages consist of movable, interrelated modules) is an attractive way to create well-ordered pages — as long as you follow the rules.

But even when you follow all the rules, confusion occasionally results from a bad juxtaposition of elements. Especially when you dummy text alongside a large vertical photograph. See for yourself:

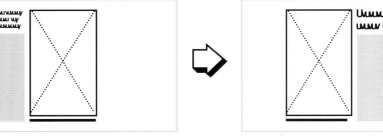

❶ Here's a simple and common story design: a big vertical photo with the text running vertically down the left side. So far, there's no problem, no confusion.

❷ Here's another common design: This time, it's a story dummied to the right of a big vertical photo. And again, it's a clean, correct layout. No problems yet.

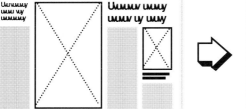
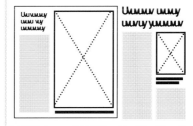

❸ But if you saw *this* page in a news-paper, how would you decide which story goes with the big vertical photo? The layout works either way. You'd have to scan both stories, then try to decide.

❹ The solution? Box one of the stories, preferably the one that deserves spe-cial emphasis. That way, all the elements in the package are bound together as a unit, and readers are less likely to be misdirected.

Later on, we'll look more closely at guidelines for boxing stories. But for now, be aware that your story designs may seem quite simple and obvious to you — but quite ambiguous and confusing to your readers.

SWIPEABLE FEATURE FORMATS

These designs are intended for special feature stories. Some of them will need fancy head-lines, long decks or text wraps to work effectively.

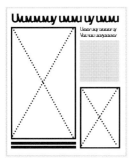

A wide headline, a photo at the bottom, a small amount of text: It's risky, but will work if boxed or run at the bottom of the page.

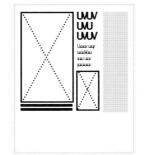

This odd design puts three vertical stacks side by side: 1) lead art and joint cutline; 2) sidesaddle head, deck and small photo; 3) text.

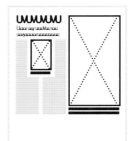

Another 1-column second-ary photo. But here, the photo is centered between the two columns, and the text wraps around it.

This design insets the small photo over the corner of the lead photo and fills in the other elements from there. Beware — this one's risky.

TWO HORIZONTALS

Pairing two horizontal photos is more common — and a bit less limiting — than pairing two verticals. Remember, however, that it's important to vary the shapes of the photos you use. So avoid running two horizontals together if a better combination is available.

Which of these two photos should be dominant? Most designers would choose the guy nuzzling the piglet, since it's more appealing and better composed. Keep in mind, however, that the second photo — the row of piglets — won't read if it's too small (as you see it here, it's about a column-and-a-half wide). That means it *must* run at least two columns wide.

DESIGN OPTIONS

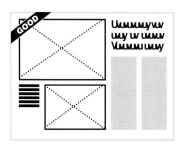

Stacking the photos vertically works well. Note the shared cutline; there's a danger of wasted white space in the lower left corner if that bottom photo is too narrow or if the cutline is too short.

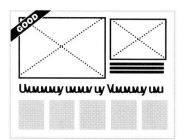

Stacking the photos horizontally also works well. A shared cutline like this will generally butt tightly against both photos. It's OK if it comes up a bit short, but aligning tightly is better.

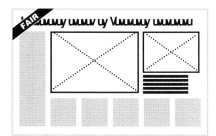

Stacking the photos horizontally works well in this configuration, too -- though you need the full width of a 6-column page for this layout. Note how we've indented the cutline a half-column to add some white space.

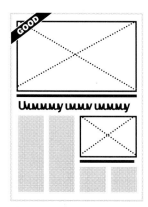

Another common solution. The smaller photo is dummied into the upper-right corner of an L-shaped text block. . .

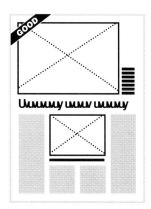

. . . or here, the smaller photo is centered. Note the cutline treatment for the lead photo, an option offering more flexibility.

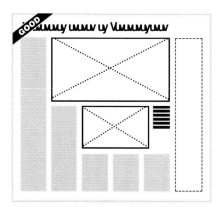

Again, you see the added flexibility of sharing a cutline: in this case, the smaller photo can be 2-3 columns wide. You also have the option of adding another leg of text along the far right.

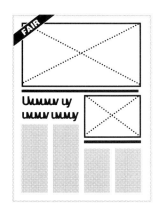

This raw-wrap headline treatment is acceptable, but not preferable. Use it if you're avoiding a horizontal headline.

TWO HORIZONTALS

SOME ODD OPTIONS — & WHY THEY DON'T WORK

Throughout this chapter, we've offered common solutions to common design situations. If we wanted to, we could easily fill several pages with rejects — designs which, for one reason or another, are too ugly to print.

Instead, we'll take a moment here to analyze a few close calls. These layouts are well-intentioned, but still wrong enough to be avoided.

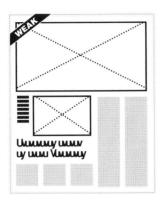

This layout illustrates the basic problem with text shaped like a backward "L": Too many readers won't know where the story starts. Even if the headline ran horizontally between the two photos, your eye would ignore those short legs on the left and assume the story starts in that fourth column.

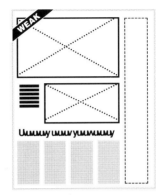

Here's a design with a very subtle flaw— it gives us a package in two totally independent chunks: a photo chunk at the top and a story chunk below. Since it's so far down to the story, the elements just don't work together. In fact, those photos could mistakenly be paired with any story running in an adjacent column.

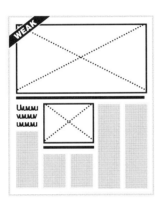

There are two things wrong with this design: 1) The headline is too small, thin and insignificant (a very unnecessary raw wrap). 2) Too many readers will think the story starts to the right of that second photo. Remember: Readers often assume that the *tallest* leg is the one that starts the story.

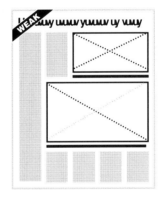

Here's a configuration that looks magazine-y, somehow. But in newspapers, you're smart to avoid confusing layouts like this. Where does the reader go at the end of that first leg: under the big photo, or all the way back up to the top? This is the risk you take whenever art interrupts the flow of the text.

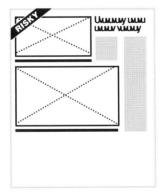

With the right photos in the right place on the right page, this design might look pretty hip. But as a rule, resist the temptation to run photos *under* text or to run the dominant photo *under* the secondary photo. It might work on features — especially if they're boxed — but be careful with hard news.

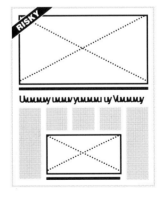

Here's another layout that would seem at home in a magazine. It might even work, boxed, on a feature page. But for most news stories, avoid dummying photos at the bottom of a story. Readers assume that that's an ad position. Or that any photo parked below one story belongs to the next story. Why risk confusing readers if you don't have to?

SWIPEABLE FEATURE FORMATS

These designs are intended for special feature stories.

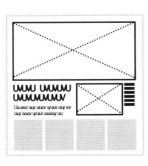

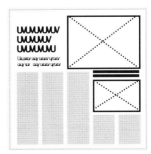

Here are three variations of the same idea: Put the small photo below the lead, then square off the headline beside one of the photos. All three will work, depending on the headline wording and photo cropping.

ADDING MUG SHOTS

Most of the photos you'll dummy with news stories will be *live* (meaning they're timely and unstaged). Mug shots, on the other hand, are *canned* (that is, shot at some neutral time and place, then put in the can — stored — until you need them).

And though it's a good idea to add mug shots to stories whenever possible, try not to confuse the reader by mixing live and canned photos. Add mugs — but dummy them slightly apart from news photos, as a signal to readers.

Also, consider adding liftout quotes to mugs whenever possible. Combining someone's face with his words connects him to the story, provides extra commentary, and creates a graphic hook to attract more readers.

MORE ON:

■ **Mug shots:** Tips for dummying them with stories......... 32

■ **Liftout quotes:** How to design and dummy them effectively............... 114

With a big vertical photo, text usually runs alongside. An added mug — or mugs — can be dummied at the top of any leg except the first. In this case, a liftout quote was added alongside the mug (assuming that the quote is either *by* or *about* the person pictured).

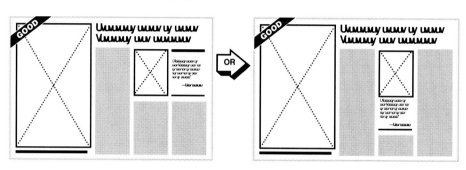

Here, the quote runs below, rather than beside, the mug shot. Either way is acceptable. An additional mug shot — with its own lift quote — could even be parked alongside this one.

With a big horizontal photo, the text will usually run underneath. The most logical spot for a mug shot (with or without an added lift quote) is in one of the middle legs, to help break up the repetitive grayness of the text.

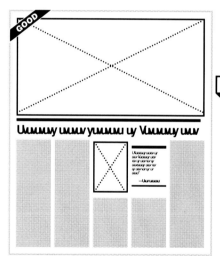

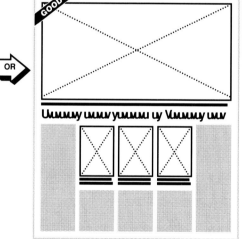

If appropriate, two or three mugs can run alongside each other at the top of those middle legs of text. Those mugs, all evenly sized, work together as a unit. And the headline helps distance them from the live photo at the top of the story.

With a dominant vertical and a secondary horizontal, a mug can be dummied into the far corner of the text. Note how this layout helps distance the mug from the two live photos. And even with this growing number of elements, the whole story holds together as a unit.

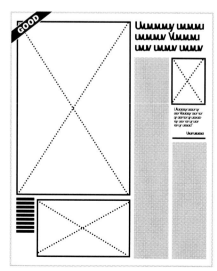

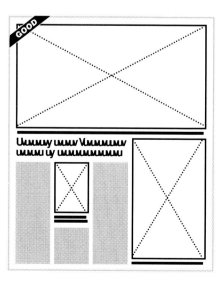

With a dominant horizontal and secondary vertical, you can, as in the examples above, add a mug in the middle leg. Again, in this design the two live photos are dummied tightly together, while the mug is kept separate by either the headline or text.

EXERCISES

Designing newspaper pages is like playing the piano: You can't learn how to do it simply by reading a book. You've got to practice.

Doing these exercises gives you a chance to practice what you've learned so far. If you want to use a dummy sheet, you can trace or copy the sample dummy on page 24.

Exercise answers are on page 164.

1 What are your two best options for dummying a 5-inch story without any art? How would you code the headline for each option if it were dummied at the top of Page One? At the bottom of an inside page?

2 You've got a 9-inch story with one mug shot (assume your newspaper runs its mug shots 3 inches deep). What are your three best options for dummying this story? Will this story work in a 3-column format?

3 Here's a layout that uses two mug shots. There are several things wrong with it. How many problems can you identify?

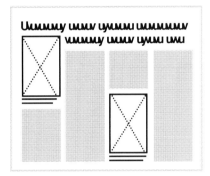

4 Today has been a busy news day, and your top story is a 12-inch piece about a fire that destroyed this man's home. Here's the photo that accompanies that story:

■ HINT: As printed here, this photo is 29 picas wide and 17.5 picas deep. Assuming you work at a paper where columns are roughly 12 picas wide, here's how deep this photo would be if it were sized for:
• 1 column: 7.3 picas
• 2 columns: 15 picas
• 3 columns: 23 picas
• 4 columns: 31 picas
• 5 columns: 38.5 picas
• 6 columns: 47 picas
For more on sizing photos by using a proportion wheel, see page 92.

There are a number of ways you could dummy this story for a 6-column broadsheet newspaper. But which would you recommend?

EXERCISES

5 Here are two photos from last night's Springsteen concert. The editor wants you to run them both. Which one should be the dominant photo?

The review that accompanies these photos is 20 inches long. There's space on the Arts page for a deep layout that's 5 columns wide. What's your strongest design if you use the horizontal photo as dominant art? If you use the vertical?

To make this exercise easier, don't worry about sizing these photos exactly. Instead, dummy them using their rough shapes and assume you can crop them slightly to fit the layout that works best.

6 What's wrong with each of these news story designs?

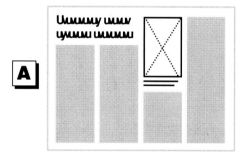

A

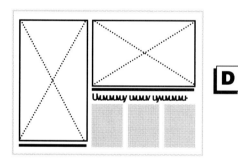

D

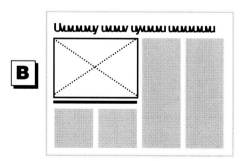

B

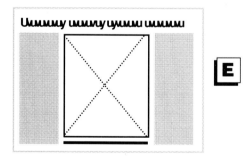

E

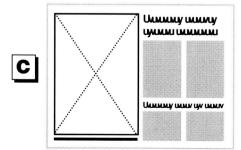

C

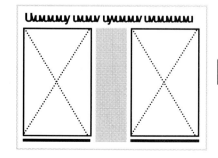

F

Exercise answers are on page 166.

Newspaper trends come and go. What's hip today will probably look hopelessly out-of-date in a decade or two. Tastes change; newsroom philosophies change, too.

The same goes for theories of page design. Some design experts once insisted that the upper-left corner is a page's prime position, and that you should put your top story there. Others claimed that the upper *right* corner is the best-read spot on the page, and that you should put your best story *there*. Still others advised putting *strong* elements in *weak* positions (like the bottom corners) to ensure that readers will read all over the place.

Confusing, isn't it? Forget what the experts say, then, and remember this: Readers will look where you *want* them to look. If you know what you're doing, you can create a page that's logical, legible and fun to read — and you can guide the reader's eye wherever you choose.

This chapter explores current principles and techniques of page design. Now that you've looked at stories as independent units — modules — we can begin examining ways you can stack those modules together to form attractive, well-balanced pages.

Once you understand how these principles work, you can adapt them to any pages you design — whatever the style of those pages.

CHAPTER CONTENTS

■ **Broadsheet formats:** Basic page and column configurations for broadsheets.......................56

■ **Tabloid formats:** Basic page and column configurations for tabloids.....................................57

■ **Pages without art:** Designing pages using only headlines and text. With sections on butting headlines, boxing stories, bastard measures, raw wraps and alternative headline treatments.......58-63

■ **Pages with art:** Designing pages using photos. With sec- tions on dominant photos, balanc- ing and scattering art, and butting headlines............................. 64-65

■ **Modules and modular design:** A look at one well- designed page — and what hap- pens when you rearrange the story modules..................... 66-67

■ **Page One design:** Some examples of well-designed broad- sheet and tabloid front pages... 68

■ **Flow chart, Page One design:** A step-by-step guide to the design process.................. 69

■ **Making stories fit:** What to do when a story comes up long or short................................... 70-71

■ **Inside pages:** Working with ads to create pages............. 72-73

■ **Double trucks:** Special lay- outs for facing pages.......... 74-75

■ **Bad juxtapositions:** How to keep story modules from colliding and overlapping....................... 76

■ **Rules of thumb:** A quick guide to layout principles................... 77

■ **Exercises**............................ 78

BROADSHEET FORMATS

When you start thinking about designing full pages, the first question you need to ask is: What size page will I be working with?

Newspapers, you'll recall, come in two basic sizes: broadsheet and tabloid. Many designers prefer broadsheets because there's more room to play in (they're twice the size of tabloids). They can use more stories, bigger photos, more expansive headline treatments. And color is more often available.

Virtually all broadsheets now use a 6-column format (especially on inside pages). But page formats change from paper to paper, often from page to page, depending on each paper's philosophy and personality. For instance:

Most broadsheets use a 6-column format throughout the paper — including Page One. Each leg is 12.2 picas, though some stories may use bastard widths.

Years ago, most papers used 8 or 9 narrow columns on Page One. Today, The Daily Oklahoman is one of the few papers still using an 8-column format.

In this 5-column format, the left-hand leg is used for promos and briefs. This format is usually limited to section fronts and special pages; inside pages use 6 columns.

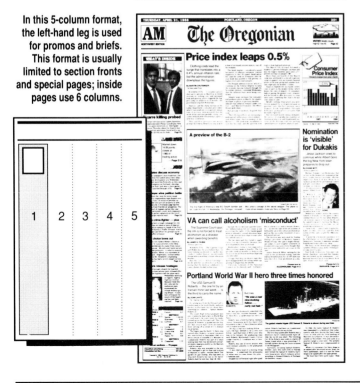

This page is a carefully calculated 7-column format that can accept only minor changes day to day. Note how those 2 left-hand legs become 1 wide column of briefs.

TABLOID FORMATS

Though big-city dailies are usually broadsheets, many other papers — including weeklies, student newspapers and special-interest journals — prefer the advantages of the tabloid format:

■ Their smaller size makes tabs easier to produce and cheaper to print.

■ They're popular with readers — handier, less bulky, faster to scan.

■ Editors and advertisers find that their stories and ads can dominate a page more effectively than in a broadsheet.

■ It's easier to create separate sections (sports, features, opinion) in a tighter space.

Tabloids are roughly half the size of broadsheets. If you took broadsheet paper, turned it sideways and folded it, you'd create two tabloid pages:

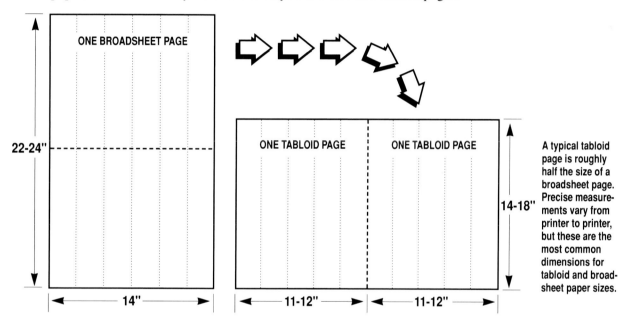

ONE BROADSHEET PAGE

22-24"

14"

ONE TABLOID PAGE   ONE TABLOID PAGE

14-18"

11-12"   11-12"

A typical tabloid page is roughly half the size of a broadsheet page. Precise measurements vary from printer to printer, but these are the most common dimensions for tabloid and broadsheet paper sizes.

Like broadsheets, tabloids come in a variety of design formats. Some tabs use 4 columns to a page — most, however, prefer the 5-column format, since it offers more design flexibility and conforms to most common ad sizes:

This is an opinion page from The Minnesota Daily. It uses a 4-column format. Elsewhere inside the paper, a 5-column format is used to conform to ad sizes. (Note the placement of the art within the atheism story.)

This is an open inside page from The Christian Science Monitor. It uses a 5-column format. On special themed pages like this one, the Monitor uses that first column for liftout quotes, lists, small pieces of art — or simply leaves it blank.

PAGES WITHOUT ART

NOTE:

Throughout this chapter, all of our examples of page design — like the one below — use a 5-column broadsheet format. In other words, these examples will have the shape and depth of a broadsheet page, but (like many tabloids) will have 5, not 6, columns.

Until now, we've looked at different ways of designing *stories*. Now, we're ready to design *pages*. And a well-designed page is really nothing more than an attractive-looking stack of stories. Sounds simple, right?

So we'll start simply. With just text — no photos. That way, you'll be able to see that, with or without art, you build a good page by fitting rectangles together with as much order, balance and variety as you can.

In the old days, they built pages by stacking stories side by side in deep vertical rows. Today, the trend is more horizontal, and it's possible to build pages in long, horizontal rows (as in the example below). Simple as it is, a page like this works pretty effectively:

MORE ON:

■ **Headlines and headline sizes:** A quick guide for both broadsheet and tabloid..................16

■ **Designing pages with art:** Guidelines for adding photos to gray pages like this one.......................64

■ **Inside pages:** Creating modular designs, working with ads.......................72

This page layout is simple, but it still observes some basic design principles:

■ **STORY PLACEMENT:** The strongest story goes at the top of the page. By "strong," we're referring to news value, impact or appeal. As you move down the page, stories become less significant.

■ **HEADLINE SIZING:** Page position dictates headline size. The lead story will have the biggest headline; headlines then get smaller as you move down the page.

■ **STORY SHAPES:** As we've already learned, stories should be shaped like rectangles. And here, you can see how keeping stories rectangular keeps pages neat and well-organized. Whether stories are stacked vertically or horizontally, whether they use art or not, that principle always applies on open pages like this. (Later on, when we look at inside pages with ads, you'll see it's not always this easy to keep stories rectangular.)

The design of this page is clean, but its impact on the reader is probably weak. Why? It's too gray. There's nothing to stop the reader's eye. The only contrast comes from the headlines.

In a perfect newspaper, every story would have some sort of art: a photo, a chart, a map or — at the very least — a liftout quote. In reality, though, actually *producing* that much art would take a colossal amount of work and might actually be too distracting for readers.

A better rule of thumb is: *Make every page at least one-third art.* In other words, when you add up all the photos, graphics, teasers and display type on a page, they should take up at least a third of the total real estate. Some pages should use even more art than that (sports, features, photo spreads).

There are times, however, when photos just don't exist. When there are no quotes to lift. When there's no time — or no artist — to add a chart or graph. Your page may be gray, but it doesn't have to be bland. Instead of simply stacking stories in rows (as in the example above), you can add variety by:

■ **Butting headlines.**

■ **Boxing stories.**

■ **Using bastard measures.**

■ **Using raw wraps and alternative headline treatments.**

In the pages ahead, we'll see how these techniques work on pages without art.

PAGES WITHOUT ART

BUTTING HEADLINES

Pilot Gridsters Set for Pacific at Stadium Today

Pilot Pulverizer—the Zenner Man

OPENING KICKOFF SLATED FOR 2:30

FISCHER, M'LEAN PLAY FOR TITLE

Missing Bearcats Arrive at Salem; Prospects Bright

BEAVERS CLINCH SEATTLE PLAYOFF

MORE ON:

■ **Headlines:** Fonts, sizes and determining number of lines................17

■ **Butting heads:** How to avoid them by using photos and raw wraps............65

Ugly heads can be dangerous. And it took newspapers years to figure out how to slap headlines onto every story without making them collide in a chaotic jumble (as in the example above). Up until the 1960s, most newspapers ran vertical rules in the gutters between stories. And when their headlines stacked alongside each other, they looked like tombstones (hence the term *tombstoning,* another name for narrow, butting heads).

For years now, the First Commandment of Page Design has been: *Never bump headlines.* That's good advice. When one headline reads into another, this is the sort of confusion that can result:

Princess Diana meets pope at Dover Beach

By Robin Fox/ **The Times**

Frisbee title-holder to challenge record

By John Hamlin/ **The Times**

Occasionally, though, you'll want to park two stories alongside each other. When you do, their heads may butt. But you can minimize the damage by:

■ **Mixing styles, fonts or sizes.** The idea here is: If headlines butt, make them *very* dissimilar. If one is boldface, make the other light or italic. If one is a large, 1-line horizontal, make the other a small, 3-line vertical.

■ **Writing short.** Let a little air separate the two headlines. That means the headline on the left should be written a few counts short, just to be safe.

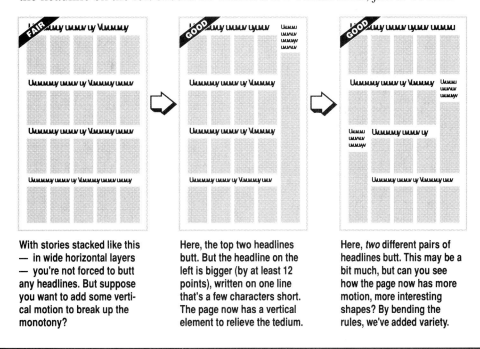

With stories stacked like this — in wide horizontal layers — you're not forced to butt any headlines. But suppose you want to add some vertical motion to break up the monotony?

Here, the top two headlines butt. But the headline on the left is bigger (by at least 12 points), written on one line that's a few characters short. The page now has a vertical element to relieve the tedium.

Here, *two* different pairs of headlines butt. This may be a bit much, but can you see how the page now has more motion, more interesting shapes? By bending the rules, we've added variety.

PAGES WITHOUT ART

BOXING STORIES

Another way to break up monotonous gray page patterns is by boxing stories. As we saw on page 49, putting a box around a story (with a photo) is one way to keep readers from getting confused by ambiguous designs:

MORE ON:

■ **Bad juxtapositions:** How they happen and how to avoid them..........76

■ **Rules and boxes:** Where (and where not) to use them..................121

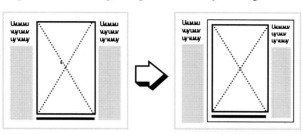

Which story does this photo belong to? Hard to tell; you'd have to scan the stories and the cutline to figure it out.

If you put a box around the story and its photo, you join them into one package — and avoid confusing readers.

Boxing a story is also a way to give it visual emphasis. It's a way of saying to the reader, "This story is *different* from the others; it's *special.*"

Don't box a story just because you're bored with a page and you need to snazz it up. Or because you want to add extra air between two butting heads.

Instead, save boxes for when you need extra emphasis for:

■ A light feature on a page that's full of hard news.

■ Small sidebars that are attached to bigger stories.

■ Standing columns (news briefs, opinion, etc.) that appear regularly.

■ Stories with risky or complicated designs whose elements might otherwise bump into *other* stories and confuse the reader.

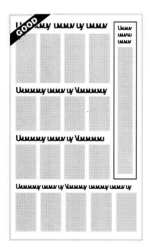

Boxing this long vertical story breaks up the monotony of the page and says to the reader, "This story is different." Give this treatment, then, *only* to special stories or columns.

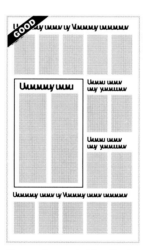

Here, we've created the effect of two lead stories on one page: one across the top and one that's boxed. See how these story shapes move your eye around the page?

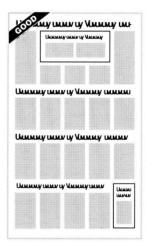

At the top, we've boxed the lead story's sidebar — and it's obvious that the two stories work together as a unit. At the bottom, we've given a graphic nudge to a small feature.

Whenever you put text inside a box, you'll need to calculate the width of the columns inside it. To figure out how wide those legs should be:

1) **Measure** the width of the box (in picas);

2) **Decide** how many legs of text you want inside the box;

3) **Subtract** 1 pica for each gutter inside the box (including the two gutters on the outside edges); and

4) **Divide** by the number of legs.

PAGES WITHOUT ART

OK, stop snickering. Bastard measures are *serious* typographic devices. They're handy, too — especially when you need extra flexibility in sizing photos. (More on this later.)

As we've already seen, most papers use a fixed number of columns on each page. Bastard measures let you deviate from the standard text width:

MORE ON:

■ **Bastard mea-sures:** How they add extra flexibility in sizing art...........**71**

At left is a broadsheet page using a 5-column format, where each leg is roughly 14.5 picas wide. If you changed the number of legs in each story, you'd have these bastard widths instead:

3 legs of 25 picas
(rounded off)

4 legs of 18 picas
(rounded off)

6 legs of 12 picas
(rounded off)

7 legs of 10 picas
(rounded off)

Bastard measures give graphic emphasis to a story by breaking it out of the rigid page grid. (In the above left example, see how the columns and gutters create a strict vertical grid?) Changing text widths is a subtle but effective way — like boxing — to show that a story is special or different:

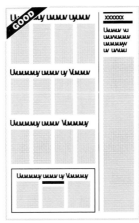

A good combination: a box with a bastard measure. This adds emphasis to the lead story and helps set it apart. The page is orderly; the relative news value of each story is clear.

A wider measure can enhance a columnist or other special piece (right column and bottom). Note, too, how the cutoff rule helps to separate that right column from the other stories.

Notice how confusing too many unnecessary bastard measures can be. Why create two competing lead stories? Why run that bottom story in wide legs? In short: Don't overdo it.

Bastard measures destroy the overall column grid on a page — which can be either good (relieving monotony) or bad (creating chaos). Some papers don't allow any bastard measures; some allow them only when a story is boxed. Like any tool, bastard legs can cause damage if used carelessly.

A warning about something that should be obvious by now: *Never change column widths within a story.* Widths may change from story to story, from page to page — but once you start a story in a certain measure, every leg of that story on that page must be the same width. No cheating.

PAGES WITHOUT ART

RAW WRAPS

Raw wraps let you park two stories side by side *without* butting their headlines. But use them with caution. They work only at the top of a page or beneath a boxed story; otherwise, as you'll see in the example below, they'll collide with other columns of text and confuse your readers:

Here's our typical photoless page again. You can see how this raw-wrapped headline adds variety to the story shapes. But see how the second leg of that raw-wrapped story runs right into the bottom of the leg above it? That's the danger of raw-wrapping stories in the middle of the page.

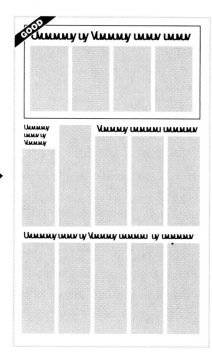

A better combination. Here, the lead story is boxed in a bastard measure. That gives it extra emphasis while staggering the column alignment, making it unlikely that readers will get misdirected. You *could* box the raw-wrapped story instead, but remember: Save boxes for stories whose content is special. Don't use boxes to salvage weak designs.

MORE ON:

■ **Types of head-lines:** A summary of non-standard options.................15

■ **Raw wraps:** How to use them with photos to keep headlines from butting.................65

OPTIONAL HEADLINE TREATMENTS

No one ever said that all headlines must look the same. Adding variety to your headlines will add life to your page designs. But don't overdo it. Save special headline treatments for special stories. If you use more than one offbeat headline on a page, their styles may clash and you'll lose the impact.

At the top of the page: a raw wrapped headline inside a boxed story (in bastard measure). Many papers raw-wrap headlines at the top of the page simply to avoid an excess of long, 1-line banner heads.
At bottom, a hammer head (with deck) gives extra oomph to what *should* be a special analysis or feature story. Avoid using hammers on ordinary news.

At the top of the page: a sidesaddle headline. Like raw wraps, these must be used carefully to avoid collisions between legs of different stories. Note, too, that if the story's legs are too deep, the headline will float in too much white space.
At the bottom of the page, a liftout quote helps lure readers as it breaks up the gray text.

PAGES WITHOUT ART

A DIFFERENT SOLUTION: PACKAGING

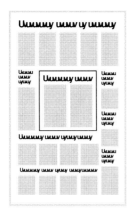

If your pages consistently look like the page at left — a gray hodgepodge crowded with short stories — you may need another photographer. Or you may need to explore a different design solution: packaging columns of short, related items. The advantages:

■ Instead of randomly scattering news briefs or event listings through the paper, you anchor them in one spot: a cleaner, better-organized approach.

■ You create more impact for your main stories by keeping those smaller ones out of their way.

■ You appeal to reader habit (most of us prefer finding the same material in the same spot every issue).

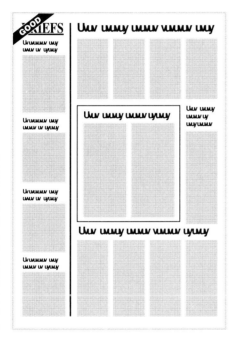

"Roundup" packages like this one usually run down the far left-hand side of the page. By running them vertically, it's easier to add or cut material to fit precisely. The column shown here runs in a wider measure, separated from the rest of the page by a cutoff rule in the gutter. A box would also work well to isolate these briefs.

By flopping that page design at far left, you can see how the page looks when you run a special column down the right-hand side. Here, a "man-in-the-street" interview uses mugs and quotes to anchor and enliven an otherwise gray page.

Some papers run news roundups horizontally across the top of the page, though the text often wraps awkwardly from one leg to another. Note the raw wrap at the bottom of the page. This is how it looks when you box a raw-wrapped story (in bastard measure) below another story. Does that solution seem clean enough?

Here's how a roundup column looks when it's stripped across the bottom of the page. Again, the biggest drawback is the awkwardness of wrapping short paragraphs from one leg to the next. In this example, a header reversed in a black bar labels the column and separates it from the rest of the page.

PAGES WITH ART

As a page designer, your job isn't just drawing lines, stacking stories and making sure things don't collide. It's *selling* the stories to the reader. People won't consume food that looks unappetizing; they won't consume information that looks unappetizing, either. And that's why you gotta have art.

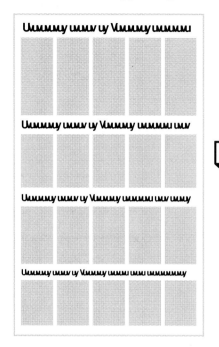

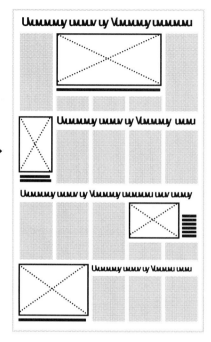

Here's that gray page again. Sure, it's clean, well-ordered, packed with information. But it's dull. Flat. Lifeless. Nothing stands out. Nothing grabs your attention or stops your eye. The stories may be beautifully written, but they may never get read.

Here's that same page, with art. There's less room for text now — so stories must either be shortened or jump to another page. But it's worth it. Remember, readers are like shoppers: They'll keep browsing until something gets them to stop. By adding photos, maps or charts, you stop their eyes — then deliver the information.

Art is essential. And *informational* art — not just decorative art — is the very heart of newspaper design. Adding art to your pages:

■ Supplements the *verbal* information in the text with *visual* information.
■ Adds motion, emotion and personality that's missing in text alone.
■ Lures readers who might otherwise ignore plain, gray type.
■ Provides a wider range of design options for each page.

GUIDELINES FOR PAGES WITH ART

When you add art to page designs, you increase their appeal to readers. You also increase the risk of clutter and confusion. So move slowly at first. Once you feel comfortable adding art to stories, keep adding it. It's better to make a page too dynamic than too dull. Or as one prominent New York graphics editor put it: "I like to take a page right to the edge of confusion, then back off just a bit."

There's a dizzying number of rules and requirements to remember when you lay out pages. The most important guidelines are these:

■ **Keep all story shapes rectangular.** You've already heard this a dozen times. But it's the key to good modular design.

■ **Emphasize what's important.** Play up the big stories, the big photos. Place them where they count. Let *play* and *placement* reflect each story's significance as you guide the reader through the page.

■ **Vary your shapes and sizes** (of stories as well as art). Avoid falling into a rut where everything's square. Or vertical. Or horizontal. Or where all the stories are 10 inches long. Give readers a variety of text and photo shapes.

On the next page, we'll look more closely at three crucial guidelines:

■ **Give each page a dominant photo.**
■ **Balance and scatter your art.**
■ **Beware of butting headlines.**

PAGES WITH ART

GIVE EACH PAGE A DOMINANT PHOTO

We've previously seen how, in stories using two or more photos, one should be dominant (page 42). The same holds true for pages: If there are two or more photos on a page, one of them should dominate.

Even if there's only *one* photo on a page, it should run big enough to provide impact and interest — to visually anchor the page.

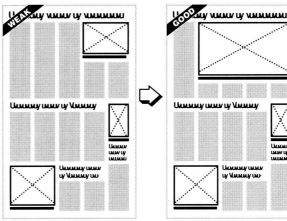

Here's a layout where no photo dominates. As a result, the page is gray. Meek. Unexciting.

Here, we've made that top photo 2 columns wider. *Now* it dominates a dynamic page.

BALANCE & SCATTER YOUR ART

Use photos to anchor your pages, but remember to use text and headlines to *separate* photos. When photos collide, you get a page that's:

■ **confusing** (when unrelated art intrudes into stories where it doesn't belong), or

■ **lopsided** (when photos lump together in one part of the page, and text collects in another).

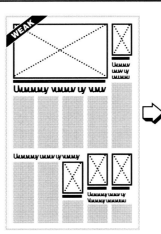
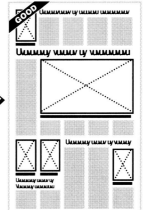

This layout seems to pair the lead photo and top mug, as well as the three mugs below. It's confusing — and top-heavy.

With smarter photo placement, there's no collision, no confusion. And the page is better-balanced when the art's apart.

BEWARE OF BUTTING HEADLINES

We've seen how you can bump heads (carefully) when you *need* to. But on most well-designed pages, head butts are unnecessary. Clumsy. And confusing to readers.

Instead, think ahead: Use art to separate stories anytime headlines collide. That's where raw-wrapped headlines can often offer a smart design solution for a crowded page.

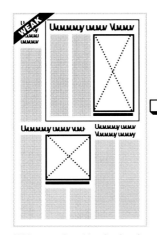
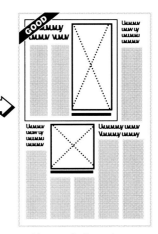

With two pairs of butting headlines, this layout is clumsy and confusing. But if you use the photos to separate stories. . .

. . .it's a much cleaner layout. Notice how the raw wrap (bottom left) provides an easy way to run two stories side by side.

MODULES AND MODULAR DESIGN

We've mentioned the term "modular design" before. And as you begin designing full pages, the idea of treating stories as modules — as movable, interchangeable units — takes on new meaning.

For instance, take a moment to study the attractive-looking page below. Notice how every story is a rectangle — and how all the rectangles fit together into a well-balanced, well-organized whole:

C section | The Orange County Register | Tuesday, July 26, 1988

Sports

MARK WHICKER

Giants nearly let Dodgers off the hook

SAN FRANCISCO — So it happens that the Dodgers don't always win when they score one run, don't always beat a right-handed pitcher, don't always win road games, don't always bail out Fernando Valenzuela, and don't always get the guy home in the top of the ninth.

Almost, but not always.

Down 3-1 and thankful it wasn't 8-1, Los Angeles conspired to get pinch-runner Alfredo Griffin to second base, with one out left, and sent Mike Davis to the plate. Kelly Downs of the Giants threw him a 3-1 split-finger and Davis swung and the ball jumped to right field and ...

"My heart stopped for a minute," Downs said.

But Candy Maldonado, straddling the warning track, made the catch, and the Dodgers are now 25-10 on the road against right-handed starters and 11-4 in two-run decisions. They're also 5½ games ahead of Houston and six ahead of the defending National League West champions, with a doubleheader tonight.

The Giants are a little more realistic than Angels manager Cookie Rojas, who was quoted as saying he'd be happy with beating Oakland two out of three this week. That would leave California a snug 12 games out. Then again, the Giants are just coming off a pennant and know what that entails.

Manager Roger Craig, who joined General Manager Al Rosen in such a string of preseason guarantees as to make Pat Riley look diplomatic, said this 97th game of the campaign was absolutely critical. "Let's face it," he said. "We need three out of four or four out of four. But we've stayed close enough that, if they do that, we can win."

Still, the Giants must question the dynamics at work here. They aimed the consistent Downs (135 innings, 106 hits) at such a desperate Valenzuela that he's fiddling with the stirrups on his socks and removing his glasses in the fifth inning. Yet their windmilling body shots kept missing.

In the second, Mike Aldrete got hung up and picked off when Bob Melvin apparently missed a hit-and-run. In the third Aldrete zapped a bases-loaded liner right at Kirk Gibson, who caught it. In the first Gibson didn't catch a much easier missile, and in the sixth John Shelby kicked away a single, but both of them recovered to throw out Giants — Shelby relaying to Sax to Mike Scioscia blocking the plate, with Donell Nixon's sliding hand fastening itself to Scioscia's shin guard as perfectly as a key goes into a lock.

"We kept letting Fernando off the hook," Downs said. "I can't think about that, as a pitcher, but it was in the back of my mind."

Please see WHICKER/4

America's Cup is on for September

Judge rules US must face New Zealand

■ **PART OF THE TEAM:** Randy Smyth is hoping to play a part in a successful America's Cup defense/**8**

From staff, news-service reports

Competitors in the embattled America's Cup race will set sail in September, a New York judge ruled Monday.

State Supreme Court Justice Carmen B. Ciparick ordered in New York City that the feuding San Diego Yacht Club and Michael Fay's New Zealand challenger begin racing Sept. 19 off the coast of San Diego. However, the date, which conflicts with the 1988 Summer Olympics in Seoul, South Korea (Sept. 17-Oct. 1), might be moved to Sept. 3.

The ruling also cleared the way for the San Diego club to use its controversial two-hulled 60-foot catamaran in defense of the title it reclaimed for the United States in 1987. New Zealand will race a 132-foot carbon-fiber hull sloop that measures 90 feet at the waterline and has a 16-story mast.

In San Diego, Tom Ehman, executive vice president of Sail America, the organization managing the defense for the yacht club, said his group was "very pleased because this gives certainty to the event."

"As the judge said at the end of her decision, 'Let's get the sailors back on the water.' " Ehman said. "That's the bottom line."

Fay, chairman of the New Zealand challenge, still maintained that the Americans have an unfair advantage sailing their catamaran against his single-hull sloop. He said multihulls are inherently faster than monohulls in similar conditions, but that he would go through with the race anyway.

"The judge hasn't decided anything," Fay said in a hastily organized news conference Monday in San Diego. "If she was convinced a multihull should be raced in the America's Cup, she would have said so."

The judge did not rule on whether San Diego could use its catamaran, but she ordered both sides to proceed with the competition and bring any complaints to court when the race was over.

"Nothing in this decision should be interpreted as indicating that multihulled boats are either permitted or barred under the America's Cup Deed of Gift," the judge said.

Fay said his Mercury Bay Club will protest the race and file an appeal after the race begins. If the catamaran is declared illegal by the courts, San Diego could face a forfeit if it wins the race.

"We will go out and race to win," Fay said. "We were here to race, and we would like to win on the water. A monohull doesn't beat a multihull on the water, but that's what we'll try to do."

Dennis Conner, skipper of the Stars and Stripes defender, said he hopes the San Diego Yacht Club and Fay can "forget the old wounds."

"Both parties have erred in this race," Conner said. "It is not a one-sided deal.

Please see AMERICA'S CUP/8

The Associated Press

Catcher Mike Scioscia stops the Giants' Donell Nixon from scoring with a body block, but the Dodgers couldn't stop San Francisco, losing, 3-1.

Safety's wish is granted

Rams give Cromwell release after 11 years

By Don Seeholzer
The Register

FULLERTON — The Nolan Cromwell era officially came to an end Monday as the Rams announced they had released their veteran safety by mutual agreement.

Owner Georgia Frontiere, in a prepared statement, called Cromwell "a true inspiration who will be sorely missed."

"Nolan is loved by his teammates and followers of the game," Frontiere said.

"He is a model of integrity and character. Nolan is the quintessential Ram. He has a thorough knowledge of the game and unequaled athletic ability. I consider him a close friend and hope he will always be affiliated with the Rams."

The Rams have offered a one-year position as assistant coach to Cromwell, who asked to be released so he can look for a team willing to let him compete for a starting job.

"If I can't find one," he said Sunday night, "I'll probably retire."

Seattle could be such a team, but Seahawks coach Chuck Knox — who was entering his final season with the Rams when they made Cromwell their second-round draft choice in 1977 — said Monday that he doesn't know yet if they're interested.

Rams coach John Robinson said he could see some team giving the 33-year-old Cromwell the opportunity he seeks, under the right conditions.

"I think a lot of those things depend on injury," Robinson said.

"I think if somebody starts playing preseason games and has two, three injuries in the secondary, then all of a sudden the veteran looks good. Tim Fox came in here and helped us for a period of time. Nolan, I think, would be of value to somebody in that kind of light."

Cromwell, who was unable to adjust to his new role as a definite non-starter, played 11 seasons for the Rams, going to the Pro Bowl four straight times from 1980-83.

The former Kansas quarterback finishes his Rams career as the team's all-time leader in intercep-

Please see CROMWELL/3

Mitchell's homer sinks Dodgers

Giants break through against Fernando, 3-1

■ **GRIFFIN:** Shortstop is activated and utilityman Mike Sharperson is sent down/**5**

By Tom Keegan
The Register

SAN FRANCISCO — The concurrent droughts of the Dodgers' highest-paid pitcher and top-salaried hitter droned on Monday night.

Once again, Fernando Valenzuela pitched but didn't win, running his winless streak to seven starts. And once again, Dodgers manager Tommy Lasorda had to fill out a lineup card that excluded Pedro Guerrero.

Valenzuela (5-8), winless since June 14, worked out of what seemed like more jams than the Lakers throw down in average practice. But he ultimately was outpitched by Kelly Downs.

Consequently, the San Francisco Giants won the first of a four-game series at Candlestick Park, 3-1, in front of 29,947 live witnesses and a national television audience.

Downs (10-8) went the distance, allowing five hits. He struck out eight, walked two and became the winning pitcher, thanks to third baseman Kevin Mitchell's tie-breaking, two-run homer to left-center with one out in the seventh.

Valenzuela, who worked out of bases-loaded jams twice, pitched seven innings, allowing nine hits, three runs and five walks, and striking out three.

"He made a bad pitch to Mitchell, but he pitched well enough to win," Lasorda said. "We just didn't get enough hits."

Downs saw to that. Guerrero, who is 7 for 14 with one career homer against Downs, wasn't around to do anything about it.

The Dodgers had hoped he might be back for the series, but Guerrero, who played Saturday and Sunday at Albuquerque on an injury-rehabilitation assignment, woke up "sore" Monday morning, according to General Manager Fred Claire. It was a spring-training type of soreness from not having played since June 4, and it kept Guerrero out of the lineup Monday at Albuquerque.

"It didn't sound to me like he will be back tomorrow," said teammate and friend Mario Soto, who spoke with Guerrero shortly before the game. "But you never know. He might surprise us. Wouldn't that be something if he walked in

Please see DODGERS/5

INSIDE

Irvine boxing: Paul Gonzales scores a unanimous decision over Javier Diaz in a flyweight bout/**2**

Starting call? Quarterback Jim Plunkett, at age 40, is optimistic about his fate with the Raiders/**3**

Jets sign Cadigan: Ex-USC lineman Dave Cadigan agrees to a four-year, $2 million deal with New York/**3**

The AL East: New York overtakes Detroit for first place; Boston, behind Roger Clemens, wins 12th in a row/**4**

Double duty: Several jockeys will commute between Del Mar and Los Alamitos race courses to ride at both tracks/**6**

DC Tennis Classic: Jimmy Connors beats Andres Gomez in straight sets, his first singles title since 1984/**7**

Sports Today/**2** The NFL/**3**
Baseball/**4-5** Sports Etc./**7**

The SportsLine, (714) 953-7723

Chris Covatta/The Register

Third baseman Jack Howell fails to stop Jose Canseco's line drive in the Angels' 2-1 victory over Oakland.

McCaskill, Angels come out on top, 2-1

He throws three-hitter to beat Stewart, A's

■ **ANGELS FOCUS:** Ailing pitcher Mike Witt declares himself fit and will start tonight's game/**5**

By Peter Schmuck
The Register

ANAHEIM — It is a showdown only to the Angels, who have been waiting a long time for another chance to go one-on-one with the first-place Oakland A's. But it was a showcase for both pitchers, who went at the series opener as if the division title hung in the balance.

Right-hander Kirk McCaskill, suddenly one of the hottest pitchers in baseball, threw a three-hitter Monday night to defeat Dave Stewart and the A's, 2-1, before 30,928 spectators at Anaheim Stadium.

"That might have been his best performance of the year right there," said Angels manager Cookie Rojas, "and the other guy didn't pitch too bad, too."

Stewart went all the way for the A's and gave up five hits. The game was decided on a run-scoring double by Wally Joyner in the fourth inning. From that point on, both starters combined to give up just two hits.

"These are the games pitchers look for," said McCaskill. "You want to be able to go out there and pitch like that. It feels good to be in a groove and know that you can put the ball where you want to."

He has been doing that with some consistency the past six weeks, winning six straight decisions to improve to 8-5. In July, he is 4-0 with a 2.31 ERA. Quite a turnaround since the June 11 loss that dropped his record to 2-5.

Please see ANGELS/5

MODULES AND MODULAR DESIGN

Could that page have been assembled differently — or better? Let's re-arrange the modules to see how other options might have turned out instead:

If you flop those two center stories, you end up with two thin vertical stories side by side, their heads nearly butting. That's a clumsy juxtaposition, even though the rest of the page looks OK.

Suppose you move the dominant photo to the very top of the page. Not bad – but you now have two gray text blocks running horizontally across the middle of the page. Otherwise, it's fine.

To break up that gray (example at left), you could move that bottom story up and dummy the America's Cup story along the bottom. *Now* your art is balanced again: a good mix of art and text.

Could that small photo run at the top of the page somehow? Well, not like this. The two photos collide too strongly – and now there's no art at all in the bottom third of the page.

Here's a better way to balance the photos if you lead with the smaller one. Does this page layout feel a bit odd, though? That's because big photos usually play better when they're near the top.

In this version, everything is flopped. There's nothing wrong with it. But traditionally, columnists have run down the left-hand side of the page. Is that a tradition worth preserving?

PAGE ONE DESIGN

Every paper has its own news philosophy. And that news philosophy is most visibly reflected in its Page One design: in the number of stories, the play of photos, the types of headlines, the variety of graphics, and so on.

Designing the front page is no tougher than designing any other page. The standards are simply higher (and the deadlines are often tighter). Here are a few current examples of Page One design, both broadsheet and tab. Study them closely. Have they observed the design principles we've discussed?

When The San Francisco Examiner redesigned in 1988, it added traditional elements in a distinctive way — including column rules, decorative cutoff rules, and a more vertical design format that's not strictly modular. Note, for instance, how that jackpot story fits into the lead story's dogleg. And note how that 1-column map in the middle of the page could accompany any one of three stories — but the cutoff rule shows you where it belongs.

The Colorado Springs Gazette Telegraph runs its front-page stories ragged right and boxed — and every box is labeled ("CRIME," "SPORTS," "HEALTH," etc.) to help readers quickly identify topics of interest. Does that device succeed — or does this design style seem too boxy and busy?

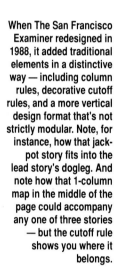

The Minnesota Daily, a college tabloid respected for its handsome design, uses typography and layout that give it an overall appearance similar to a broadsheet. This page uses a strong dominant photo — but should it have run in the middle of the page, with a vertical story on each side? Note, too, the headline placement for the story along the bottom.

Each month, U, The National College Newspaper, reprints features culled from student newspapers across the country. This colorful tabloid's design style relies upon rules, screens and boxes to keep stories organized. The front page makes extensive use of briefs and teasers to attract new readers. One question: Is that dominant photo dominant enough to create impact?

FLOW CHART: PAGE ONE DESIGN

START HERE

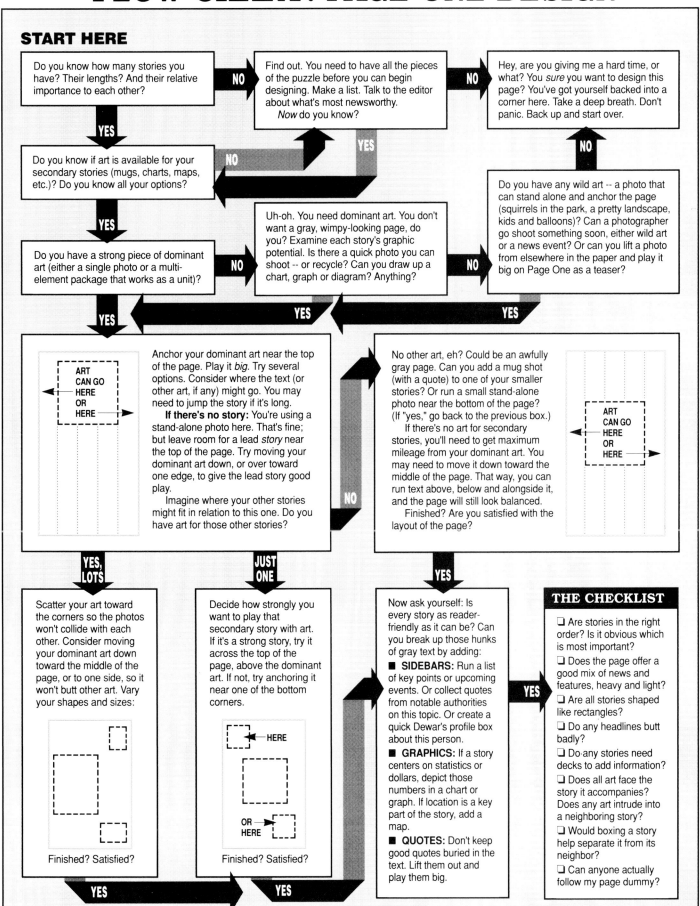

Do you know how many stories you have? Their lengths? And their relative importance to each other? — **NO** → Find out. You need to have all the pieces of the puzzle before you can begin designing. Make a list. Talk to the editor about what's most newsworthy. *Now* do you know? — **NO** → Hey, are you giving me a hard time, or what? You *sure* you want to design this page? You've got yourself backed into a corner here. Take a deep breath. Don't panic. Back up and start over.

YES ↓

Do you know if art is available for your secondary stories (mugs, charts, maps, etc.)? Do you know all your options? — **NO** ← (to previous box) / **YES** →

YES ↓

Do you have a strong piece of dominant art (either a single photo or a multi-element package that works as a unit)? — **NO** → Uh-oh. You need dominant art. You don't want a gray, wimpy-looking page, do you? Examine each story's graphic potential. Is there a quick photo you can shoot -- or recycle? Can you draw up a chart, graph or diagram? Anything? — **NO** → Do you have any wild art -- a photo that can stand alone and anchor the page (squirrels in the park, a pretty landscape, kids and balloons)? Can a photographer go shoot something soon, either wild art or a news event? Or can you lift a photo from elsewhere in the paper and play it big on Page One as a teaser?

YES ← **YES** ← **YES**

ART CAN GO HERE OR HERE

Anchor your dominant art near the top of the page. Play it *big*. Try several options. Consider where the text (or other art, if any) might go. You may need to jump the story if it's long.

If there's no story: You're using a stand-alone photo here. That's fine; but leave room for a lead *story* near the top of the page. Try moving your dominant art down, or over toward one edge, to give the lead story good play.

Imagine where your other stories might fit in relation to this one. Do you have art for those other stories?

No other art, eh? Could be an awfully gray page. Can you add a mug shot (with a quote) to one of your smaller stories? Or run a small stand-alone photo near the bottom of the page? (If "yes," go back to the previous box.)

If there's no art for secondary stories, you'll need to get maximum mileage from your dominant art. You may need to move it down toward the middle of the page. That way, you can run text above, below and alongside it, and the page will still look balanced.

Finished? Are you satisfied with the layout of the page?

ART CAN GO HERE OR HERE

YES, LOTS ↓ | **JUST ONE** ↓ | **NO** | **YES** ↓

Scatter your art toward the corners so the photos won't collide with each other. Consider moving your dominant art down toward the middle of the page, or to one side, so it won't butt other art. Vary your shapes and sizes:

Finished? Satisfied?

Decide how strongly you want to play that secondary story with art. If it's a strong story, try it across the top of the page, above the dominant art. If not, try anchoring it near one of the bottom corners.

HERE

OR HERE

Finished? Satisfied?

Now ask yourself: Is every story as reader-friendly as it can be? Can you break up those hunks of gray text by adding:

■ **SIDEBARS:** Run a list of key points or upcoming events. Or collect quotes from notable authorities on this topic. Or create a quick Dewar's profile box about this person.

■ **GRAPHICS:** If a story centers on statistics or dollars, depict those numbers in a chart or graph. If location is a key part of the story, add a map.

■ **QUOTES:** Don't keep good quotes buried in the text. Lift them out and play them big.

→ **YES** →

THE CHECKLIST

❏ Are stories in the right order? Is it obvious which is most important?

❏ Does the page offer a good mix of news and features, heavy and light?

❏ Are all stories shaped like rectangles?

❏ Do any headlines butt badly?

❏ Do any stories need decks to add information?

❏ Does all art face the story it accompanies? Does any art intrude into a neighboring story?

❏ Would boxing a story help separate it from its neighbor?

❏ Can anyone actually follow my page dummy?

YES → | **YES** →

MAKING STORIES FIT

Someday, all newspaper pages will be created on computer screens using a process called pagination. The computer will count the *exact* number of lines in each story, measure the *exact* sizes of photos, and dummy everything *exactly* into place.

Until then, things may get a little sloppy.

No matter how hard you try, no matter how carefully you calculate, no matter how simple and goof-proof your page designs may seem, your stories will still come up short. Or long.

Once a page is pasted up, minor adjustments are easy. Major repairs, however, can be tricky and time-consuming. You may need to back up and re-dummy a story or two. But first, find out what went wrong. Ask yourself:

■ **Is there an error on the dummy?** Did you make a mistake dummying the depth of the text? Sizing the photos? Writing a headline code? Were any ads sized wrong on the dummy? Omitted? Killed?

■ **Did someone make a mistake pasting up the page?** Was the dummy misread? Was a photo trimmed wrong? Was copy lost? Are all elements — bylines, cutlines, refers, lift quotes, logos — where they're supposed to be?

■ **Was I given incorrect information?** Did someone change a story's length without telling me? Did someone swap photos? Is there machine error (a computer or typesetter that consistently mismeasures story lengths)?

If a story's close to fitting — say, within a few inches — try some of these options, either before you dummy the page or after it's pasted up:

MORE ON:

■ **Sizing photos:** How to use a proportion wheel...... 92

■ **Liftout quotes:** Some basic styles & guidelines.......... 114

■ **Decks:** Sizing and dummying guidelines.......... 116

IF A STORY'S TOO LONG

■ **Trim the text.** As a rule of thumb, all stories are cuttable by 10%. For instance, a 10-inch story can usually lose an inch without serious damage; a 30-inch story can lose a few inches. (Your readers may thank you, too.)

■ **Trim a photo.** Shave a few picas off the top or bottom, if the image allows it. Or, if necessary, re-size the photo so you can crop more tightly.

■ **Trim an adjacent story.** If you find that a story is trimmed to the max, try tightening the one above or below it.

■ **Drop a line from the headline.** But be careful — headlines that make no sense can doom an entire story. (See chart, page 17).

■ **Move an ad.** Either into another column or onto another page.

IF A STORY'S TOO SHORT

■ **Add more text.** If material was trimmed from the story, add it back in. Or break out a small sidebar with tight, highlighted information.

■ **Enlarge a photo.** Crop it more loosely. Or size it a column larger.

■ **Add a mug shot.** But be sure it's someone who's relevant to the story.

■ **Add a liftout quote.** Make it provocative, enticing. Don't just play up meaningless words to fill space.

■ **Add another line of headline.** Or add a deck, if the story lacks (and needs) one.

■ **Add some air between paragraphs.** This old composing-room trick lets you add a few points of space between the final paragraphs of a story. Go easy: If you overdo it, those floating text blocks become unreadable.

■ **Add a filler story.** Keep a selection of optional 1- or 2-inch stories handy to drop in as needed.

■ **Add a house ad** (a 1- or 2-column in-house promotion for your paper).

■ **Move an ad.** Either from another column or from another page.

In addition to these quick fixes, there are two more techniques — using bastard measures and jumping stories — that are a bit more complicated:

MAKING STORIES FIT

BASTARD MEASURES

Most of the time, photos fit fine using the standard column widths. But on some pages, they're just too small in one column measure — and just too big in another .

At times like those, bastard measures are the answer — especially for feature pages, where photos often dominate.

Take this column you're reading right now, for instance. Most text in this book is set 29 picas wide. But to accommodate the four illustrations at right, we're running this leg in a bastard width (9 picas) alongside the diagrams.

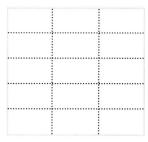

❶ Suppose you're dummying a 6-inch story with a mug. You need to fill a space that's 3 columns wide, 5 inches deep. What are your best options?

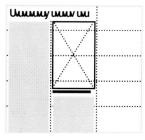

❷ With a 1-column mug, the story fits in 2 legs. Which leaves 1 column empty. (A 2-line headline would force text into the third leg, but wouldn't fill it.)

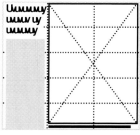

❸ You could try running the mug 2 columns wide, but it wastes way too much space. Only 3.5 inches of text will fit into that left-hand column.

❹ The solution? Running 2 bastard legs in place of the usual 3. The text is 4 inches deep, but it's half-again as wide as a 1-column leg — so it fits.

JUMPING STORIES

There will be times — many, many times — when you'll need to fit a 30-inch story into a 10-inch hole. When that happens, you can either:

1) Cut 20 inches from the story (lots of luck), or

2) Start the story on one page and finish it on another.

When stories runneth over like that, they're called *jumps.* Interesting critters, jumps: Many editors hate them. Many readers hate them, too. But most page designers love them, because they give you the freedom to yank, jerk, stretch and slice stories in otherwise unimaginable ways.

(That age-old journalistic question — "Do readers actually follow stories that jump?" — has yet to be answered definitively. The conventional wisdom suggests that readers will faithfully follow a story *anywhere* if it's important, well-written, engrossing, etc. Otherwise, they'll use the jump as an excuse to quit reading.)

When you dummy a jumping story, keep in mind:

■ It's pointless (and annoying) to jump just a few short paragraphs at the end of a story. Make it worth the reader's while. Jump *at least* 6 inches of text, unless the story is simply uncuttable and there's no other option.

■ Start the story solidly — with *at least* 4 inches of text — before you jump it. Otherwise, readers may think it's too insignificant to bother with.

■ Jump stories to the same place as often as possible. Readers will accept jumps more easily once they're trained to always turn to the back page, the top of Page 2, the bottom of Page 3, etc.

■ Jump stories once — and once only. You'll lose too many readers if you jump a few inches to Page 2, then snake a few more inches along Pages 3

Please turn to **JUMPS,** *Page 123*

INSIDE PAGES

ADS: THREAT OR MENACE?

News stories exist to inform readers. Ads exist to make money for publishers. Can you guess which is more important?

Right. Ads.

The big difference between a front page and most other inside pages is that, on inside pages, you're co-existing with a loud, pushy, messy heap of boxes — ads — stacked upwards from the page bottom. Some stacks look better than others. But whatever format they use, ad stacks are dummied onto pages before the news is — and thus, they dictate the shape of the news hole you're stuck with.

Today, these three formats are most often used for dummying ads:

Stair-step (or pyramid)   *Well*   *Modular*

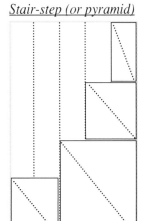

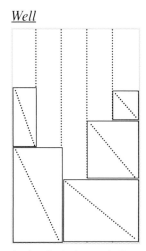

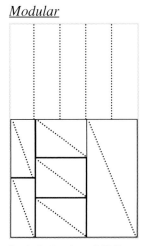

This traditional format allows every ad to touch news copy, which is important to some advertisers. But for page designers, it creates some ugly-looking news holes. It's also used to create a pyramid effect on two facing pages.

As the ads stack up on both sides of the page, a deep well forms in the middle — hence the name. Though some advertisers insist on parking their ads alongside text, this approach too often results in Ad Stacks From Hell.

Looks better, doesn't it? By arranging ads in modular blocks, some get buried. But overall, it's a more orderly, appealing arrangement. This fairly recent innovation will become increasingly popular in the years ahead.

As you can see, those two old-fashioned ad configurations — stair-step and well — offer some tough challenges for page designers. What's the best way to squeeze stories into those oddly shaped spaces? Here's some advice:

GUIDELINES FOR AD LAYDOWN

Many pages are doomed to fail long before you even begin dummying. That's usually because the ad staff and the newsroom aren't communicating. As a result, ad laydowns may be unwittingly awkward, forcing you to waste valuable time trying to overcome some obvious obstacles.

To avoid unnecessary headaches in advance, work with the ad staff to:

■ **Use modular ad formats.** Snaking stories around steeply stair-stepped ads punishes both readers and advertisers. Square off ads whenever possible.

■ **Use house ads** to smooth out any small, awkward holes.

■ **Establish guidelines for key pages.** Negotiate dependable news holes where you need them most. Reach an agreement that Page 2 will always be open, for instance, or that Page 3's left-hand column is off-limits to ads.

■ **Establish limits.** If ads are stacked too high — say, an inch from the top of the page — dummying even the simplest headline and story is impossible. Ideally, ads should stack either clear to the top or start at least 2 inches down.

■ **Get permission to move ads.** Ad positions aren't etched in stone. Reserve the right to move ads if necessary. Just don't abuse the privilege.

INSIDE PAGES

GUIDELINES FOR PAGE DESIGN

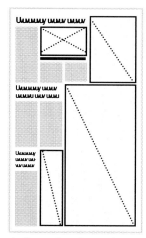

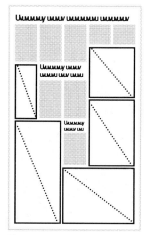

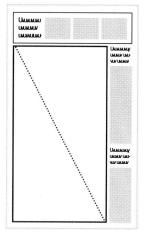

As these ads stair-step down the page, the stories square off alongside. You may need to trim the stories to fit these modular shapes, but the resulting page will be much more readable than one full of doglegs.

The more crowded the page, the less necessary (and more difficult) it will be to dummy photos. Note how this page plays up one dominant story — and how slight doglegs around ads are not a problem.

With a banner headline, that top story would have looked shallow and awkward. But by using a sidesaddle head, the elements fit together smoothly. The box and bastard measures are both optional.

■ **Give every page a dominant story.** On crowded pages with tiny news holes, this may be impossible. And on other tight pages, even squeezing in a small photo may be difficult. But try to anchor each page with the strongest possible element. Don't just crowbar clumps of cluttered copy together.

■ **Work with the ad stacks.** Yes, it's best to dummy stories into rectangles — but on pages crowded with ads, that may not work. Doglegs are common on inside pages, and often they're your only option.

But before you begin dummying, explore how best to subdivide each page. Work *with* the ads to block out clean, modular story segments. Start at the bottom, if necessary; sometimes you can smooth things out by stretching one wide story atop an uneven stack of small ads. Or try working backwards from an awkward corner. But wherever possible, square off stories along the edges of ads.

■ **Use alternative headline treatments.** When ads crowd up near the top of a page, you may barely have enough depth for a headline and an inch of text. That's where sidesaddle headlines come in handy (see example above, at far right). Boxing the story or running the legs in a bastard measure is optional.

On other occasions, a raw-wrapped headline will let you dummy two stories side by side at the top of a crowded page. Proceed with caution, however.

■ **Avoid dummying photos on top of ads.** Ads are boxes. Photos are boxes. And readers can't always tell one box from another. So unless you want your photos mistaken for ads, always keep a little text between the two (see example at right).

■ **Avoid boxing small stories beside ads.** Again, the more your stories look like ads, the more you'll confuse your readers (see example at right). Ads are boxed; so whenever you've got ads in the vicinity, keep your stories *un*boxed.

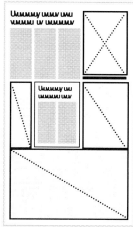

Two problems here: At top, the photo sits on an ad — and could easily be mistaken for an ad itself. In the middle of the page, a boxed story is sandwiched between ads — and, like the photo, seems to turn into another ad.

DOUBLE TRUCKS

This two-page "Tall Ships" spread, printed on the front and back pages of the Upfront feature section, was published by the Rochester (N.Y.) Times-Union in 1984. Designed by art director Ray Stanczak, this double-truck design lifted many of its ideas from a "tall ships" page previously done at The Boston Globe. It took several artists several days to research and execute this layout, which heralded the arrival of a fleet of sailing ships by showing readers fun facts, a diagram, a map of the route, etc. This "Tall Ships" page became a favorite of many Times-Union staffers . . .

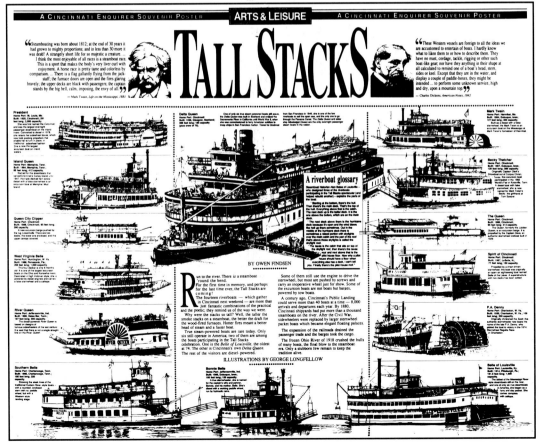

. . . Years later, a Times-Union feature editor, Felix Winternitz, got a job at The Cincinnati Enquirer. Though he hadn't worked on the original "Tall Ships" page, Winternitz said, "I always loved it, and I thought, 'Someday I'm gonna find a way to use this.' " And one of his last projects in Cincinnati — before leaving the paper in 1989 — was to help design the "Tall Stacks" page at left.

The design and illustrations for the "Tall Stacks "page took three months. Like the "Tall Ships" spread, it used the front and back pages of the feature section. Unlike "Tall Ships," it printed in black and white ("Tall Ships" originally ran in color) to achieve a more antique effect.

As Winternitz said: "Ideas are made to be stolen."

DOUBLE TRUCKS

This double truck spread from The Christian Science Monitor ties together three arts stories in a handsome, magazine-style package. Note how the photos are balanced across the page; in the lead story, they're dummied in modules entirely separate from the text.

When two facing pages print across the gutter on one sheet of newsprint — say, the front and back pages of a section, or the two pages in the very center — it's called a *double truck*. A double truck is fun to design and will work best if you:

■ **Clear off all ads**. Keep it one big, modular, editorial block. Any ads will either intrude, get buried, or be mistaken for editorial matter.

■ **Treat both pages as one horizontal unit**. If you're used to dealing with vertical formats, this is a good chance to rethink your approach. Ignore the gutter between pages; spread your elements from left to right in a balanced, orderly way. Keep the flow of text clean. Anchor the design with a bold headline and big photo. But above all, package only *related* topics together.

■ **Save it for special occasions.** Readers expect these packages to be special; don't let them down. Use double trucks for news features, infographics, photo layouts or major events. Add color and graphic effects. Have fun.

FACING PAGES

You can also apply special treatment to two facing pages anywhere in the paper (these are sometimes called "double trucks out of position").

As with true double trucks, it's important to view facing pages as one wide unit and balance your elements accordingly. If you're careful, you can even run some elements across the gutter. Big photos will work best, but smaller elements — especially type — will seldom align evenly. Readers are a bit forgiving, but don't push your luck.

This well-balanced photo spread from The Times (Beaverton, Ore.) ran on two facing pages — not a true double truck. We've printed it here the way many readers would have seen it: with the pages slightly out of alignment and a gutter opening up through the lead photo and headline. It's a problem, but only a minor one.

BAD JUXTAPOSITIONS

As newspaper designer Phil Nesbitt once said: People and puppies must both be trained to use a newspaper.

In olden days, readers were trained to read newspapers *vertically* — and since every story on every page ran vertically, readers were rarely confused about which photo went with which story.

Today, however, stories run in vertical and horizontal modules that change from page to page. And on every page — even with every story — we expect our readers to instantly deduce which photo belongs to which story.

We don't always make their choices easy (as in the example at right: Is Nixon the escaped lunatic? Is that goril-

Ax-wielding lunatic escapes from asylum

Ex-president Nixon visits new grandson

Gorilla gives birth at city zoo

Killer ape goes bananas, destroys daycare center

la photo a portrait of Nixon's new grandson?) So it's especially important to analyze every page design as objectively as you can, to determine:

■ If a photo sits at the intersection of two stories in a way that confuses or misdirects the reader.

■ If an advertisement seems to comment upon a neighboring news story.

■ If two stories — or their headlines — seem tasteless together on the same page (in the above example, those two ape stories create an awkward combination).

It's easy to embarrass yourself, your readers and the subjects of your stories (both apes *and* humans) by dubious dummying. When in doubt, either *move* it or *box* it — whatever it takes to make your design perfectly clear.

OVERLAPPING MODULES

The most common blunder, as shown in the Nixon layout above, occurs when you dummy two separate story modules that seem to overlap. Beware of modules that overlap either horizontally (on both sides of a photo) or both vertically *and* horizontally (beside and below a photo).

Horizontally

Two stories, one photo — and the reader must decide where the photo belongs. To fix:
■ Box or screen one of the stories;
■ Divide them with a cutoff rule; or
■ Run a big headline across the top of the photo and its text.

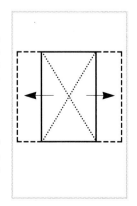

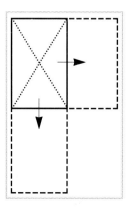

Horizontally and vertically

Dummying photos into corner intersections can be dangerous. To avoid confusion:
■ Box or screen one of the stories;
■ Make sure any story *below* an unrelated photo is at least 1 column wider or narrower.

RULES OF THUMB

On this page, we've gathered together the most basic design principles discussed in this book. Use this list as a handy reference; the numbers running along the right margin are the pages where you can find more information.

LAYOUT & DESIGN

- All stories should be shaped like rectangles. Pages should consist of rectangles stacked together. [30]
- Avoid placing any graphic element in the middle of a leg of type. [32, 115]
- Avoid placing art at the bottom of a leg of type. [32]
- Text that wraps below a photo should be at least one inch deep. [33]
- In vertical layouts, stack elements in this order: photo, cutline, headline, text. [32]
- Every page should have a dominant piece of art. [42]
- A well-designed, well-balanced page is usually at least one-third art. [58]
- Avoid dummying a photo directly on top of an ad. [73]
- Avoid boxing stories just to keep headlines from butting. Box stories only if they're special or different. [60]

TEXT

- Avoid changing typefaces, text sizes or column widths within a layout. [61]
- Type 8 point or smaller is difficult to read. Use it sparingly, and never print it behind a screen. [18, 137]
- Avoid dummying legs of text more than 20 picas wide or narrower than 10 picas. [19]
- The optimum depth for legs of text is from 2-10 inches. [19]
- Use italics, boldface, reverses, all caps or any other special effects in small doses. [18]

HEADLINES

- Every story must have a headline.
- Headlines should get smaller as you move down the page. Smaller stories get smaller headlines. [16]
- 5-10 words is optimum for most headlines. [17]
- Never allow an art element to come between the headline and the start of a news story. [37]
- Avoid butting headlines. If you must, run the left head several counts short, vary their sizes, and vary the number of lines. [59]

JUMPS

- Run at least 4 inches of a story before you jump it. [71]
- Jump at least 6 inches of a story (to make it worth the reader's while to follow the jump). [71]
- Jump stories once and once only. Whenever possible, jump to the same place in every edition. [71]

PHOTOS

- Directional photos should face the text they accompany. [36, 37]
- When in doubt, run one big photo instead of two small ones. [43, 98]
- When using two or more photos, make one dominant — that is, substantially bigger than any competing photo. [42, 65]
- Try to vary the shapes and sizes of all photos (as well as stories) on a page. [64]

CUTLINES

- For best results, run one cutline per photo. Each cutline should touch the photo it describes. [23, 99]
- When cutlines run beside photos, they should be at least 6 picas wide. [23]
- When cutlines run below photos, they should square off as evenly as possible on both sides of the photo. They should never extend beyond either edge of the photo. [23]
- Cutlines wider than 30 picas should be divided into two legs if they're more than one line deep. [23]
- Avoid widows in any cutline more than one line deep. [23]

EXERCISES

Exercise answers are on page 167.

1 You need to dummy text in a box that's 40 picas wide. How wide will each leg be if there are 4 legs? If there are 3 legs? If there are 2 legs?

2 You're laying out an inside page in a 5-column format. The ads stack up pretty high; your available space for news is 6 inches deep and the full page (5 columns) across. You need to dummy two stories: one 15 inches long, the other 10 inches. Neither has art. You can trim one inch out of either story, if necessary — but no more. How many design options do you have?

3 There are several things wrong with each of these three page designs. Like what, for instance?

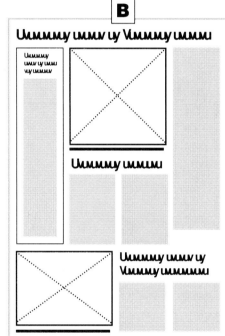

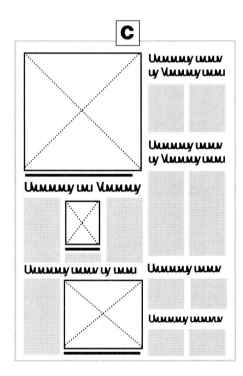

4 The four layouts below all use the same story elements. Which of the four is the best, and why?

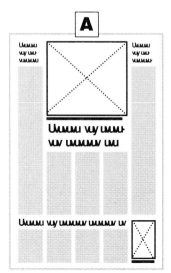

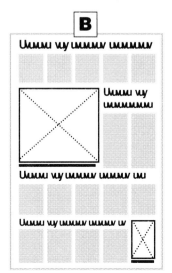

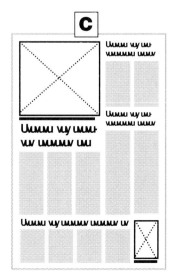

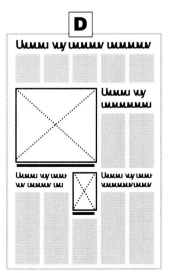

EXERCISES

5 When the layout above ran in the newspaper, some editors complained that the Campaign '88 promo box was positioned poorly. It appears as if it's part of the Hyundai story to its left. How would you redesign this part of the page to avoid that problem, using the sizes shown here?

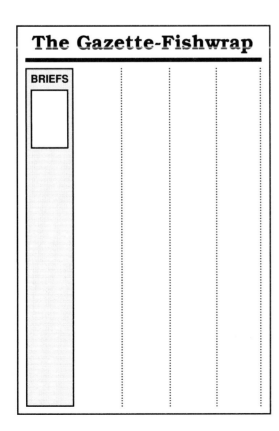

6 At left is Page One of a typical tabloid. It's a 5-column format; the left-hand column is used for news briefs.

Design this page with the following three elements:

1) A 10-inch lead story with a good horizontal photo;

2) An 8-inch story with a horizontal photo; and

3) A 4-inch bright (an upbeat, offbeat feature).

Exercise answers are on page 168.

On March 4, 1880, the New York Daily Graphic became the first newspaper to print a photograph. And from that day to this, newspaper photographers have repeatedly asked themselves: "Will they *ever* give us any respect?"

You can't blame photographers for feeling a little paranoid. Newsrooms, after all, are dominated by editors who were once reporters, who believe *news* means *text,* who think photos are a nice accessory to stories — but if space gets tight, and they need to cut an inch out of either the story or the photo, you know which way they'll vote.

Trouble is, those editors are badly mistaken. Our society is becoming more and more visually oriented. In today's media, images are strong; text, by comparison, is weak. If you want to convey information, photos can be as valuable as text. If you want to hook passing readers, photos are even *more* valuable than text.

Until now, this book has treated photos as simple boxes parked on the page. But there's more to it than that. Photographs are essential for good design — and good design is essential for photographs.

In this chapter, we'll take a closer look at the art and science of photo-journalism.

CHAPTER CONTENTS

■ **General guidelines:** Basic photographic principles every designer should know............. **82**

■ **Good photos:** A portfolio of striking images from five professional shooters....................**83-87**

■ **Bad photos:** How to salvage botched photo assignments and avoid dangerous cliches..... **88-89**

■ **Cropping photos:** Tips for getting maximum impact from photo images.....................**90-91**

■ **The proportion wheel:** A fast way to calculate the dimensions of resized photos.....................**92**

■ **Halftones and line shots:** Two ways to reproduce photos on the printed page.......................**93**

■ **Stand-alone photos:** Running single photos alone.................**94**

■ **Photo spreads:** Getting started designing photo pages... **95-97**

■ **Photo spread guidelines:** Tips for planning and designing a successful photo page........ **98-99**

■ **Studio shots:** Adding photo-graphic freedom to layouts **100**

■ **Photo illustrations:** What to look for when creating feature ideas in the studio.................. **101**

■ **Illustrations:** A look at the different ways newspapers use drawings **102-103**

■ **A feature art checklist:** Where to go for ideas when stories are a little vague...................... **104-105**

■ **Risky business:** A few artsy gimmicks to avoid.................. **106**

■ **Exercises** **107**

GENERAL GUIDELINES

There's a lot to learn about cropping photos, scaling them for reproduction and positioning them in photo spreads — but before we study those techniques, let's summarize a few guidelines:

■ **Every photo should have a clean, clear center of interest.** A good photo, like a well-written story, is easy to read. It presents information that's free of clutter and distractions. To do that, it must be sharply focused and cleanly composed, so that its most important elements stand out instantly.

■ **Every photo should get a cutline.** You'd be surprised how often editors will think, "Well, *everyone* knows who this is: It's Elmo T. Quarp!" Never assume readers are as smart as you are, or that they've even read the text. Give IDs to every photo. Make sure all faces, places and activities are clearly labeled.

This photo has a clean, clear center of interest: an old war veteran caught in a nostalgic salute. It's a sharp, strong image, with no background clutter to distract us. And it seems to be an honest portrait — not posed or artificial.

■ **Every photo should be bordered.** Don't allow the white tones of a photo to blur into the whiteness of the page. Frame each image with a border — a plain, thin rule running along the edge of the photo (1-point is standard).

This excellent portrait uses a natural, informal pose to capture the subject's personality. But notice how the white background blends into the whiteness of the page. Without a border to frame this image, the crop at the top of the photo looks awkward.

Don't overdo it, though; if you *box* each photo and cutline to be fancy, readers may think they're separate from the stories they accompany.

■ **Every photo should look natural.** In amateur snapshots, people smile stiffly at the camera; in professional news portraits, they're loose, relaxed, engaged in activities. Whenever possible, shoot *real* people doing *real* things, not gazing blankly into space or pretending to be busy.

■ **Every photo should be relevant.** Readers don't have time for trivia in text; they don't want to see it in photos, either. Run only images that have a direct connection to the story (the woman who heads the protest, the punch that caused the knockout). Photos must provide information, not decoration.

■ **Every face should be at least the size of a dime.** It's rare that photos are played too big in newspapers, but they're often run too small — especially when the key characters shrink to insect-size. If you want photos to have impact, shoot individuals, not crowds. Then size the photos as big as you can.

This engaging portrait of a cleaning crew was shot from an appropriate perspective. But if you ran this photo this small, all its impact would be lost. It needs to be played at least twice this size, so that every face is at least the size of a dime.

GOOD PHOTOS

What makes a good photograph? In the pages that follow, five photographers from The Oregonian present some of their favorite images — and explain, in their own words, what makes these photos strong.

Kraig Scattarella:

"This is the aftermath of a fatal fire where a relative has just come on the scene and realized that her grandson was killed. The emotion overwhelmed her, and all she wanted to do was run inside and see the body. The fireman stepped in to hold her back and comfort her.

"The news editor was adamant about NOT using this picture.* He felt that it was an invasion of these people's privacy — which it is. It's their moment of grief. My selling point for this picture was that these people didn't have any smoke detectors in their house. In the story it mentions that; they had just moved into the house a day or two before. And anybody that sees that picture is going to think of himself in that situation and think, 'I don't want this to happen to me.'

"This is the picture you dream about, that all photojournalists strive for — when all the elements fall together to make a complete picture that can stand alone, without words. If you can capture a moment like this, then you've done your job 100 percent."

* The photo DID run.

83

GOOD PHOTOS

Randy L. Rasmussen:

"This is Patricia Kent. She was in her 70s or early 80s when I photographed her for a series The Oregonian did on poverty and unemployment in Oregon. For this series, I traveled throughout western Oregon for two weeks of shooting.

"She lived near Woodburn in a little one-room house that had no central heating system, no running water. . . . She had subsisted that way for years. When I met her, she was chopping her own fire-wood. She embodied a sort of pioneer spirit, yet she also symbolized the victim-ization of older people. She was a gutsy lady; she didn't want any help.

"I photographed her a couple different times. In this picture, she was stand-ing in her doorway. She's out in the light, and the doorway falls off dark behind her. I think we were saying goodbye. It just seemed to characterize the loneliness and depression that was going on around the state at that time.

"The photo ran with the story in the opening of the series, then was picked up and incorporated in the logo for the series, which was called 'Sorrowful Spring.' It fit perfectly.

"It's one of the few assignments that's stuck with me through the years. To me, it's classic portrait-ure. It captures everything about this lady in a quick read. You can really see the suffering she's gone through."

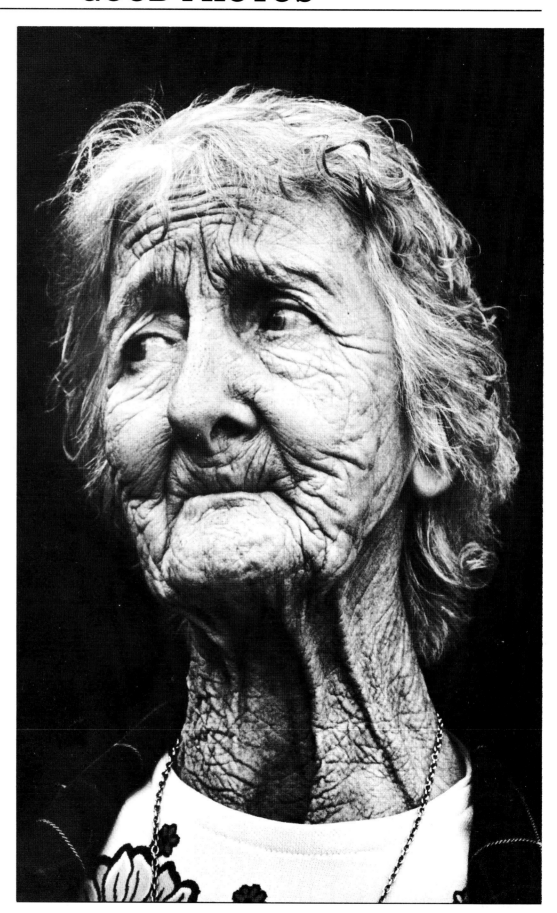

GOOD PHOTOS

Michael Lloyd:

"This picture is from the Portland State University women's volleyball championship — a successful defense of their national title for the second year in a row.

"A lot of sports action pictures — say, of the volleyball game itself — are quite ambiguous. Even a great action picture really doesn't tell you who wins or loses. But in this case, this moment said it all. It wasn't an action moment; it was after the game was over. It required a lot of quickness and preparation, to see this happening and get there in time to shoot it. Which all comes from experience, from covering a lot of things like this over a long time.

"When I shoot sports, I try to tell a story through the emotions of the people. Sometimes that's in action; a lot of times it's not.

"This ran real well (because I was picture editor for Sports). It ran at least three columns. One picture. Didn't need to clutter up the page with a lot of photos. This one said it all."

GOOD PHOTOS

Steve Nehl:

"In 1978, a United Airlines DC-8 crashed right in the middle of a residential area (in Portland). The pilot had fuel gauge trouble and landing gear trouble at the same time; as they tried to fix the landing gear, they ran out of fuel on approach. The aircraft was destroyed. No one on the ground was injured. There were 12 people killed on the plane, and about 80 survivors.

"For this photograph, I got up to the front of the plane, where there was quite a bit of activity. Some of the people were still being evacuated. I saw this stewardess way back up in the plane, and I said, 'Well, she's gonna have to come out the front.' So I got in the best position I could, to show the destruction of the plane, and just waited for her. Pretty soon, out she came, and the firemen were helping her out through the wreckage. I made a number of frames, and this is the best of the bunch.

"There was not a whole lot of luck involved in this picture. I was trying to keep a calm head in an extremely tense situation. There were dead people nearby — in fact, there's one person here in the corner of the frame. But I knew the picture was going to be that stewardess coming out of there. I just had to wait for it, and I got it."

GOOD PHOTOS

Ross Hamilton:

"I've always been a boxing fan. And being able to appreciate an event has a lot to do with what you come up with.

"This is a perfect example of one of those sports shots you always hope for, where lots of elements come together: timing, luck, focus. Probably the same could be said for the guy hitting the other guy. It's a powerful shot. By me AND the boxer.

"Some of it is luck. But you have to be prepared to take advantage of lucky events. There was a photographer next to me, shooting the same stuff, and he didn't get that shot. He might have been changing film, or changing lenses, or changing cameras — he may even have shot it, and it was out of focus. But there I was. Lucky.

"We were both being sprayed with sweat, blood and water. We were constantly wiping off our lenses as we were shooting. So he might have been wiping sweat and blood off his lens while I got the shot.

"It wasn't until I got back and saw the shot that I went, 'Damn, I got one.' I remember feeling confident, but I didn't realize until I saw the film that I had such a crucial moment.

"I love the guy's face. I love the fact that he's just getting blasted. I love the swirl of sweat coming off his head. It's a successful, powerful sports image."

BAD PHOTOS

Scratches and assorted darkroom crud.

Print is under-exposed (too dark).

Distractions in the background.

Clumsy composition. Subject is off center, awkwardly cropped. No center of interest.

Light pole sticking out of subject's head (poor mix of foreground and background).

Harsh shadows on subject's face.

Poor depth of field. Subject is out of focus.

Unflattering and unnatural pose.

Photos can be bad in a mind-boggling number of ways. They can be too dark, too light, too fuzzy, too tasteless, too meaningless or too *late* to run in the paper. They can, like the photo above, show blurry blobs of useless information. They can even show, with frightening clarity, a person with a utility pole growing out of his head.

So be thankful, then, whenever a photographer hands you a sharp, dramatic, immaculately printed photograph. And avoid turning good photos into bad ones by cropping them clumsily. Or playing them too small. Or dummying them where they compete with another photo — or intrude into the wrong story.

Remember, photographers often use terms like "hack," "mangle," "kill" and "bury" to describe what editors do to their photos. So be careful. People who talk like that shouldn't be pushed too far.

SALVAGING BAD PHOTOS

What can you do to salvage a bungled photo assignment?

■ **Edit for the best image.** Find the most informative frame on the roll. Is there one that shows more than the rest? With a telling face, gesture, action?

■ **Crop carefully.** Focus our attention on what *works* in the photo — not what doesn't. Play up what's important and eliminate the rest.

■ **Run a sequence.** Sometimes two small photos aren't as bad as one big, nasty one. Consider pairing a couple of complementary images.

■ **Reshoot.** Is there time? A willing photographer? An available subject?

■ **Try another photo source.** Was there another photographer at the scene? Would older file photos be appropriate?

■ **Use alternative art.** Is there another way to illustrate this story? With a chart? A map? A well-designed mug/liftout quote? A sidebar?

■ **Retouch mistakes.** With a pencil, grease pencil, airbrush or paint, tone down distracting backgrounds, sharpen contrast, add highlights. But go easy.

■ **Bury it.** By playing a photo small, you can de-emphasize its faults. By moving it further down the page, you can make it less noticeable.

■ **Mortise one photo over another.** It's risky, but may help if there's an offensive element that you'd like to eliminate or disguise. (See page 135.)

■ **Do without.** Remind yourself that bad art is worse than no art at all.

BAD PHOTOS

There are certain photojournalistic cliches that have plagued editors for decades. Some, like "The Mayor Wears a Funny Hat," have at least *some* redeeming value (either as entertainment or as a peculiar form of revenge).

Others, like the four types shown below, have almost no redeeming value — except for friends, relatives and employees of those in the photo. Shoot them if you must, but look for alternatives (for instance, a revealing portrait of an interesting person in a *real-life* situation) every chance you get.

GRIP & GRIN

Who's involved: Club presidents, civic heroes, honors students, school administrators, retiring bureaucrats.

Where it occurs: City halls, banquets, school offices — anyplace civic-minded folks want to glorify their gratitude.

Variations: Awarding diplomas, passing checks, cutting ribbons — any symbolic ceremony where nothing happens.

THE EXECUTION AT DAWN

Who's involved: Any clump of victims lined up against a wall to be shot: club members, sports teams, award winners, etc.

Where it occurs: Social wingdings, public meetings, fundraisers. Also occurs, pre-season, in the gym.

Variations: Standing on a stage, sitting at a conference table. Sometimes known as The Yearbook Photo.

THE GUY AT HIS DESK

Who's involved: Administrators, bureaucrats, civic organizers — anybody who bosses other people around.

Where it occurs: The office. (Some of us suspect that only one office is ever used for these photos, and people keep taking turns posing in it.)

Variations: The Guy on the Phone. The Guy in the Doorway. The Guy Standing by the Sign in Front of the Building.

ME & MY PROP

Who's involved: Artists holding art, workers holding tools, farmers holding pumpkins, quarterbacks holding footballs.

Where it occurs: Location is irrelevant, since we only notice a) the person, and b) the prop.

Variations: Pointing at it. Leaning on it. Smiling at it. Monkeying with it. (Also appears as a variation of the Grip & Grin Photo, usually immediately following some ceremony.)

CROPPING PHOTOS

Most photographers shoot 35mm film, which produces a frame like the one at left. But that doesn't mean all your photos must be shaped like that — or that you're required to use the entire image that a photographer shoots.

To get the most out of a photograph, you *crop* it. Cropping lets you re-frame the image, creating a new shape that focuses attention on what's important — and deletes what's not.

Three ways to crop the same photograph:
- Full frame (left), we see the entire photo image. By showing us this man's books, his furnishings and his dog, the photo gives us clues to his character.
- A moderately tight crop (above) focuses on the man, not his environment, and reduces the distractions in the background.
- An extremely tight crop (below) lets us study the subject's face to explore his personality — though enlarging small details from large photos may produce grainy, fuzzy images.

CROPPING PHOTOS

Yes, a photo can be cropped to fit into almost any space, regardless of its shape. But designers who do that are insensitive louts. That's like taking a 40-inch story and cramming it into a 6-inch hole — not a popular idea.

As a rule, you should edit and crop photos *first,* before you dummy the story. Once you've made the strongest possible crop, *then* select a layout that plays off the photo cleanly and attractively.

To do all that, you must learn where to crop — and where to stop:

This is the photograph as it was originally shot, full frame. Notice the excessive amount of empty space surrounding the central action.

Here's the proper crop for that photo. Note how it focuses tightly on the action without crowding — and without cropping into the hoop, ball or feet.

This is a bad crop because it goes too far. We've chopped off the top of the ball, amputated feet, and crammed the action against the edge of the frame.

A good crop:

■ Finds the focal point of a photo and enhances it. A good crop adds impact by making the central image as large and powerful as possible.

■ Eliminates unnecessary air, people or distractions from the background.

■ Leaves air where it's needed. If a photo captures a mood (loneliness, fear, repose, etc.), crop loosely if it enhances that mood. If a photo is active and directional, don't cram the action against the edge of the frame.

A bad crop:

■ Amputates body parts (especially at joints: wrists, ankles, fingers) or lops off appendages (baseball bats, golf clubs, musical instruments, etc.).

■ Forces the image into an awkward shape just to fit a predetermined hole.

■ Changes the meaning of a photo by removing information. By cropping someone out of a news photo or eliminating an important object in the background, you can distort the meaning of what remains.

■ Violates works of art (paintings, drawings, fine photography) by re-cropping them. Any artwork *not* printed in full should be labeled "detail."

■ Damages the original photo. Never cut photographs or mark them with ink. Instead, make crop marks with a grease pencil, write notes in the margins, or attach a sheet of paper with cropping instructions.

THE PROPORTION WHEEL

Before you can dummy a photo onto a page, you've got to rescale it: that is, you've got to calculate what its new dimensions will be (its height and width) after it's enlarged or reduced. That's why you need a proportion wheel.

THE PROBLEM

7
4
?
12

Take the small gray box above. It's 7 picas wide and 4 picas deep (always give the *width* first). Suppose you want to enlarge it so that it measures 12 picas deep. How *wide* will the box then become?

THE SOLUTION

1 Find the original depth (4) on the inner wheel. Got it? Now turn the wheel so the 4 (the old depth) lines up with the 12 (the new depth) on the outer wheel. Remember: The inner wheel is the *original* size; the outer wheel is the *reproduction* size.

2 Now, without turning the wheel, look at the original width (7) on the inner wheel. It's lined up against 21 on the outer wheel. That means the new width of your reproduction is 21.

3 At some papers, you may need to tell the production department the *percentage* of enlargement or reduction. Look in the window here for that figure: In this case, you'll enlarge the photo 300%.

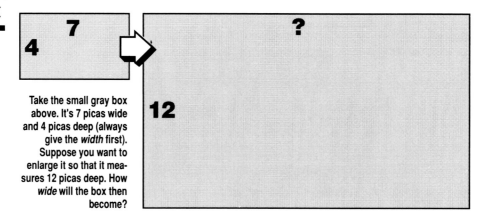

NOTE: This proportion wheel is marked in inches. But don't let that throw you. Your proportions will hold true whether you're measuring things in inches, picas, yards or miles.

IF YOU'D RATHER USE A CALCULATOR...

A proportion wheel is just a mathematical shortcut, a way of showing that the *original width* is to the *original depth* as the *new width* is to the *new depth*. If you'd rather do the math on a calculator, use this formula:

$$\frac{original\ width}{original\ depth} = \frac{new\ width}{new\ depth}$$

For our example above, you'd use this equation to find the new width:

$$\frac{7}{4} = \frac{x}{12}$$ 7 is to 4 as *what* is to 12? To find that missing number, multiply the diagonals (7 X 12 = 84) . . .

$$4x = 84$$ . . . then divide that total by the remaining value (84 ÷ 4) . . .

$$x = 21$$ . . . to find the missing width.

HALFTONES & LINE SHOTS

HALFTONES

Once a photo has been cropped and marked for rescaling, it must be re-photographed by a *copy camera*. There are three reasons for this:

1) The photo may need to be reduced or enlarged to a new size.

2) The contrast or exposure of the original photo may need fine-tuning to improve the way it reproduces on newsprint.

3) Printing presses *cannot print gray*. They can only create the illusion of gray by changing the photo into a pattern of dots called a *halftone*.

Halftone dots are created by re-shooting the original photo through a halftone screen. Most newspapers use screens with 85 lines to the inch. (Those lines, as you can see in the enlargement at right, run diagonally.) Finer screens, with more lines to the inch, produce finer dots and cleaner images. (This book, for instance, uses 100-line screens.)

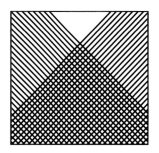

If you examine a halftone with a magnifying glass, you can see how different-sized dots create the range of shades from black to white.

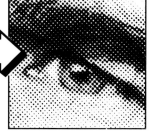

The halftone at left was created by re-shooting the original photo through an 85-line screen. In the enlarged area above, you can see how those dot patterns create the gray tones in George Bush's eye.

LINE SHOTS

As we've seen above, halftone screens are necessary to preserve gray tones when photos are printed on newspaper presses. But what would happen if you printed a photo *without* using a halftone screen?

You'd create something called a line conversion or *line shot*. All dark

tones turn black, while light tones turn white — and as you can see, the result is a dramatic, high-contrast image.

Line shots are used to copy any art that has no gray (pen-and-ink drawings, type treatments, etc.) But since line shots distort the honesty of photo images, they're best reserved for features, not hard news.

STAND-ALONE PHOTOS

Seattle girl
attacked
by killer rat

Mickey says hello

Seattle girl
attacked
by killer rat

In the example at left, you'd assume that's an actual photo of the Seattle girl being attacked by a rat, like the headline says. But it's not. It's a sweet, funny, *stand-alone photo* that's completely unrelated to the story. In the layout at right, the photo is boxed separately, to show readers it's a separate element. (Actually, it's in very poor taste to dummy these two items alongside each other — but we're trying to make a point.)

The point is this: Photos often run independently. You don't need text or a newsworthy hook to justify running a strong photo image. These photos, sometimes called "wild" art since they're so free-form and unpredictable, help designers add life to pages where stories are dull and gray (sewer commission meetings, budget conferences, etc). Stand-alone photos should be encouraged, but they must be packaged in a consistent way that instantly shows readers that the photo stands alone.

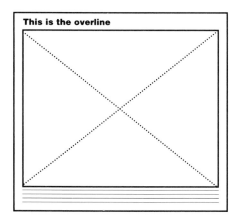

Some papers create a stand-alone photo style that uses an overline (a headline over the photo). The text, underneath, is larger than a standard cutline.

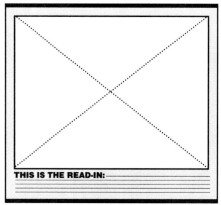

Some papers box the photo with bold rules or run a screen in the background. Some start the cutline with a boldface read-in instead of an overline.

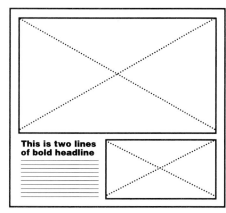

Stand-alone boxes can be used with two or more photos. But as boxes grow bigger, you'll need to follow the guidelines for photo spreads.

PHOTO SPREADS

This photo page from
The Virginian-Pilot and
The Ledger-Star tells
the story of an
American boxer train-
ing for a title fight in
Paris. Note the variety
of photo shapes and
sizes; note the balance
and flow of the layout.
(This is actually a well-
packaged jump page.
Papers often begin
stories on a section
front, then jump to a
photo page inside.)

Unlike the rest of the newspaper, where photos compete for space with text (and usually lose), photo spreads are self-contained visual packages that give good photos the big, bold play they deserve. They're usually used for:

■ **Covering a major event** (a disaster, election night, The Big Game) from a number of different angles — often from several photographers.

■ **Exploring a topic or trend** (the homeless, neo-Nazis, a skateboarding craze), taking readers on a tour of people and places they've never seen.

■ **Profiling a personality** (an athlete, a disease victim, a politician), painting a portrait by capturing a person's moods, actions and surroundings.

■ **Telling a story** with a definite beginning, middle and end (the birth of a baby, a Marine's ordeal in boot camp, an artist in the act of creation).

■ **Displaying objects/places** (a tour of a new building, fall fashions, hot toys for Christmas), where photos present an inventory of items.

Photo spreads are different from standard news layouts. They bend and break the rules. They let you play with headlines, decks and cutlines. They let you create your own customized widths for photos and text.

In fact, text often becomes a minor element on photo pages. Some pages use only a short (under 6-inch) text block; others use long stories, but jump most of the text to another page to allow maximum display for photos.

This Halloween photo page from The Oregonian displays an assortment of customized pumpkins and their creators. Since there's no storytelling here — no dramatic beginning, middle or end — the biggest design consideration is fitting all the photos onto the page in an orderly, attractive way.

PHOTO SPREADS

At many papers, photographers shoot special assignments, then design their own photo pages. Usually, however, the layout is done by an editor or designer who's handed some photos, given a headline and asked to leave room for a certain amount of copy. Here's a typical example of how it works:

A DESIGN EXERCISE

Let's design a photo page for a tabloid. The photos were shot at a folk music festival, so the head can simply say "Folk Fest." There's no story, but we'll assume someone will write a short text block (3-4 inches) to describe the event. Here are the four best photos; we'll use all four. Cutlines can be written later.

1 This is the photographer's favorite shot. He wants it to be the lead. What you're looking at here — for all four photos, actually — is a work print that's cropped the way he'd like it cropped. You can make slight cropping changes to suit your layout, but be careful not to damage the composition suggested by the photographer.

3 Another nice shot. This little girl was a real crowd-pleaser, so be sure to run this photo big enough that we can see her.

4 This is the scene-setter (sometimes called an "establishing shot") showing the stage platform. As these four photos demonstrate, a good photo layout provides a mix of close-up, mid-range and wide-angle scene-setting shots to tell the whole story.

2 This shot provides "color," showing the types of folks attending the folk festival. It's a charming alternative to the performance shots. And besides, it's a vertical, and the layout will probably need at least one alternative to all those horizontals.

PHOTO SPREADS

Here are six layouts using those photos from the facing page:

This layout alternates the sizes of photos — big, small, big, small — to achieve good balance. Note how the page is bordered by two sets of outer margins: 1) a thin margin outside all the elements, and 2) a wider indent beside the text and photo #2. Balancing two sets of indents gives you more flexibility in sizing photos and keeps the page from getting too dense.

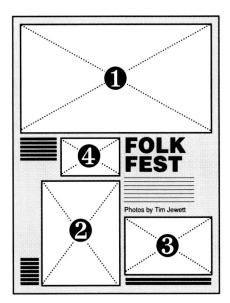

This layout is a flopped variation of the page at far left; the biggest difference is that photo #3 (a horizontal) is the second-biggest photo instead of photo #2 (a vertical). The text runs in two legs instead of one, and there are now two pairs of shared cutlines. Notice how, of all the layouts on this page, this one is the most tightly packed. All the others have been designed with more air in their outer margins.

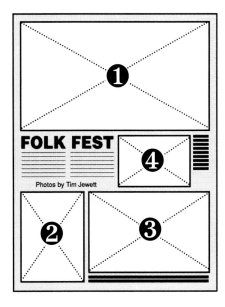

This layout treats the headline as an independent art element, placing it squarely in the center of the page, aligned with the two photos below it. The leg of text then runs beside it — an arrangement that would never work in a standard news story, but it seems to fit neatly here. The only problem with this page is that all the open space is shoved to the left edge of the page.

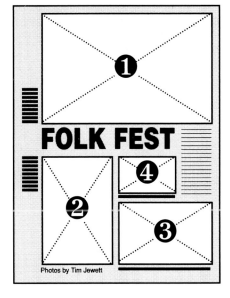

This layout forces the text into a bottom corner. Since there's not enough text to fill the hole, it's indented (to match the photo indents on the right side of the page), and the photo credit is used to pad the remaining space. Note how the text is indented more than the headline; that's called a hanging indent. A final note: Placing cutlines in a top corner can sometimes be awkward, but here it balances the cutline in the bottom corner of the page.

This design is a variation on the layout directly above. This version is a little less effective, since putting the headline and text in the center of the layout divides the photos into two separate groups. It's well balanced, however — though photos #2 and #3 are very similar in size.

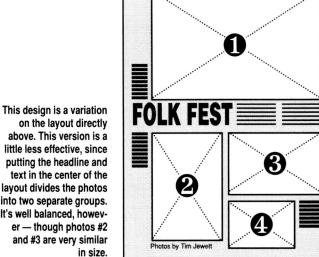

This approach is an old favorite: Park a scene-setter (photo 4) beside the headline at the top of the page, then smack readers with the loud lead photo. The text then starts below the lead photo, directly below the headline. That breaks the usual rule about keeping headlines with text — but it seems to work here. Note how the elements above and below the lead photo align with each other; all are indented equally along the right and left edge of the page.

PHOTO SPREAD GUIDELINES

The following guidelines apply not only to photo pages but to feature sections and special news packages as well. You'll find many of the same principles will apply whether you're using photos, illustrations, charts or maps.

Note: Photo pages are often designed with gray background screens. We've added screens to the examples below to make the photo shapes easier to see.

PHOTOS

■ **Talk to the photographer (and the reporter).** Learn about the story. Find out which photos they prefer — which should be the lead, which are expendable. Make sure the page presents their material fairly and accurately.

■ **Mix it up.** Use different shapes. Different sizes. Different perspectives. Tell the story with a variety of visuals: horizontals and verticals, tight close-ups and wide-angle scene-setters. Keep things moving. Surprise our eyes.

 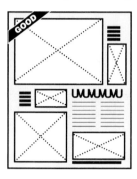

The layout at left feels static and dull because the photos are all similar in shape and size. Nothing grabs your attention. The layout at right uses a variety of shapes and sizes. As a result, the page looks interesting and inviting.

■ **Design for quality, not quantity.** Yes, you want variety — but one good picture played well is worth two small ones played weakly. Mix it up, but be a tough judge. If you overcrowd the page, all your photos lose impact.

■ **Position photos carefully.** Are photos strongly directional? (Don't let them collide or face off the page.) Are they sequential or chronological? (Give the page order — a beginning and an end, a setup and a punchline.)

■ **Make one photo dominant.** Play it big. Give it clout. Plant it in your layout first, *then* play the other photos off of it. And remember: Dominant photos usually work best in the top half of the layout:

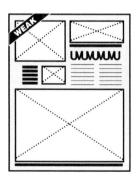 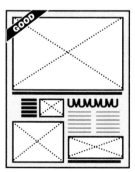

In the layout at left, the page seems bottom-heavy and poorly balanced. Compare that to the effect of the page at right. It uses all the same elements, but here the lead photo has been dummied on top.

HEADLINES

■ **Get your headline first.** Pages look better and come together easier if you have a headline before you start dummying. If you dummy a hole for someone to fill later, you may get a dull headline that doesn't quite fit.

■ **Use the headline to anchor the page.** Don't be shy. Make it bold. But use it to tie elements together; don't just float it in a corner or across the top.

■ **Use a display headline (with a deck) if appropriate.** Don't limit yourself to standard news headline formats. Try something with more personality.

PHOTO SPREAD GUIDELINES

TEXT

■ **Don't run too much — or too little.** Most photo pages need text to explain why they're there. But anything under 3 inches may get buried; huge text blocks, on the other hand, turn the page gray and crowd out photos.

■ **Keep text blocks modular.** Never snake text over, around and through a maze of photos. Keep text rectangular. Park it in a neat, logical place.

■ **Ask for leeway on story sizes.** Sure, you dummy as closely as you can, but sometimes that 13.3-inch story will just *have* to be cut — or padded — to fit. Make sure writers and editors give you a little flexibility on story lengths.

MORE ON:

■ **Cutlines:** Basic guidelines on sizing and placement.... **23**

■ **Dominant photos:** Why they're important and how to choose them... **42**

■ **Photo credits:** Style and placement options............ **119**

■ **Screens:** What they are, where to use them.......... **136**

■ **Display headlines:** Tips on how to build them..... **138**

CUTLINES & PHOTO CREDITS

■ **Give every photo a cutline.** Two photos may share a cutline if the layout requires it, but make it very clear which words describe which photo.

■ **Remember, cutlines can run beside (or between) photos.** But don't float them loosely — plant them flush against the photo they describe. If cutlines use ragged type, run ragged edges *away* from the photo.

■ **Push cutlines to the outside.** In bad designs, cutlines butt up against headlines or text. In good designs, cutlines move to the outside of the page where they won't collide with any other type elements:

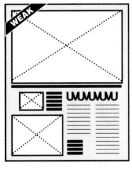 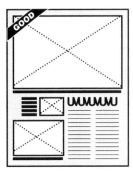

In the layout at left, one set of cutlines butts against the headline, while another runs into the bottom of a leg of text. Both problems have been fixed in the layout at right, where the cutlines have been moved to the outside.

■ **Credit photos properly.** This is usually done either by running a separate photo credit line along the edge of the design, or by attaching credit lines to each photo (or just to the lead, if they're all by the same photographer).

OTHER DESIGN ADVICE

■ **Design in white space.** Don't cram text and photos into every square pica. Let the page breathe with what's called "white space" or "air." But don't trap dead space between elements; push it to the outside of the page:

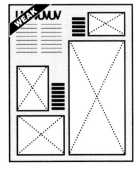 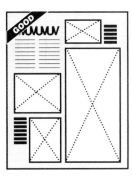

Note how pockets of dead space seem scattered through the page at left. At right, all the extra space has been pushed to the outer edges of the layout. As a result, the elements fit more neatly.

■ **Keep margins consistent.** Decide how you'll align elements (1-pica gutters? Two picas outside the whole page?) to maintain underlying order.

■ **Use screens sparingly.** A gray background screen can help organize and enhance layouts. But too much gray makes pages drab — so be careful.

■ **Draw life-size dummies.** Many pros design special pages on full-size grid sheets. It's a good way to get an accurate feel for shape and proportion.

STUDIO SHOTS

Photojournalism is an honest craft. It captures real people in real situations, without poses or props. But what if you need a photo of a hot new bikini? A plate of food? A book jacket? Will that photo be *real, honest* photojournalism?

Not exactly. It's a studio shot. And unlike news photos, where shooters merely observe events, studio shots let shooters manipulate objects, pose models, build props and control lighting.

Studio shots — or any other set-up photos, whether they're shot in a studio or not — are used primarily in features, and primarily for:

■ **Fashion.** Clothes by themselves are dull; clothes worn by a model who smiles, struts or flirts will yank readers right into the page.

■ **Food.** Making food look delicious in a 2-column black-and-white photo is tougher than you think, but absolutely necessary for food stories.

■ **Portraits.** Special faces deserve special treatment, and studio shots let you glamorize someone celebrated in an in-depth personality profile.

■ **Incidental objects.** Don't forget: It's important to show readers the miscellaneous items mentioned in features or reviews (album covers, book jackets, new products, etc.).

MORE ON:

■ **Photo cutouts:** How to turn studio shots (like the fashion model at left) into silhouettes......... **134**

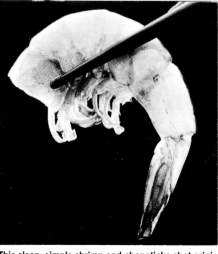

This clean, simple shrimp-and-chopsticks shot originally ran in color on a food page in The Oregonian.

This magazine-cover portrait of Portland's mayor added a reversed headline to the background.

PHOTO ILLUSTRATIONS

To illustrate this story on credit cards and debt, an artist turned a mousetrap into an **American Excess** credit card, and the headline tied it all together. By combining the humor of parody with the pain of debt, you create an attention-getting image.

This photo illustration ran on the Business page of the Sacramento Bee. Note how the photographer manipulates cliches: The boss (a model) is a gruff, middle-aged, cigar-smoking, business-suited man. (Yes, women are bosses, too — but making a woman the main character here might have given many readers a different message altogether.)

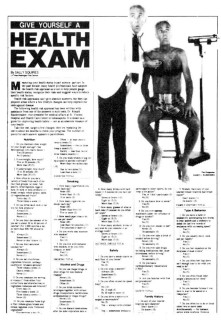

Again, this photo-illustration is a simple depiction of the story's headline: The head of the seated model has been pasted onto the doctor's body.

Sometimes the best way to illustrate a feature story is to shoot a photograph, yet manipulate the composition as if it were a drawing. The result: a *photo illustration.*

Photo illustrations are usually studio shots (see previous page). But unlike fashion photos or portraits, photo illustrations don't simply present an image; they express an idea, a point of view. They use lighting, props and special effects to capture moods, symbolize concepts, tell visual jokes.

As a result, photo illustrations are often excellent solutions for topical features where the themes are abstract — depression, love in the workplace, junk-food junkies — stories where real photos of real people would be too difficult to find or too dull to print.

A good photo illustration:

■ **Instantly shows what the story's about.** A photo illustration shouldn't confuse or distract readers. It should present one clean, clear idea that requires no guesswork (and avoids misleading meanings). And it must match the tone and content of the text.

■ **Should never be mistaken for reality.** Most newspaper photos are honest: They show real people doing real things. Readers expect that. So if you're going to change the rules and present a false image, make it immediately obvious. Distort angles, exaggerate sizes, manipulate lighting, use odd-looking models — do *something* to cue the reader that this photo isn't authentic. It's dishonest to pass off a posed photo (someone pretending to be a drug addict) as the real thing. Even warning readers in a cutline isn't good enough; once a photo makes its impact on a reader, the damage is done.

■ **Works with the headline.** The photo and the headline must form a unit. They must work together to convey one idea, not two.

■ **Performs with flair.** A good photo illustration shows off the photographer's skill and cleverness with lighting, special effects, poses and props. In a world where newspaper graphics compete against slick TV and magazine ads, you either excel or you lose. If your photo illustration looks bland and ordinary, you lose.

ILLUSTRATIONS

Newspapers are full of illustrations. Some exist purely for amusement (comics, for instance). Some appear in ads, selling tires or TV sets. Some are used to jazz up logos; some run in teasers to promote stories.

And then there are bigger, more ambitious illustrations, the ones that require more space, more collaboration between artists and page designers — and bigger budgets.

Below are some of the most common types of newspaper illustrations:

COMMENTARY & CARICATURE

The first illustration ever printed in an American newspaper was an editorial cartoon in Ben Franklin's Pennsylvania Gazette. It showed a dismembered snake, with each section representing one of the 13 colonies. It carried the caption "JOIN or DIE".

Editorial cartoons have gotten a lot funnier since then. Today, they're expected to be humorous, yet thoughtful; provocative, yet tasteful; far-fetched, yet truthful. That's why editorial cartooning is one of the toughest jobs in journalism — and why successful editorial cartoonists are a rarity.

This editorial cartoon, by Jack Ohman of The Oregonian, relies on a hip drawing style, crisp hand lettering and a wicked sense of satire.

A similar type of illustration, the commentary drawing, also interprets current events. Like editorial cartoons, commentary drawings usually run on a separate opinion page. Unlike editorial cartoons, commentary drawings accompany a story or analysis, rather than standing alone; they don't try as hard to be funny, but still employ symbols and caricatures to comment on personalities and issues.

Taking a cue from the story's headline, this caricature by Joe Iula of the Rochester Times-Union makes the most of comedian Sam Kinison's screaming mouth and "bad boy" image.

Caricatures, however, aren't limited to opinion pages. They're often used on sports or entertainment pages to accompany profiles of well-known celebrities. A good caricature exaggerates its subject's most distinctive features for comic effect. Like editorial cartooning, it's a skill that's difficult to master, and should be avoided if:

■ The subject's face isn't very well-known.

■ The story is too sensitive or downbeat for this brash style of art.

■ The artist's ability to pull it off is doubtful.

ILLUSTRATIONS

FLAVOR DRAWINGS

This comical cartoon of a happy hiker ran in The Oregonian. It immediately tells readers what the story's about: an upbeat IQ test for campers heading off to the woods. A hiking photograph would not have been as appealing or effective as Pat McLelland's drawing.

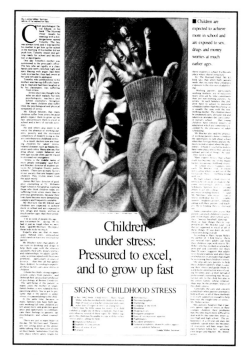

Children under stress: Pressured to excel, and to grow up fast

Childhood stress is a difficult topic to depict. A set-up photograph might look phony or make readers wonder, "Is this child featured in the story?" This effective drawing by Paul Compton in The Washington Times captures the serious tone of the story.

Feature pages often focus on abstract themes: drugs, depression, dreams, diets, etc. And many of those themes are too vague or slippery to capture in a photograph.

That's where illustrations can save the day. Flavor drawings — drawings that capture the tone of a topic — can add impact to the text while giving focus to the design.

Finding the right approach to use in an illustration takes practice — both for artists and editors. But flavor drawings can be silly or serious, colorful or black-and-white. They can dominate the page or simply drop into a leg of text to provide quick diversion. Be careful, however: Readers can sense when you're simply filling space.

Readers read newspapers for information. Don't just give them decoration.

GRAPHICS

As we'll see three chapters from now, there's a hot trend afoot in newspapers these days:

Infographics.

Blending information and illustration, infographics take the form of charts, diagrams, maps and tables. Often, art is essential to the graphic. It might reconstruct how a news event unfolded, or analyze how a complicated gizmo operates. In smaller graphics (like the one at right), art is more decorative, cuing readers to the topic without becoming an integral part of the data.

For more on the art of infographics, turn to the chapter that begins on page 143.

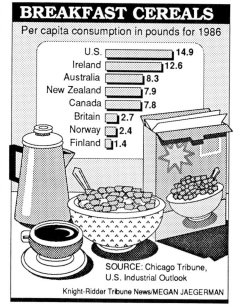

In this bar chart, the important data — 1986 cereal consumption — is represented by different-sized bars. The breakfast-table drawing adds visual appeal to a graphic that would otherwise look pretty dull.

A FEATURE ART CHECKLIST

Feature pages require good art. To create good art, you need good ideas. And you need those good ideas *before* stories are written, *before* photos are shot, *before* you sit down to design the page. Begin your idea search *before* deadline pressures force you to take shortcuts.

Stumped on how to illustrate a page? The following checklist will help guide you (and your colleagues) to the graphic heart of a feature story:

PHOTO SOLUTIONS

❑ **Can we <u>shoot</u> photos?**
Can we illustrate this story photojournalistically — showing real people in real situations? Look for:

■ *Events:* What events/actions are connected with this story? What do the main characters *do* that's interesting? (A reminder: Talking, thinking and sitting at a desk are *not* interesting.)

■ *People:* Who is the key player? Are there several? What kind of portrait tells us the most about them? What emotions do they experience in this story? Can one mood-oriented portrait convey the idea? Is there a situation where emotions and actions intersect?

■ *Places:* Can location/setting help tell the story, either:
 • With a main character posed in a dramatic location? (Avoid desks, doorways, couches and signs in front of buildings.)
 • With several of the main characters working or interacting?
 • Without people (focusing instead on buildings, scenery, environments)?

■ *Objects:* What items are integral to the story? Machines? Equipment? Works of art? Vehicles? Clothing? Can they be used as lead art? Turned into a diagram? Explained in detail in a sidebar?

❑ **Can we <u>find</u> photos (from an outside source)?**
 ■ From a wire service?
 ■ From the newsroom library? A local library?
 ■ From organizations (government offices, museums, clubs, stores, companies mentioned in the story)?
 ■ From other media (TV networks, other newspapers, film studios)?
 ■ From books (with proper approval from the publisher)?
 ■ From the people in the story?

If photos won't tell the story, then you should consider:

ART SOLUTIONS (including photo illustrations)

❑ Does the story focus on an abstract theme? Can one strong image capture that theme and anchor the page? Or are several smaller images needed?

❑ Should we create a:
 ■ *Drawing?* (Is an artist available? Or do we prefer the realism of a photo?)
 ■ *Photo illustration?* (Is a photographer available? Or do we want a freer, more fanciful solution?)

To pull strong images out of the story, try to:

❑ **Write a headline.** A clever headline will often inspire a graphic hook. Before you begin sketching art ideas, wander through the story and look for key words and phrases. Loosen up and noodle around with:
 ■ *Puns.* ("Give Peas a Chance." "The Noel Prizes." "Art and Sole.")
 ■ *Alliteration and rhyme.* ("FAX Facts." "High-Tech Home Ec.")
 ■ *TV, movie or song titles.* ("Born to Run." "The Right Stuff.")
 ■ *Well-known quotes, proverbs or slang expressions.*
 ■ *A quote or phrase lifted from the text.*
 ■ *A key word from the story.* (Someone's name. A place. An emotion.)

A FEATURE ART CHECKLIST

No headline yet? Or is it clever, but still vague?

❏ **Brainstorm images.** Wander through your topic again, but this time compile a list of words, activities, symbols, visual cliches. Analyze the story in terms of:

■ *Who.* What types (or stereotypes) are involved? How can you exaggerrate their personalities? Are there victims? Villains? Are there props or symbols you can use to represent people in the story?

■ *What.* What objects, feelings or actions are involved? What cliches or symbols come to mind? Isolate them. Mix 'n' match them. What happens if you exaggerate or distort them? See anything humorous? Dramatic?

■ *When.* When does the action occur? Are there moments when the topic is most dramatic or humorous? At what times does the topic begin or end?

■ *Where.* Where does this subject occur? Where does it start? End? If you were filming a movie, what dramatic angles or close-ups would you use?

■ *Why.* What does this story mean? What's the end result, the ultimate effect? What's the reason people do it, dread it, love it? And why should we care?

Once you've compiled a list of images, try to combine them in different ways. View them from different angles. Or try these approaches:

■ *Parody.* There's a world of symbols and cliches out there waiting to be recycled. Some are universal: an egg (frailty, rebirth), a light bulb (creativity), a test tube (research), a gun (danger), an apple (education). You can play with the flag, dollar bills, road signs, game boards. Or parody cultural icons: The Statue of Liberty. The Thinker. Uncle Sam. "American Gothic."

■ *Combination.* Two images can combine to form a fresh new idea. If your story's about people *trapped* by *credit cards,* create a *credit-card mousetrap.* If your story's about some *puzzle* at *City Hall,* create a *City Hall jigsaw puzzle.* And so on.

■ *Exaggeration.* Distort size, speed, emotion, repetition. Is there a BIG problem looming? Is something shrinking? Fading? Taken to an extreme, what would this subject look like? How would affected people look?

■ *Montage.* Arrange a scrapbook of images: photos, artifacts, old engravings from library books. Try to create order, interplay or point of view.

OTHER GRAPHICS SOLUTIONS

By now, you may have found a solution that seems like pure genius to you. But beware: Ideas don't always translate into reality. Your solution must work instantly for hundreds of readers. So before you proceed, run a rough sketch past your colleagues to test their reactions. If it doesn't fly, drop it.

Remember, too: Informational art is usually better than decorational art. Will your illustration inform, or is it just a silly cartoon? Does it make a point, or convey fuzzy emotion? Is it big simply because you need to fill space?

You can still salvage your idea — but consider using it along with:

■ *Infographics.* Dress up charts, graphs, maps or diagrams as lead or secondary art. Show your readers how things work, what they mean, where they're headed. Teach — don't just entertain.

■ *Sidebars (with art).* Add enough art support (diagrams, book jackets, mugs, products, etc.) and you can make a sidebar carry the whole page.

■ *Large type effects.* Add a big display headline. A jumbo initial cap.

■ *Mugs and quotes.* Drop these in wherever pages look gray.

If you're still trying to dress things up, try a combination of boxes, screens or background wallpaper effects. This is just fancy footwork, however — a way of distracting the reader to disguise your lack of art.

❏ **A warning:** If you've come this far and still don't have a solution, rethink your story. If it's too vague for you, it's probably too vague for readers.

RISKY BUSINESS

*In your search for
The Ultimate Page Design,
you may be tempted to try
some of these effects.
But before you do, read on.*

STEALING

Before you print a picture that's "borrowed" from an outside source, be sure you're not violating copyright laws. Old art (like the Mona Lisa) is safe; copyrighted art can be used if it's part of a review or a breaking news story. But copyright laws are complex — as are laws governing the reprinting of money* — so get good advice before proceeding.

FRAMING

There are dozens of decorative border tapes. There are books full of fancy frames. And one day, you'll finally succumb to temptation and destroy an elegant photo with a gaudy, glitzy frame. Don't do it. Art and photos should be bordered with thin, simple rules. Anything thick, ornate or colorful just distracts the readers' attention from what's important.

FLOPPING

Printing a photo backward, as a mirror image of itself, is called *flopping.* Usually, it's done because a designer wants a photo facing the opposite direction, to better suit a layout. But that's dangerous. It distorts the truth of the image. *Never* flop news photos; flop feature photos or studio shots *only* as a last resort, and if there's no way to tell you've done it.

RESHAPING

As we've learned, photos work best as rectangles with right-angle corners. Cutting them into other "creative" shapes distorts their meaning, confuses the reader and messes up the page. Put quite simply: Slicing up photos is the mark of a true amateur. There's hardly ever a valid reason for doing it, so put the idea right out of your mind.

TILTING

Sometimes you get art that's so wild, so wacky, you just *have* to give it an equally nutty layout. OK — but beware. Unless you choose appropriate art, tilt it at just the right angle and skew the type smoothly, you'll trash the page. Even though the pros try it from time to time (see page 14), remember: Tilting can be treacherous.

SILHOUETTING

If a photo is weakened by harsh shadows or a distracting background, you may consider cutting out the central image and running it either against the white page or with a new background. That works well with some photos, poorly with others — but should be considered *only* for feature pages. For more advice and warnings about cutouts, see page 134.

*For instance, dollar bills can only be reproduced with black ink; they must be enlarged to 150% or more, or reduced to 75% or less.

EXERCISES

Exercise answers are on page 169.

1 Below are four photos that accompany a story about a woman jockey. Using all four, create a full-page photo layout for a broadsheet feature section, with the headline "On the fast track" (and you'll need to add a deck below the headline, as well). The story is very long, so assume you can jump as much text as you need.

Crop the photos as you see fit. But before you begin, ask yourself: Which photo should be dominant?

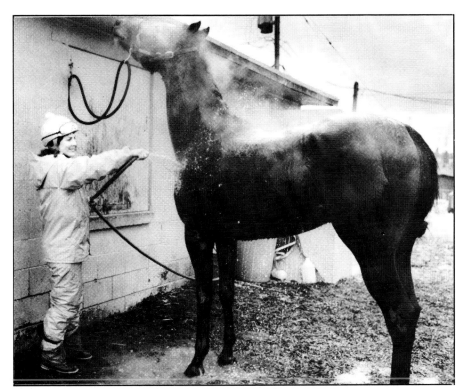

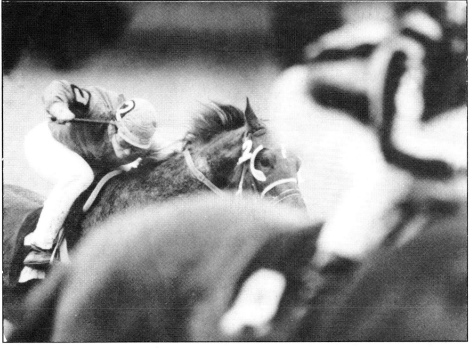

EXERCISES

2 The photos for that woman jockey spread (previous page) were good, both in content and technical quality. But if you were the photo editor for that page, and there was time to go back and shoot more photos, what might you ask for? What's missing?

3 The three layouts below were created from those jockey photos. Can you find at least three things wrong with each of these page designs?

4 **A.** At left is a full-frame photo from a local drug bust. How would you crop this shot if you were using it as your horizontal lead photo?
B. Now that you've cropped it, what will its new depth be if its width becomes 45 picas?

Exercise answers begin on page 171.

A newspaper is a product — like a box of corn flakes. Like corn flakes, newspapers are good for you. Like corn flakes, newspapers are a part of America's breakfast routine. And like corn flakes, newspapers seem pretty much alike from one brand to the next.

So how do you make your brand of corn flakes more attractive to consumers? Through *packaging.* You dress them up in a colorful box. Design a snappy-looking name. Play up a catchy promotion (FREE WHISTLE INSIDE!) or lift out some quotable phrase ("High-fiber nutrition with real blueberry goodness") to catch the eye of passing shoppers. And finally, stick in all the extras that are required to be there — ingredients, weight, date, the company's address — as neatly and unobtrusively as you can.

All of the above holds true for newspapers, too. And in this chapter, we'll explore some graphic and typographic constants used to build and sell a typical newspaper package: flags, decks, bylines, teasers, liftout quotes.

Up to this point, we've discussed the foundations of design. In this chapter, we'll examine how you can label and connect related stories. How you can break up long columns of gray text. How you can add graphic devices to sell stories to the reader.

In other words, how to put more real corn goodness into every bite.

Weather

Partly cloudy. Winds NW 10-15 mph. High 70, low 40. Details on **2A**

CHAPTER CONTENTS

■ **Flags:** Examples of different nameplate styles 110

■ **Standing heads:** How section logos help readers find their way around the paper.................... 111

■ **Logos & sigs:** How to design and dummy column logos, sigs and bugs, and series logos to label special features....... 112-113

■ **Liftout quotes:** Guidelines for using quotations as a graphic element within text............... 114-115

■ **Decks:** How to size them, where to dummy them 116

■ **Breaking up text:** Using subheads, initial caps and dingbats to break up long legs of type...... 117

■ **Bylines:** A look at different formats both for news stories and for special pages........................ 118

■ **Credit lines:** Different options for crediting photographers.... 119

■ **Spacing:** Positioning tips for

different design elements on a typical page 120

■ **Rules & boxes:** Guidelines for using them both functionally and decoratively 121

■ **Refers & teasers:** How editors alert readers to stories scattered throughout the paper 122

■ **Jumps:** Guidelines for jumping stories smoothly from one page to another 123

FLAGS

It's one of the oldest journalistic traditions: centering the *flag* (or name-plate) at the very top of Page One. Over the years, some papers have tried boxing it in a corner. Some have tried flipping it sideways. Some have tried floating it below stories partway down the page. But most papers choose the simplest solution: Park the flag at the top and give the page some dignity.

Most designers, it turns out, have little input when it comes to flags, which get overhauled maybe,once every 20 years — if that often. (Flags, incidentally, are often mistakenly called "mastheads." But a masthead is the staff box full of publication data that usually runs on the editorial page.)

There are basically two philosophies of flag design. One argues that flags should evoke a sense of tradition, trust, sobriety — and indeed, most Old English flags look downright religious. Some, on the other hand, argue that flags are like corporate logos, and should be distinctive, modern, graphically sophisticated. (Some try to play it both ways: conservative, but a bit hip.)

Here are a few examples. Do they offer clues to the papers' personalities?

Some papers float their flag in white space to give it prominence. Others add *ears* (items in the corners on each side of the flag) to fill the space. Ears often appeal to readers with weather reports, slogans ("All the News That's Fit to Print") or teasers that promote items inside the paper:

What's essential in a flag? The name of the paper. The city, school or organization it serves. The date. The price. The edition, if different versions (Westside, Sunrise) are printed. Some papers include the volume number — but though that may matter to librarians, readers aren't keeping score.

STANDING HEADS

THE OREGONIAN   **THE DETROIT FREE PRESS**   **THE WASHINGTON TIMES**

As you travel through a newspaper, you need signposts to tell you where you are. Some are like big billboards ("You are now entering **LIVING**"). Others are like small road signs that direct traffic ("Exit here for *Movie Review*").

Every paper needs a well-coordinated system of signposts — or, as they're often called, *standing heads* or *headers*. And just as highway signposts are designed to stand apart from the scenery, standing heads should be designed to "pop" off the page. They can use rules, bolder type, extra leading, screens or reverses — but it's essential that they project a personality that differs from the ordinary text and headlines they accompany.

Compare, for example, the effectiveness of these two section logos:

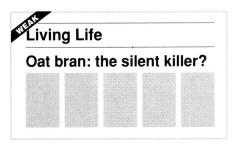

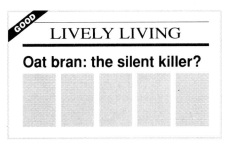

This section logo uses the same font as the headline. It has no special character to set it apart from the day's news, so it doesn't "pop" off the page.

Here, the section logo uses all-cap serifs and a thick rule to set it apart from the text. It could also have been screened, boxed or run in bolder type.

A *logo* is a word or name that's customized in a graphic way. Logos can be created with type alone, or by adding rules, photos or other art elements.

Section logos, like those above, help departmentalize the paper. In small tabloids, they should appear atop the page each time the topic changes (from Features to Opinion, for instance). Bigger papers use section logos to identify each separate section, often adding teasers to promote what's inside:

Some papers use small standing heads to label the content on every single page. Others reserve that treatment for special themed pages or news-feature packages (*Super Bowl XXXIV Preview*, for instance, or *AIDS in Our Schools: A Special Report*).

Either way, those added signposts guide readers effectively only if they're designed and positioned consistently throughout the paper, in a graphic style that sets them apart from the "live" news.

LOGOS & SIGS

As we've just seen, section logos and page headers label entire sections or pages. But labels are necessary for special stories, too. And these labels for stories are simply called *logos, bugs* or *sigs.*

Logos and sigs are usually small enough to park within the legs of a story. But whatever their size, they need to be designed with:

■ A graphic personality that sets them apart from text and headlines;

■ A consistent style that's maintained throughout the paper; and

■ Flexible widths that will work well in any design context.

It's important to put logos where they'll label the column's content without confusing the layout — which means they should never disrupt the flow of text or create confusion by butting up against other elements.

Here are some of the most common ways to dummy logos with stories:

In multi-column layouts, sigs and logos are usually dummied at the top of the second leg, so they won't interrupt the flow of the text. Avoid, if possible, running mugs or photos in that second leg — the logo will look odd whether it's dummied above or below other art, and both will compete for the reader's attention.

In vertical layouts, sigs and logos are either dummied above the headline or indented a few inches down into the text. Indenting logos is tricky, though, since text should be at least 6 picas wide — which doesn't leave much room for long words in a logo.

Instead of placing sigs and logos down within the legs of text, some papers use headers that stretch above the headline, usually running the full width of the story. This is a very clean, clear way to label special features, but takes up more space than the other formats — and doesn't do much to break up gray legs of text.

COLUMN LOGOS

Column logos are a way to label special writers, those regularly appearing personalities whose names and faces are worth remembering. These logos (also called *photo sigs*) are usually reserved for writers who express opinions — writers whose columns, for whatever reason, create a reader habit. (To support that reader habit, then, it's important to dummy the column in the same style and the same place each edition.)

Column logos usually consist of:

■ The writer's name.

■ The writer's likeness (either a photo or a sketch).

■ A catchy title *(Dear Abby, Screen Scene* or — yawn — *On the Town).*

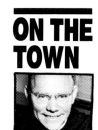

LOGOS & SIGS

SIGS & BUGS

Column logos add personality to pages by promoting the personalities of writers. Sigs and bugs, on the other hand, are more functional than decorative. They identify topics, not people; they display words, not some writer's mug.

Sigs are used to label:

■ Briefs and non-standard news columns (*Business Notes, People, Legislative Roundup*).

■ Opinion pieces that appear on news pages (*News Analysis, Movie Review*).

■ Regularly appearing non-bylined features (*NBA Notebook, Letters to the Editor, Money Matters, Action Line!*)

At some papers, there's even a trend toward labeling more and more stories by topic (*City Council, Medicine, Tennis*). That's difficult to do consistently throughout the paper, but it's a helpful idea for guiding busy readers from topic to topic.

Other papers have created sig variations that refer to stories on other pages or add capsulized information (as in the bottom movie review sig at right).

Sigs are designed in a variety of sizes and styles, using rules, screens or graphic effects to catch readers' eyes. But since every paper must use a consistent graphic treatment for all its logos, what's appropriate for POP MUSIC should also be appropriate for OBITUARIES.

MOVIE REVIEW

Ghostbusters 2
★★★

Starring: Bill Murray, Dan Aykroyd, Sigourney Weaver
Director: Ivan Reitman
Rating: PG for language, slime
Playing at: Mall City Octoplex

SERIES LOGOS

Series logos are a way to label special packages (a 5-day series on *Racism in the Classroom*) or stories that will appear more than once (a news event continuing over an extended period, like *Election '92* or *Revolt in China.*)

Series logos (called *icons* at some papers) usually consist of:

■ A brief, catchy title that creates instant reader familiarity.

■ A small illustration or photo that symbolizes the topic graphically.

■ Optional refer lines to other pages or to tomorrow's installment.

Logos incorporating refers or copy blocks are usually 1 or 2 columns wide; those standing alone are 1 column wide — or indented into the text.

LIFTOUT QUOTES

"If I repent of anything, it is very likely to be my good behavior. What demon possessed me that I behaved so well?"

— Henry David Thoreau

'I don't want to achieve immortality through my work. I want to achieve it through not dying. '

WOODY ALLEN

 I don't care what is written about me, so long as it isn't true.

— KATHARINE HEPBURN

"We are healthy only to the extent that our ideas are humane."

— Kurt Vonnegut, Jr.

"The surest way to make a monkey of a man," said Robert Benchley, "is to quote him." And the surest way to make a reader curious about a story is to plant a wise, witty or controversial quote within a column of text.

As the examples above show, *liftout quotes* can be packaged in a variety of styles, jazzed up with rules, boxes, screens or reverses. (They go by a variety of names, too: *pullquotes, breakouts, quoteblocks, quote sandwiches,* etc.) But whether simple or ornate, liftout quotes should follow these guidelines:

■ **They should be quotations.** Not paraphrases, not decks, not narration from the text — but complete sentences spoken by someone in the story.

■ **They should be attributed.** Don't run "mystery quotes" that force us to comb the text for the speaker's identity. Tell us who's doing the talking.

■ **They should be bigger and bolder than text type.** Don't be shy. Use a liftout style that pops from the page to catch the reader's eye— something distinctive that won't be mistaken for a headline or subhead.

■ **They should be 1-2 inches deep.** Shallower than that, they seem too terse and trivial; deeper than that, they seem too dense and wordy.

QUOTES WITH MUGS

Words of wisdom are appealing, but when we can see the speaker's face we're attracted even more. That's why mug/quote combinations are among the surest ways to hook passing readers.

Quotes with mugs can be boxed or unboxed. Whichever style you adopt, adapt it to work both horizontally (in 2- or 3-column widths) and vertically (in 1-column widths or indented within a column). Be sure the format's wide enough, and the type small enough, to fit long words without hyphenation.

"People have got to know whether or not their President is a crook. Well, I am not a crook."

— Richard Nixon

QUOTABLE

"It's been an extraordinary life. I just wish that I had been there to enjoy it."

— SYLVESTER STALLONE

LIFTOUT QUOTES

DESIGN GUIDELINES

■ Be sure you have a quote worth lifting *before* you dummy it in. You can't expect great quotes to materialize automatically — some stories, after all, don't even *have* any quotations.

Read the story first. Or talk to the reporter. Remember, once you get in the habit of promoting great quotes, it will encourage reporters to *find* more great quotes. As a result, both the stories and their readers will benefit.

■ Don't sprinkle liftouts randomly through the text just to kill space:

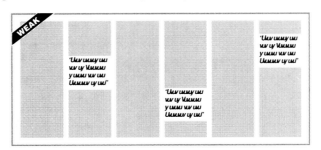

Instead, limit liftouts to one per story. That gives each quote maximum impact and keeps the design clean and well-balanced. Use two or more liftouts only if dummied symmetrically or to provide point/counterpoint:

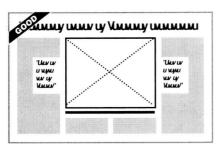 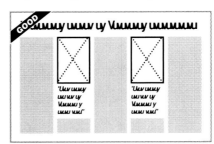

■ Never force readers to read around *any* 2- or 3-column impediment; text that jumps back and forth like that gets too confusing (below left). It's OK to interrupt a leg of text with a 1-column liftout, but use 2-column liftouts *only* at the top of the text (below middle). As an alternative, you might try indenting a window for the liftout, then wrapping the text around it (below right).

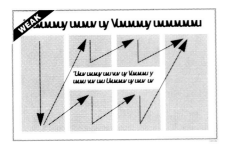  

■ Keep liftout quotes as typographically tidy as you can. Avoid partial quotes, parentheses, hyphenation, ellipses and widows.

The liftout below actually ran in a student newspaper. The editors probably thought they were keeping the quote accurate, but the distracting typography killed the quote's readability:

"... possible enhancements (such as) ... an essay as a direct measurement of writing skill ..."

MORE ON:

■ Skews and wraparounds: Guidelines for dummying special type effects.............. 133

DECKS

One of the most persistent problems in all of newspapering is The Headline That Doesn't Mean Anything:

Schools bill falls

Copy editors are only human, usually, so headlines like that are inevitable. But one way to make headlines work more efficiently — especially on important stories — is to add a *deck* (some call it a *drop head*) below the headline to explain things a bit further:

Schools bill falls
Senate vetoes plan to finance classes by taxing cigarettes

This example uses a 36-point bold headline and an 18-point light deck. Decks are usually in lightweight or italic faces that contrast with the main headline. In news stories, they're usually set flush left in the first leg of type.

MORE ON:

■ **Headlines:** Different styles of heads and how to size them....... 15-17

■ **Display headlines:** How to add variety to feature headlines.......... 139

Quite often, decks make more sense than headlines. Which shows you how valuable they can be.

Years ago, papers stacked decks in deep rows (see example, page 15). Today, most use only one deck per story. Decks for news stories are often 3-4 lines (6-12 words); decks for features are generally longer (10-30 words).

Many papers think decks are a waste of space and use them only as filler when stories come up an inch short. That's a mistake. Since most readers browse the paper by scanning headlines, it's easy to see that a good head/deck combination adds more meaning — and increases readership.

GUIDELINES

■ **Use decks for all long or important stories.** Remember, readers are more likely to plunge into a gray sea of text if they know what it's about.

■ **Use decks with all hammer or display headlines.** It's great to write a clever, punchy feature head like "Heavy Mental." But if you don't add a deck to explain what that means, readers may not appreciate your cleverness.

■ **Give decks contrast — in size and weight.** By sizing decks noticeably smaller than headlines, they'll be easier to write. They'll convey more information. And they'll look more graceful (as magazines have discovered). Most papers devise their own system of deck sizing, but as a rule decks run from 14 to 24 points, depending on the size of the headline they accompany.

For added contrast, most papers use either italic decks (with roman heads) or lightface decks (with regular or boldface heads). Whatever your paper's style, it's important to set the deck apart — both in spacing and in typography — from both the headline and the text.

■ **Stack it at the start of the story.** Don't float it in the middle of the layout, park it in some exotic corner or banner it across the full width of the page. A deck is a tool, not a toy. Put it to work where it will lead the reader into the story. Generally, that's in the first leg of text (though in wider layouts, a 2-column deck works fine).

In fancy feature layouts, you can be more creative. But that comes later.

BREAKING UP TEXT

Reading long, gray columns of text can be an intimidating chore. But if you break up the gray with occasional subheads, initial caps or dingbats, you can better organize your material — and, at the same time, provide rest stops for the reader's eye.

SUBHEADS

Subheads are the most common way to subdivide long stories (i.e., features or news analyses that run over 30 inches). They're usually inserted every 8-10 inches, wherever there's a shift of topic or a logical pause in the commentary. Avoid dropping them in at random (which won't help the reader's understanding of the material) or at the very bottom of a leg of type.

Subheads come in a variety of styles but are usually bolder than text type:

without first having his wife brought to see him; and they had sent an escort for her, which had occasioned the delay.

Under the guillotine

He immediately kneeled down, below the knife. His neck fitting into a hole, made for the purpose, in a cross plank, was shut down, by

This is a typical format for news subheads: bold type, centered, a few points larger than text type.

Sutherland's trip at 7 p.m. Thursday at Pioneer Courthouse Square. The program is free.

■ **Africa preview:** A slide presentation on Kenya and Tanzania will be shown at 10:30 a.m. Wednesday at Weststar Tour and Travel, 19888 S.E. Stark. The show is a preview of a February

This format is used to change topics in stories that consist of short, assorted bits and pieces.

$50 for Oslo, but a seven-day second-class rail pass can be bought for about $70 at rail stations.

WHERE TO STAY

The Fjord Pass program offers discounts on rates at 200 hotels. The pass costs $10 and comes with a list of hotels offering discounts for

This reversed subhead helps to organize catalog-style stories into clearly identifiable sections.

INITIAL CAPS

Initial caps are a classy way to begin features, columns or specially packaged news stories. They're also a decorative (though non-informational) alternative to subheads for breaking up long columns of text.

Be sure the large cap letter has neat spacing and alignment, whether it's indented into the text or raised above it:

This is an example of a dropped initial. These are usually tucked into the first three or four lines of the text.

Here is a raised initial, which sits above the first line of the text.

Even small graphics and sidebars can begin with initial caps to give the text extra typographic emphasis. Use them sparingly, though, as a way to anchor text blocks.

DINGBATS

Dingbat is the ridiculous-sounding term used to describe any typographic gimmick like these:

Most dingbats are too frivolous to use in a serious-minded newspaper. Some, however, are handy for relieving long legs of text (example at right).

Others, like bullets (•) and squares (■), can help itemize lists within text. Remember, however:

■ Use bullets or squares for three or more related items. Fewer than that, it looks odd.

■ Keep bullet items short and punchy. Like this.

■ Don't overdo it. Use them only for emphasis.

had left it in that instant. It was dull, cold, livid, wax. The body also.

❑

There was a great deal of blood. When we left the window, and went close up to the scaffold, it was very dirty; one of the two men who were throwing water

BYLINES

To reporters, bylines are the most important graphic element in the entire newspaper. What a shame, then, that readers rarely give bylines a glance as their eyes leap from the end of the headline to the start of the story.

It's necessary, though, to give credit where credit is due (especially when readers have complaints or questions about a story). Papers differ on byline policies, but most put reporters' names on stories of any substance — i.e., stories more than 6 inches long.

Bylines generally run at the start of the story in a format that sets them apart from the text (often achieved with boldface, italics, or one or two rules). Bylines are usually either centered or flush left. The first line gives the reporter's name; a second line tells whether he or she writes for an outside organization (The Associated Press, for example), works as a free-lancer (often labeled a "special writer" or "correspondent"), or belongs on the staff (most papers run either the name of the paper or the writer's title).

Every newspaper should adopt *one* standard byline style. Some examples:

Student newspapers often use loud, eye-catching byline styles, perhaps as a bribe to lure reporters onto the staff. Screened, reversed or indented bylines can be fun, but they risk calling too much attention to themselves — and they can get awfully difficult to read. Proceed with caution.

For short sidebars or columns of briefs, credit is often given in the form of a flush-right tag line at the end of the text. As with bylines, these credit lines need spacing and typography to set them apart from the text:

On feature pages, photo spreads and special reports, newspapers often use a more prominent byline style to credit either the writer, the photographer, or both (page designers, sad to say, rarely receive printed credit for their work). These special credit lines are either indented into a wide column of text or parked into empty space at the edge of the design. They often look like this:

Story by
STAN LAUREL

Photos by
OLIVER HARDY

CREDIT LINES

Artwork, like stories, should be credited — whether the art comes from staffers, free-lancers, wire services or library files. Credit lines come in several forms to serve several functions:

■ For photos and illustrations, they provide the name and affiliation of the photographer or artist who produced the image.

■ For old, historic photos or maps, they tell readers where the documents come from (i.e., The Bozoville Historical Society). Often, credit lines include the date a photo was taken, which is necessary for any photo that could mistakenly be considered current.

■ For charts or diagrams, an additional "source" line tells readers where the artist obtained the data that was graphicized. Citing sources is just as important for artists as it is for reporters.

■ For copyrighted material, they provide the necessary legal wording ("Reprinted with permission of. . ." or "©1988 by . . .")

Not all papers credit all photos, however. Most papers, for instance, don't bother crediting run-of-the-mill mug shots. And publicity handouts — movie stills, fashion shots, glossies of entertainers — usually run uncredited, too (probably because editors resent giving away all that free publicity).

Most papers run credits in small type (below 7-point), in a font that contrasts with any nearby cutline. There are still some papers that run photo credits at the end of cutlines, like this —

Tokyo citizens scream in terror Tuesday as Godzilla destroys the city. (Staff photo by Dan Gustafson).

— but that credit style isn't as effective as it could be. Ideally, there should be a clear distinction between cutlines and credit lines, just as there's a distinction between text and bylines.

Most papers run credit lines flush right, just a few points below the edge of the art and a few points above the cutline. Some papers run them flush left; some run them on top; some have even tried running them sideways along the right edge, though that's difficult to read and tends to jam up against any neighboring leg of text. (If a photo or graphic uses both a source line and a credit line, they should be dummied in two separate positions to avoid confusing readers.)

Below, you can gauge the effectiveness of each location:

MORE ON:

■ **Photo spreads:** Guidelines for designing special photo pages........ **99**

Some papers run credit lines above the photo, flush right — though many readers habitually look for them down around the cutline below.

Many magazines run credit lines sideways like this, but they require small, fine type and perfect paste-up technique — and still, they risk crowding into adjacent columns of text.

Most papers run credit lines flush right, a few points below the photo or art. Whatever you choose to do, keep it consistent — pick one position and run all credits there.

Not many papers run credit lines in the lower left corner. Instead, it's becoming common to run the *source line* here — that's the line in a chart, map or diagram that tells the source of the data being used. Putting that information here (or inside the box instead of outside) keeps it separate from all other credit lines.

The Oregonian/STEVE NEHL

The Oregonian/STEVE NEHL

The Oregonian/STEVE NEHL

The Oregonian/STEVE NEHL

This is the cutline (or caption). Cutlines usually run a few points below the credit line and use a bigger, bolder typeface.

SPACING

Spacing guidelines vary from paper to paper. But here's how one typical newspaper might position story elements on a typical page:

Friday, April 14, 1990 **5B**

SPORTS

in 9th inning

The Oregonian/STEVE NEHL

•me run as the Dodgers rallied in the ninth inning to win.

itcher threw,
us terrified
le ball game."
— Joe Spooner

rs." That was a signal
nized, although it had
ssed between him and his

as saying, "Pitch to the

big bum if he hammers every ball in
the park into the North River."
And so, at Snyder's request, Bentley
did pitch to Ruth, and the Babe drove
the ball deep into right center; so deep
that Casey Stengel could feel the hot
breath of the bleacherites on his back
as the ball came down and he caught
it. If that drive had been just a shade
to the right it would have been a third
home run for Ruth. As it was, the
Babe had a great day, with two home
runs, a terrific long fly, and two bases
on balls.

Ump claims
new balk rule
may be unfair

By EAMONN HUGHES
Sports editor

For the first time since the
American League instituted its

Section logos & headers
Above: Allow 3 points between logo and folio line.
Inside: Maintain 8-point margins between type and edge of box.
Below: Allow 18 points between logo and headlines/photos.

Headlines
Above: Allow 18 points under logos or unrelated stories.
Below: Allow 1 pica between descenders and text/photos.

Photos
Credit line: Allow 3 points between photo and credit line.
Cutline: Allow 3 points between credit line and cutline. Allow 3 points between photo and cutline if there's no credit line.

Text
Above: Allow 1 pica between cutline and text.
Gutters: All vertical gutters are 1 pica.
Graphic elements: Allow 1 pica between all graphic elements (liftout quotes, refers, etc.) and text.
Below: Allow 18 points between text and unrelated stories.

Boxes
Margins: Allow 1 pica between outside rules and all headlines/text/photos.

Bylines
Above: Allow 1 pica between descenders and byline.
Below: Allow 1 pica between byline and text.

120

RULES & BOXES

Newspapers use rules both functionally (to organize and separate elements) and decoratively (to add contrast and flair). Notice, for instance, how the rules in this sig and byline are both functional and decorative:

NFL ROUNDUP

By ROBIN FOX
Bugle-Beacon staff writer

Rule thickness, like type size, is measured in points. The "NFL Roundup" sig above uses a 4-point rule above the type and a 1-point rule below, while the byline uses a hairline rule (that's the thinnest size available). With so many thicknesses to choose from, most papers limit rule selection to just one or two sizes — say, 1-point and 4-point: one thin, one thick.

Rules are most commonly used in the following ways:

- ■ To build logos, bylines and other standing elements
- ■ To create boxes (for stories, graphics, ads, etc.)
- ■ To build charts & graphs
- ■ To embellish feature designs and display headlines
- ■ To separate stories and elements from each other
- ■ To border photos

This page, from U., The National College Newspaper, uses boxes and rules to organize elements.

A few decades ago, newspapers used rules primarily to separate stories from each other. Some rules ran vertically in the gutters (called *column rules*), while others ran horizontally, beneath photos or text (called *cutoff* rules). That trend faded in the '60s, but it's been making a comeback recently in newspapers like the one at left. As Harold Evans, editor of The Sunday Times in London once said: "The most backward step, under the flag of freedom, has been the abandonment of column rules and cutoffs which so usefully define columns and separate stories."

Most modern papers run most stories unruled and unboxed, reserving box treatments for big news packages, sidebars, stand-alone photos, etc. As we've said before, it's best to box stories *only* if they're special or if they need to be set apart from other stories on the page. Rules and boxes can produce handsome designs, but they shouldn't be used to compensate for butting headlines or poorly placed photos. A weak design is a weak design, regardless of whether rules are used to soften the impact of colliding elements.

You'll often be tempted to use decorative rules or borders for special effects. But like other graphic gimmicks, it's easy to use them clumsily or excessively — so use restraint.

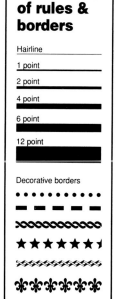

A sampling of rules & borders

Hairline

1 point

2 point

4 point

6 point

12 point

Decorative borders

This box was made with 1-point rules on all sides.

Thick frames and fat shadows leap too loudly off the page. Avoid them. Use thin rules to build boxes and border photos.

Underscoring

Someday, you'll get bored with news headlines and decide they might look better with a rule (called an *underscore)* beneath them. But avoid doing that. Use rules only in display headlines (see page 138 for more details).

Rounded corners and decorative borders were stylish 20 years ago. But they're hopelessly corny today. Avoid gimmicks; they only call attention to themselves.

REFERS & TEASERS

REFERS

Throughout this book, we've cross-referenced material by using "INSIDE" boxes. (There's one on the next page, for example). Those boxes are a handy way to show readers where to find related information on other pages.

Newspapers need to cross-reference their stories, too. And they do that by using lines, paragraphs or boxes called *refers* (see examples). Some refers are simple; others, with art, are more elaborate. Whatever style your paper uses, refers should:

■ **Stand out typographically** from the surrounding text. That's why refers often include rules, bullets, boldface or italic type.

■ **Be tightly written.** Refers are signposts, so they should simply point — not pontificate.

■ **Be specific.** Refers should index all related items — on the TV page, the opinion page, wherever — not just say, "Other stories inside."

■ **Be consistently positioned** each time they're used— i.e., above the byline, at the top of a column, at the end of the story — whatever is most appropriate and unobtrusive.

Refer line

■ **How Bush views the tax plan, Page 5A**

Refer paragraph

On Page 4A:
Turkish naval vessels were placed on alert Wednesday as Iran prepared to launch its first nuclear submarine.

Refer box (with art)

INSIDE

❏ *Why Kraft was forced to resign* **A5**

❏ *Reaction from other board members* **A7**

❏ *Highlights of Kraft's stormy career* **A7**

TEASERS

A refer is a signpost that guides readers to stories inside the paper. A *teaser* is another kind of signpost — actually, it's more like a billboard. Where refers advise, teasers advertise. They say "BUY ME: HOT STORY INSIDE."

The covers of most supermarket tabloids, for example, are loaded with titillating teasers. Most newspapers, by comparison, use a more refined approach for their teasers (also called promos, skylines or boxcars).

Teasers are usually boxed in an eye-catching way at the top of Page One (though many tabs stack them along the bottom). Some are bold and simple:

Spooner's grand slam wins it for Dodgers/D1

A better idea is to combine a catchy headline phrase, a short copy blurb and the story's page number or section. To be most effective, teasers should use art, since an arresting image is the fastest way to catch a reader's eye.

Here are two teaser styles from the competing dailies in Rochester, N.Y.:

At the Times-Union, teaser boxes change their style, shape and position each day, depending on the available art. This constant variety keeps readers from getting bored and tuning the teasers out.

At the Democrat and Chronicle, teasers are more solidly anchored, running across the top of Page One. This basic format can accommodate different types of art and varying numbers of teaser items.

Continued from page 71

and 4.

■ Avoid jumping orphans. An *orphan* (sometimes called a *widow*) is a short word or phrase that's carried over to the top of a new column or page. Like the first line in this column: "and 4."

Orphans seem clumsy. They look like typographical errors, even when they're not. And, as you may have just experienced, it's aggravating enough to reach the end of a column, then be told to go to page 123, then fish around trying to *find* page 123, then, when you get to page 123, read something cryptic like "and 4" — at which point you discover you've forgotten the rest of the sentence back on page 71.

And that's why readers dislike jumps.

■ Since jumping is so unpleasant, you must make it easy typographically. There are two ways to do this:

1) Run *continuation lines* (the lines that tell you where a story is continued) flush right, since that's where your eye stops reading at end of a column. Run *jump lines* (the lines that tell you where a story has been jumped from) flush left, since that's where your eye begins reading at the top of a column.

2) Give each jump a key word or phrase, then highlight it typographically.

Suppose, for instance, you're jumping a story on oat bran. You could run a continuation line that simply says *Turn to page 6.* But that's not too friendly. And when readers get to page 6, how will they spot the jump? You'd be wiser to run a continuation line like *See **OAT BRAN,** page 6.* And when readers arrived at page 6, they would find a jump headline like one of these:

MORE ON:

■ **Jumps:** What they are, with guidelines on how to dummy them....... 71

Oat bran: Study proves it prevents heart attacks

Continued from Page One

This is a popular treatment for jump headlines. It treats the key word (or phrase) as a boldface lead-in, then follows it with a lightface headline written in standard style. Since the key word is played so boldly, jump stories are easy to spot when readers arrive at the new page. To be effective, jump lines should be set apart from the text, both by extra spacing and type selection.

Oat bran   Continued from Page One

This is another common style for jump headlines. It uses only the key word (or phrase) to catch readers' eyes, then adds a rule both for emphasis and to separate the text from any columns running above. One problem: Readers encountering this jump story for the first time won't have any idea what it's about if all the headline says is something like "SMITH."

Study proves grain, fiber can prevent heart attacks

■ OAT BRAN, from Page One

This treatment is very straightforward: a standard news headline followed by a boldface key word in the jumpline. But is it obvious enough to readers that this is the oat bran story they're searching for? Some would argue that unless the jump headline boldly proclaims a key word or phrase, too many readers may get lost.

■ Finally, remember to package jumps as attractively as you'd package any other story. Many newspapers regard jumps as mandatory blocks of gray slop — ugly leftovers from nice-looking pages. And if your deadlines are tight, you may be forced to blow off jump-page designs. But if there's time, you can add photos. Create mug-quote blocks. Pull out charts or maps.

To summarize: Jumps will never be popular. But if you can devise a clear, consistent format for packaging jump stories, readers will regard them as minor detours — not major roadblocks. And their benefits to designers (higher story counts and increased layout options on key pages) far outweigh the annoyance they cause readers.

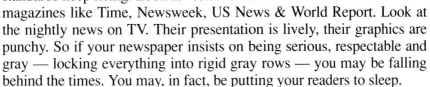

T here was a time, not too long ago, when all newspaper pages looked serious. Respectable. Gray. Paper was white, ink was black, and everything was locked in rigid gray rows.

Today, that's all changed. Newspapers are more "reader-friendly" than ever. Headlines are orange, backgrounds are blue, and photos run in eye-poppingly true colors. News pages look flashy. Feature pages look flashy. Even *business* pages look flashy.

The best page designers now carry big bags of graphic tricks. That's partly to make stories more informative, partly to make pages more lively, but mostly to keep up with a world in which *everything* competes for the readers' attention.

Thanks in part to television (and in part to innovations in computer graphics), design standards keep rising. Look at "serious" news-magazines like Time, Newsweek, US News & World Report. Look at the nightly news on TV. Their presentation is lively, their graphics are punchy. So if your newspaper insists on being serious, respectable and gray — locking everything into rigid gray rows — you may be falling behind the times. You may, in fact, be putting your readers to sleep.

In this chapter, we'll look at some graphic techniques that help pages — especially feature pages — take on new life. These techniques are optional. But as time goes by, you may see more of these graphic gim-micks finding their way onto every page in the paper.

CHAPTER CONTENTS

■ **Stretching the limits:** How some pages go beyond ordinary design guidelines to hit new heights **126**

■ **The Cosby variations:** Take one photo. One big story. One empty page. How many options are available for dummying that page creatively?.............. **127-131**

■ **Wraparounds and skews:** A look at alternatives to the stan-dard rectangular text block, with guidelines on their use.... **132-133**

■ **Photo cutouts:** How to poke body parts out of photos — or simply run entire images against the white page........................ **134**

■ **Mortises & insets:** The art of overlapping images and text blocks to dramatize layouts (and conserve space)..................... **135**

■ **Screens and reverses:** What's black and white and gray all over? Once you introduce screen options, pages take on a whole new hue................ **136-137**

■ **Display headlines:** A look at type trickery that can transform a feature headline into something flashy and splashy........... **138-139**

■ **How to build a mechanical:** A step-by-step guide to assembling overlays for screen effects...... **140**

■ **Color:** Guidelines to help you decide when color will work — and when it won't............ **141-147**

■ **Risky business:** Special effects to avoid..................... **148**

STRETCHING THE LIMITS

As we saw in the previous chapter, every newspaper needs clear, consistent design guidelines. And for most pages, most of the time, those guidelines should be rigidly enforced.

But every so often, by bending the rules just a *bit,* you create appealing pages like these:

Top left: A page from The Oregonian combines a display headline, photo cutouts, column rules and wraparounds. **Bottom left:** A food page from The Times (Beaverton, Ore.) reverses type out of a fiery studio photo. **Above:** The Washington Times uses photo cutouts to create a delightful fashion page.

THE COSBY VARIATIONS

Page design is part science, part art. And that's especially true on feature pages, where you take the basic rules of page layout, then nudge, stretch and tweak them as far as time — and your creativity — will allow.

Here's a simple exercise that will let you test your creative layout skills. Suppose you're the feature designer for the Living section. On today's page, you have this hole to fill:

Today's lead story — the one that will fill that big hole on the page — is a profile of TV comic Bill Cosby. It's a long piece, and you can jump as much as you like. There's no headline yet, but feel free to write one if you think of one (or leave a space for it if you'd prefer).

Unfortunately, there's only one photo available (left).

How would you design this story? In the next four pages, we'll explore 16 of the most likely options.

©1985, National Broadcasting Co., Inc.

THE COSBY VARIATIONS

1

This is the basic news approach: parking the photo in the top 2 legs of a 3-column layout. It works, but it's dull. The page is gray. And the headline is too meek and lifeless. In short, nothing on this page *grabs* the reader.

2

Here, we scooted the photo toward the center and enlarged it a bit. That helps. We've made the headline bigger and bolder, too. But the page still seems cautious and quiet. And there's a busy intersection where the Cosby deck collides with that headline beside it.

3

Better. The photo has moved all the way to the left. It's bigger still, and more dramatically vertical. (But does it bother you that we've lopped off Cosby's hand?) The headline is bolder, with a friendly reference to "Cos," but it's stretched awkwardly atop the photo. Note, too, the added liftout quote.

4

Now we've taken that friendly word "Cos" and turned it into a big, bold display headline: Note the use of rules and the flush-right read-in. We've added his hand back, too, allowing it to poke out of the photo and dangle above the liftout quote. All in all, this is a bolder, more modular design than the three previous pages.

THE COSBY VARIATIONS

5

Now the photo's even wider and takes up nearly half the page. (Is that too much?) Since there's now just one wide column of text, the headline has been restacked, boxed and screened. The liftout quote is now indented. And the text skews around Cosby's hand.

6

This option is fancier still, using boxes inside of boxes: The photo's in one box, the text is in another, and both rest inside a third gray-screened box. The headline is more decorative as well. Does all this make the package slick — or just more fussy and flashy? It's a matter of taste.

7

Let's move the photo back to the middle of the page to test a few other options. This layout is very symmetrical: The headline is centered, and the two quotes balance nicely on both sides of the photo. Note, too, the white space that opens up the corners of the design. Does that help the page breathe?

8

If we move the deck below the headline, we open up still more white space in the top corners. Is it too much now? Note how the quote fills the space below the photo. The reader now reaches the end of the left leg and must jump clear across the photo to continue reading. Is that a problem?

THE COSBY VARIATIONS

9

Another centered, symmetrical solution. Building this page requires a little work, since those indents at the corners of the photo must be carefully aligned. And if the legs alongside the photo were any thinner, reading the text might become an irritating experience.

10

Here, we've moved the headline down, boxing and mortising it into the middle of the photo. It doesn't cover up any essential information in the photo — but does it seem too crowded? Some may say the headline is too low on the page, but it's a fresh alternative.

11

Here, the headline is even lower, sitting nearly at the bottom of the story. Will it be clear to most readers that they should begin reading at the top of the left leg? Note the bold decorative rules; note, too, how we've poked not only Cosby's hand out of the photo frame, but the top of his head, too.

12

We've poked out most of Cosby's head in this option. And we've returned to a variation on our first design, parking the photo at the top right and wrapping the text below. This time, however, the photo uses 3 legs of a 4-column format, and the headline gets a more featurized treatment.

THE COSBY VARIATIONS

13

Since we've started cutting Cosby silhouettes, we might as well cut him out completely. Here, we've reverted to an earlier variation, with one wide leg of text. The liftout quote is now used to fill the white space behind Cosby's head. One problem: The skewed text may be a bit hard to read.

14

It's not often you get the chance to park art at the bottom of a design. Usually, it doesn't work. But here it anchors the page pretty well. Cosby's head pokes into the middle column pretty neatly, as his fingers dangle into the story below. Not a bad touch — a bit offbeat, but still engaging.

15

Instead of cutting away the photo's background, here we've cut a hole in the photo — and around Cosby — and we've mortised in the text block. It works well. There's enough room for a small quote and one leg of text. The only drawback: a lot of dead space floating around near the top of the page.

16

This treatment is a bit tacky. We've given up trying to work with the background of the photo and have instead created a background of our own. Some would argue it's a clumsy treatment, and certainly the headline is louder than it needs to be. But the design *does* create impact.

WRAPAROUNDS & SKEWS

As we've previously seen — both in the Cosby variations and in the swipe-able feature formats used in Chapter 3 — text isn't always locked into rigid gray rows. It can, instead, dodge occasional liftout quotes, flow around photos, and indent around logos and bugs. When a column of text does that, it's called a *wraparound.* (Some papers call it a *runaround.* And when it snakes around a jagged piece of art, it's often called a *skew.*)

Wraparounds can be used with a variety of graphic elements:

MORE ON:

■ **Liftout quotes:**
Using them with wraparounds..... 114

■ **Photo cutouts:**
Guidelines for using them with wraps and skews............... 134

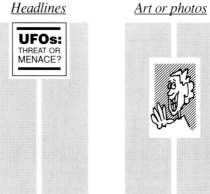

Mugs   *Liftout quotes*   *Headlines*   *Art or photos*

Until a few years ago, wraparounds were common in books and maga-zines, but not in newspapers. That's because they usually require a lot of time, patience and tricky typesetting codes. But with the current generation of personal computers and publishing programs, type wraps have become a toy that's much easier to play with.

Wraparounds add flair and flexibility to story designs in three ways:

■ They let you put graphic elements in the middle of a layout without dis-rupting the flow of the text.

■ They let photos and illustrations interact with the words.

■ Best of all, they allow you to run graphic elements at their optimum sizes, rather than locking you into strict column widths.

As you can see in the example below, wraparounds can help you save space by letting you crop photos more economically:

In the layout at left, we've cropped to the edge of the photo frame. But unless we crop into the model's skirt, we're forced to create a layout that's mostly empty white space. The layout at right, however, fits two legs of type where only one fit before. How? By cropping more tight-ly, poking both cor-ners of the skirt into the text by using wraparounds.

WRAPAROUNDS & SKEWS

GUIDELINES

■ Don't overdo it. Any graphic gimmick will annoy readers if they see it too often, and wraparounds are *very* gimmicky. That's why they're best saved for occasional features — not hard news.

Remember: The text of a story is like a road the reader travels; a wraparound is like a pothole in the road. Steering around *one* pothole is fun, but who wants to drive a road that's *loaded* with potholes?

■ If you plan on using several wraps and skews on one page (like this one), begin by anchoring the text block as solidly as you can. Then start poking art into it at carefully determined intervals. As soon as the art starts overwhelming the text, back off.

In other words, never use wraps as an excuse for a dizzying layout. Be sure to "grid off" the text legs solidly, then add the skews as enhancement.

■ Observe the basic guidelines for text width and depth (see example at right).

■ Be sure there's plenty of contrast between the main text block and the object that's poking into it. As you can see here, the sidebar box at right is screened and set off with a drop shadow — and the window for the art is parked on the wrapping side, as well.

■ Don't silhouette a photo simply because you want to skew around it. That makes photographers very angry. (For more on photo cutouts, see next page.)

> ■ When you indent any art into a leg of text, be sure to run at least three lines of text *above* and *below* the indented art.
>
>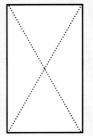
>
> ■ Allow a 1-pica gutter between the edges of the art and the text.
>
> ■ Run all text at least 6 picas wide (that's our width here). And keep in mind how tired you can get reading a long, skinny totem pole of text. Try to limit all thin, indented legs to a few inches of depth, max.

■ Smooth out your skews as much as you can. Abrupt shifts in the width of the text are awkward-looking — and awkward to read, too.

■ When a wraparound is centered between two legs of text, position it carefully. Don't make it lopsided on either side.

■ Skews on the *right* side are preferable to skews on the *left*. Here's why:

This is a text block with a skew along its *left* edge. It looks appealing, but notice how tired your eye gets bouncing back and forth as you finish one line and try to find the beginning of the next one. That gets annoying very quickly, and it turns readers off.

When text skews along the *right* edge, it's not nearly as frustrating to read. Even though each line ends in a different place, your eye always knows exactly where to go to begin the next line. It's like an exaggerated ragged right. So skew on the *right,* if you can.

■ And finally — as we've said many times before — don't ever force readers to jump back and forth across any graphic element. No matter how simple or clever the layout may seem to you, your readers will get confused, lost or angry.

Take this example, for instance. It may seem obvious to me, the designer, that you're supposed to start reading each line, then jump across this cattle-crossing sign to finish it — but most readers will probably try to read each column separately, get frustrated and quit without ever getting this far. You still trying to decipher this? Well, it must be nice to have so much free time. . . .

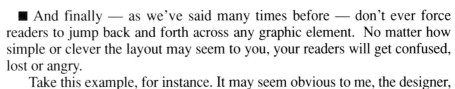

PHOTO CUTOUTS

We said earlier that photos come in three shapes: horizontal, vertical and square. And that's usually true. But occasionally, feature photos may break out of the confines of the rectangle:

This fashion photo is run with background intact, cropped in a conventional vertical rectangle.

This is a partial cutout, in which the model's head and part of his arm poke out of the frame.

This is a complete cutout, in which the entire gray background has been cut away from the model.

Many photographers and editors hate this kind of treatment. They think it's abusive, that it destroys the integrity of the photographic image. They call it "cookie-cutter art."

Artists and designers, on the other hand, find it a handy, sophisticated technique. They call these photos *cutouts* or *silhouettes*.

Why create cutouts? It's mainly done for dramatic effect. A photo that's boxed and framed seems flat and two-dimensional. A cutout, by contrast, seems almost 3-D. It pops off the page and creates an element of surprise.

It's also a good way to eliminate an unwanted, distracting background from a photograph. And it can help tighten up a story design by letting the text hug a photo's central image instead of parking several inches away.

When creating cutouts, remember:

■ Respect the photograph (and the photographer). A bad crop or a silly silhouette can ruin a good photo. So work *with* the photographer. Discuss cutout treatments in advance. When in doubt, leave it alone.

■ Use cutouts on features — not hard news. If you distort or violate a photo, you damage its credibility. That may be OK for celebrity photos or fashion shots, but you're not allowed to change the meaning of news photos.

■ Use only images with crisp, dark edges. White skin and clothes will fade like ghosts into the background, so be careful. And be especially careful trimming faces, fingers and frizzy hair. Crude cutouts look amateurish.

■ If you use a cutout as lead art, play it strong. Don't let cutouts swim meekly in a sea of white space. Do it with gusto — or don't do it.

■ Don't ever cut up actual photographs. Instead, either trim away the background from a halftone or see your printer for advice on cutting overlays.

MORTISES & INSETS

NOTE: This page is being included despite nearly hysterical protests from some of my colleagues, who believe mortises are downright *evil.* One of them even wrote me a letter that went something like this:

> The presidentboard said todfficialshat met to the neprotest taxes

to demonstrate how you'd never stack one leg of text atop another — so why do it with photos?

I say: Lighten up. If you don't like it, *don't do it.* NYAH!

When one text block or photo overlaps another, it's called a *mortise* or *inset.* And on this page, you can see three types of mortises: photo on photo, photo on text, and text on photo.

When creating a mortise:

■ Inset small elements onto bigger ones.

■ Overlap *only* into dead space, or to cover up something questionable or distracting in a photo. Avoid crowding or covering any informational part of a photo (hands, feet, background details, etc.)

■ Mortise only photos of different scale. Never mortise any object that might mistakenly be perceived as belonging in the main photo.

■ Maintain contrast between overlapping elements: dark onto light, light onto dark. If photos have similar values, add a gutter or shadow around the inset photo.

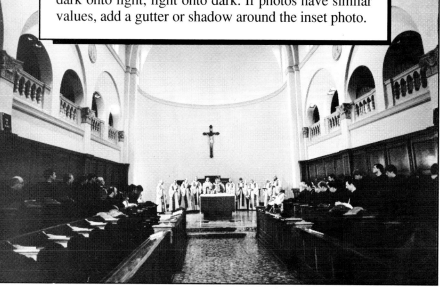

The three photos on this page are from a photo-essay on a monastic order. Note how the inset into the top photo uses a white gutter to keep the dark areas of both photos from blurring into each other; the text box at left adds a 4-point shadow to keep the white areas separate. In each case, the inset is relatively unobtrusive and doesn't violate either photo's center of interest (though the photographer would much prefer running both photos *without* insets).

SCREENS & REVERSES

Ink is black. Newsprint is white. So how do we create shades of *gray?*

We do it by fooling the reader's eye. Instead of using gray inks, we create the illusion of gray by printing row upon row of tiny black dots in a *dot screen.* And the bigger those dots are, the darker the gray is. We've seen how this works in halftones (page 93), but here's how dot screens create tints:

| 0% | 10% | 20% | 40% | 60% | 80% | 100% |

As these examples show, dot screens are measured by percentages. A 50% screen will be half-filled with black dots, while a 100% screen is solid ink. (That ink doesn't have to be just black, either. You can create lighter screens with any color ink, or with any combination of inks — for instance, if you look closely at a color newspaper photo through a magnifying glass, you'll see it's actually just a mass of red, yellow, black and blue dots.)

Screens can be used for printing gray type: Or they can create gray rules, bars and boxes: Or they can provide background tints behind type:

When screens are used to create background tints, they impair the legibility of type. As we've seen in the examples above, it's easy to read black type on light screens (10-20%). On medium screens, it gets harder. And it's nearly impossible to read type on dark screens unless the type is *reversed* — that is, printed white instead of black.

| This is 10-point type on a white background. It's easy to read, no matter how long the story is. | This is 10-point type on a 10% black screen. It's easy to read, but works best in small doses. | This is 10-point type **reversed** on solid (100%) black. It's easy to read, but only in small doses. |

Screens and reverses dramatically expand the range of contrast on any black-and-white page. Because they're so conspicuous, they call attention to themselves and are best used to emphasize headers, logos, headlines and sidebars — especially on feature pages. They can also be integrated with photos and illustrations to create a tighter, more striking package, as in this example:

In this feature layout, the photo illustration sits above the text and its sidesaddle headline. But there's empty space in the photograph that could be put to use. . .

Here, the headline is reversed into that empty space in the photo. This connects the headline to the photo image and frees up extra space in the columns below.

SCREENS & REVERSES

GUIDELINES

■ Don't overdo it. Don't splatter screens and reverses at random, or your paper will look like a cheesy circus poster. Use special effects *only* to highlight items that are special or different: a feature headline, a column logo, an infographic. Readers regard these effects as cosmetic options, so use them only on optional items; never screen hard news stories.

■ Never compromise the readability of type. *Any* screen or reverse slows the reader down (and should therefore be used only in small doses), but some combinations of fonts and screens create obstacles that are impossible to overcome:

MORE ON:

■ **Halftones:** How dot screens are used to reproduce photographs................. 93

■ **Display headlines:** Examples of different screens at work................... 138

■ **Color:** When to use color tints and screens....... 142-147

Not legible

| This is 8-point serif type. It's too small. And serif fonts are hard to read when they're printed against gray screens. | Sometimes you ask for a light screen, but it prints like this instead. It's too dark, too hard to read. | When type is reversed out of a gray screen, the screen dots break up the type characters. |

Legible

| This is a 9-point sans serif font. Sans serif fonts, **especially bold**, are easier to read against screens, but use 9-point or larger. | This is a true 10% screen. It's easy on the eyes. With a darker screen, either gray or in color, you risk losing legibility. | When type is reversed out of solid black, the type characters keep their shape and remain much easier to read. |

■ Never screen text type, unless you want it to look like this. Gray headlines are OK, but be sure the font is big and bold, since the dot screen will give it a slightly ragged edge.

■ Avoid violating a good photo composition with a crowded reversed headline or cutline. Always give the photo room to breathe. Any added type should complement, not compete against, the central image.

This reversed headline fits poorly. Not only does it butt against the right edge of the frame, but it crowds the portrait and disrupts the photo's elegant composition.

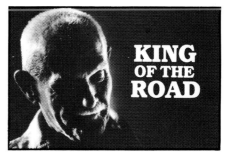

Here, the words in the headline have been re-stacked and centered, and the subject's head has been scooted farther left. The elements are now better balanced.

■ Avoid printing type against a mottled, inconsistent background. In such cases, a *drop shadow* behind the type will often improve legibility, but try it at your own risk. Remember: Type is legible *only* when it's dark against light or light against dark.

You can see how a distracting background affects (1) black type, (2) reversed type and (3) reversed type with a black shadow. There should always be at least a 50% difference in value between the type and any part of the background.

Drop shadows are made by sandwiching layers of type, one behind the other, like this:

See page 140 for more detailed instructions.

DISPLAY HEADLINES

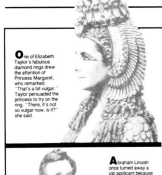

QUIPS, QUOTES & CLEVER RETORTS

More than just sayings, anecdotes provide the human side of history

By DON HAMILTON

One of Elizabeth Taylor's fabulous diamond rings drew the attention of Princess Margaret, who remarked, "That's a bit vulgar." Taylor persuaded the princess to try on the ring. "There, it's not so vulgar now, is it?" she said.

Abraham Lincoln once turned away a job applicant because he didn't like his face. Aides were critical, saying that wasn't a satisfactory reason. "Every man over 40," Lincoln explained, "is responsible for his face."

While arguing women's rights with Winston Churchill, Nancy Astor became exasperated and sputtered, "Winston, if I were married to you, I'd put poison in your coffee." Churchill responded, "And if you were my wife, I'd drink it."

A drunk stumbled up to Groucho Marx, slapped him on the back and said, "You old son-of-a-gun, you probably don't remember me." Marx glared at him and said, "I never forget a face — but in your case I'll be glad to make an exception."

Anecdotes sometimes tell more about people than some people really want to know.

They are the human side of history, both the good and the bad. An anecdote is a slip of the tongue, a well-turned phrase, a foot in the mouth. Here are a few familiar examples:

• Dorothy Parker, a writer famous for her quick wit, once was asked to use the word "horticulture" in a sentence. She pondered the word for a moment before saying: "You can lead a horticulture but you can't make her think."

• Charlie Chaplin once anonymously entered a Charlie Chaplin look-alike contest in Monte Carlo. He came in third.

• Johnny Weissmuller had a two-word response when it was suggested he try out for the movie role of Tarzan. "Me? Tarzan?" he said.

• A woman once sidled up to President Calvin Coolidge and told him she had made a bet she could get him to say more than two words. True to form, Silent Cal said only: "You lose."

Now those and other snippets of history and personality have been gathered in a new volume: "Little, Brown Book of Anecdotes" (Little, Brown and Co., $29.95). Clifton Fadiman, general editor of the 751-page volume, spent more than five years collecting the vignettes, tales, yarns and stories. There are more than 4,500 items from more than 2,000 people.

Many in the volume are recorded for more than one anecdote. Churchill is quoted most often, with 49 anecdotes. Next is Abraham Lincoln, who is so honored with 38.

Anecdotes are an unheralded but crucial element in the way stories are told. They are an important part of biography that add flesh and substance to accounts of the official acts of public people and by helping to understand private people. They can be trivial and important.

"One anecdote of a man," said William Ellery Channing, "is worth a volume of biography." Winston Churchill said he considered anecdotes the "gleaming toys of history."

Anecdotes have not been held in great esteem by historians, who may dismiss a piece of information as "merely anecdotal" or "anecdotal evidence" unless substantiated by traditional historical sources. They fall somewhere between scholarship and trivia.

The "Little, Brown Book of Anecdotes" includes a massive bibliography including books, periodicals, radio programs and television shows. There also is a long index of subjects. When the editors are unable to substantiate adequately an item or suspect it to be apocryphal, they say so in the text.

Despite the research, there are some mistakes. Joe DiMaggio and Marilyn Monroe, for example, were married in 1954, not 1946; Henry Kissinger didn't become secretary of state until 1973; and the legendary Alabama football coach was named Bear Bryant, not Bryan. And some wonderfully creative characters whose stories would have contributed admirably to the book are sadly missing, including musician John Lennon and baseball entrepreneur Bill Veeck.

Despite the criticisms, the "Little, Brown Book of Anecdotes" remains an excellent collection. Its real value is in its great delight as a volume perfect for casual or serious browsing. Open any page, and gems will emerge.

There's Winston Churchill being reminded by a woman that he was drunk and responding that yes, he was, but she was ugly and at least he'd be sober in the morning. Groucho Marx is here talking about his cigar and Babe Ruth reminding his boss that he'd had a better year than President Hoover.

It's a delightful tour through human imagination and creativity and helps bridge the gap between strict history and strict quotations.

Ordinary news stories use ordinary headlines.

And then there are features.

Some newspapers give designers total freedom to create loud, lively feature headlines. Other papers demand that feature headlines follow the same rules (and use the same fonts) as the rest of the paper. So before you get too fancy, be sure you know the limits of your editors' tastes.

And even if you're restricted to one type family, there are lots of creative options available. Here, for instance, are some common headline treatments using screens, reverses and rules:

Solid black type →

Widely spaced type centered between 1-pt. rules →

Solid black type →

← Solid black type over a 15% screen, enclosed in a 1-point box with a 4-pt. drop shadow

← Widely spaced type reversed out of a solid black bar

Solid black type →

Solid black type, 20% gray bar with 1-pt. border →

Solid black type →

← Type reversed out of a 30% screen with a black drop shadow

← Solid black type enclosed in a 1-point box with a 2-pt. drop shadow

← 1-pt. box

30% black type →

Type reversed out of a solid black bar →

30% black type with a solid black shadow →

← Type reversed out of a solid black box with a 1-point reversed inline

← Solid black type over a 20% gray bar

← Type reversed out of solid black

DISPLAY HEADLINES

■ Use display headlines only on big feature stories, special news packages or photo spreads. Don't overuse them.

■ Give each headline focus: one or two key words with impact. Think of popular book or movie titles *(Jaws, Star Wars, Dirty Dancing, The Naked and the Dead),* and keep your headlines equally punchy and uncluttered. Play with the phrase to figure out where to place graphic emphasis.

MORE ON:

■ **Headlines:** A look at the fundamentals of news headlines....... **14-17**

■ **Decks:** How they work with display headlines........... **116**

■ **Risky business:** Headline effects you should avoid **142**

NO: This headline is too long, too wordy. It's written in a stilted news style. Nothing *hooks* the reader.

LIFE TOUGH FOR MOMS BEHIND BARS

YES: This headline is much punchier. It focuses on two key words, playing them BIG to hook the reader.

MOMS BEHIND BARS

■ Grid it off. That's design jargon for aligning your type so it fits neatly into your story design. Don't just float the words in an artsy way; instead, enlarge, reduce, stretch or stack the words so they're neatly organized.

NO: This headline floats too much. It's not anchored; none of the words align. It wastes space and calls too much attention to itself.

Singin' in the Rain

YES: Each of these headlines is neatly stacked, gridding off along either one or both sides. Some words have been resized to ensure a clean fit.

Singin' IN THE *Rain*

Singin' in the *Rain*

Singin' in the Rain

■ Work with the words. Where are the natural breaks in phrasing? Will it play better wide (run horizontally)? Narrow (stacked vertically)? Wide horizontal treatments may look like typical news banners; if you use all caps, an innocent feature head may become a "PRESIDENT DEAD!" screamer:

BABY BUNNIES SPREAD EASTER JOY

Stacked vertically, a display headline may work best in all caps, depending on the typeface you're using. And you may want to run a word or line in a different weight or font — be careful here — for extra emphasis or variety.

NO: This headline is all lower case. But the characters don't stack well vertically; the contours of the ascenders leave ragged holes. And there's no punch to the word "wild."

Born to be wild

YES: Words in all caps align evenly when they're stacked atop each other. And note the contrast gained by changing fonts: the bold "wild," the serif "to be."

BORN TO BE WILD

■ Add contour to all-cap headlines, if the layout allows it, by enlarging the first letter of a key word (or words). But don't overreach:

MARIO MANIA

SUNDAY SCHOOL

THE BOSS

YES: The first letter of a proper noun or title is usually capitalized; when *all* the letters are caps, you can still create the same effect by enlarging the first letter about 20%. Be careful, though, how you stack words vertically.

NO: Enlarged caps can add a decorative touch. But don't push them too far: trying to share one jumbo letter can be confusing (SUNDAY *CHOOL?*). Beginning *and* ending a word with enlarged caps too often looks clumsy. Don't get gimmicky.

HOW TO BUILD A MECHANICAL

How do you create logos like the one at right? You can build them on a computer — or you can combine type, rules and screens in a series of overlays called a *mechanical,* which your printer re-shoots on a copy camera to create the final print. Here's how it works:

1 Typeset METROWEST and SOUND OFF. Make sure all the type is the size you need. Make two copies of SOUND OFF exactly the same size — in the finished logo, one will become white (reversed), while the other will be used to make the black shadow.

2 On a grid sheet, paste up all the elements that will print solid black. Lay down a 1-point border. Cut a black bar to hold the word METROWEST and place that at the top. Finally, position the type that will become SOUND OFF's black shadow.

3 Tape a clear plastic overlay to the grid sheet. On it, you'll paste up the reverse elements (those that will print white). Lay down a 4-point inline. Place the word METROWEST over that black bar. Place the word SOUND OFF so it's slightly offset from the black SOUND OFF below.

This is the reverse overlay. The type and rules will *knock out* all the black or gray images from the layers below, becoming white in the final print. On this overlay, you'd write instructions like these to the copy camera operator: *REVERSE OUT OF EVERYTHING.*

This overlay will produce the gray screen. It will overprint gray on the layer below, but the white elements above will be dropped out of it. To get a 20% gray tint, you'd write: *20% BLACK.*

The elements pasted on the grid sheet will print in black. When finished, the background will be overprinted in gray and the reverse overlay (top layer) will knock out white rules and type. On this sheet, you'd write: *SOLID BLACK.*

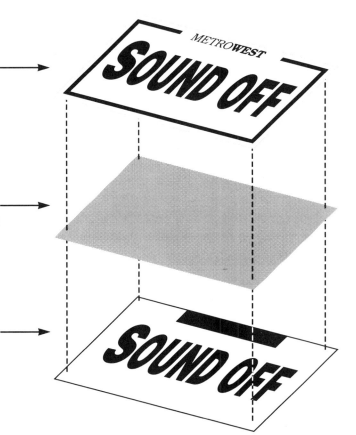

4 Now tape down a second overlay for the background screen. Trim either amberlith, rubylith (these are special red/orange overlays printers use) or black paper into the exact shape of the box. When re-shot in camera, this overlay will produce a gray dot screen.

5 Finally, register all three overlays (this will ensure that the elements align exactly when they're sandwiched together in the copy camera). To do that, stick two register marks in opposite corners of the grid sheet. Then place two more on each overlay, making sure they match the register marks below.

COLOR

For years—for *decades*—newspaper editors viewed color with suspicion. Color, they stubbornly believed, was fine for the Sunday funnies, but *news* pages should be black and white and read all over.

Time passed. TV went full color. Magazines went full color. And in the '80s, after USA Today caught on, newspapers realized that color isn't just decoration; it attracts readers as it performs a variety of design functions:

Advertising & promotion

There are no ads on this page, since most papers keep Page One off-limits to advertisers. But there's a color teaser, prominently located, that's designed to catch the reader's eye. And there's surely a color ad on the back page of this section, since sharing color printing positions with advertisers helps lower the cost of newsroom color production.

Standing elements:

Many papers create an identity by applying color in a consistent way to various standing elements: the flag, headers, screens, reverse bars. Some papers use a specific hue to label each section of the paper (the Sports header is red, the Money header is green, etc.). Others use colors to label each edition (in this example, the morning paper uses blue reverse bars; the evening paper uses red).

Quality control

Sharp, consistent color printing isn't easy. If inks aren't properly balanced, faces turn orange; the sky turns purple. That's why many papers print color control bars like this one, which mixes tints of three different inks — 10% blue, 10% yellow and 10% magenta. When the press is properly inked, this bar prints a neutral gray.

Illustrations

Colorizing art is one of the easiest ways to add appeal to a page. It's just like taking crayons to a coloring book: An artist can layer one, two or a dozen colors over any black line drawing. Color illustrations can be used as standing elements (like this weather icon), as logos, as supporting art in infographics, or to illustrate features. And, of course, there's always the Sunday funnies. . . .

Photographs

Prior to 1980, photojournalism — in both magazines and newspapers — was primarily a black-and-white craft. But at many modern papers, color photos on section fronts have now become mandatory. Good-quality reproduction is still difficult and expensive, but that cost is offset by the appeal color photos have — and the added information they convey.

Infographics

Charts, graphs and maps rely on screens and rules to separate elements and enhance readability. And adding color makes them even more effective. In maps, for example, readers see at a glance that blue means water, tan means land. And large-scale infographics like this one can become the centerpiece of a page — particularly when no photos are available.

TYPES OF COLOR

SPOT COLOR

Ordinarily, printers use just one color of ink: black. But for a little extra money, they'll add a second ink to the press — a *spot color* — to let you create effects in a new hue.

(For even more money, you can add several spot colors to your paper. But unless you can coax an advertiser into sharing the color and footing the bill, you could blow your whole printing budget on a few flashy pages.)

Any single color — green, orange, purple, brown, you name it — can print as a spot color. But because readers are so accustomed to basic black and white, any added color has instant impact. So proceed with caution. Some "hot" colors (pink, orange) seem more cartoony than "cool" ones (blue, violet) — so choose hues that suit your news.

At left is a *duotone,* a photograph reproduced using both black and a spot color. As you can see in the enlargement below, the duotone combines different-sized black and blue screened dots to create the blue-gray effect.

Like basic black, spot colors can print as either solid tones or tints. Here, for instance, are some screen percentages for a spot blue:

| 10% BLUE | 20% BLUE | 50% BLUE | 100% BLUE |

You can add richness and variety to spot colors by mixing in black:

| 10% BLUE + 10% BLACK | 100% BLUE + 20% BLACK |

Pastels work best for background screens; solid tones work best for borders and headlines:

THIS IS A 100% BLUE / 20% BLACK HEADLINE INSIDE A 100% BLUE BOX

PROCESS OR FULL COLOR

But what if you want to print *all* the colors — the whole rainbow — instead of just one? You could add hundreds of separate spot colors, but that would cost a fortune (and you'd need a printing press a mile long). Instead, you can create the effect of full color by mixing and matching these four *process colors:*

CYAN MAGENTA YELLOW **BLACK**

By layering these four colors in different densities, a printing press can create almost any hue.

Running process color is expensive— not just for the extra ink, but for all the production work needed to prepare pages for printing. To reproduce a color photo, for instance, a special scanner must separate the image into the four process colors — and afterwards, those negatives must be carefully registered into place. (For more on color separation, see next page.)

At left is a full color photograph, which has been reproduced using all four of the process colors. As you can see in the enlargement below, the image combines different-sized cyan (blue), magenta (red), yellow and black screened dots to create the effect of full color.

Process colors can print as either solid tones or screens. Here, for instance, are the four process colors reproduced as 20% screens:

| 20% CYAN | 20% MAGENTA | 20% YELLOW | 20% BLACK |

Combining different values of process colors creates new hues:

| 50% CYAN / 50% YELLOW | 10% CYAN/ 40% MAGENTA / 50 YELLOW |

Pastels work best for background screens; solid tones work best for borders and headlines:

THIS IS A 50% CYAN / 100% MAGENTA HEADLINE INSIDE A 100% CYAN BOX

CREATING COLOR ART

How do you print full-color art using just four inks? The technology is brain-bogglingly complex, but the overall process is easy to understand. Here's how it works for a typical color illustration:

MORE ON:

■ **Building a mechanical:** How to add spot color to a page by cutting overlays 140

Original art

STEP ONE: The artist draws this color illustration on a Macintosh computer. As he draws, he creates custom colors from the computer's internal color palette, viewing the results on a color monitor. (A black-and-white monitor would work, too — it's less expensive, but it forces you to guess your color values.) When completed, this image exists *only* in electronic form — the artist will never actually hold the full-color illustration in his hand until it prints in the paper.

If this were a drawing on paper or a print of a color photo, it would be separated into process colors by either a process camera or a laser scanner, which use color filters to re-image the art.

Cyan printout   *Magenta printout*   *Yellow printout*   *Black printout*

STEP TWO: The artist transmits his artwork to a typesetter. Since a typesetter uses only black ink, it won't print the drawing in color. Instead, the computer electronically separates the drawing into the four process colors and produces printouts for each color using black ink.

         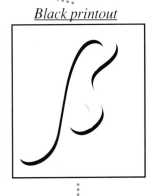

Cyan plate   *Magenta plate*   *Yellow plate*   *Black plate*

STEP THREE: A process camera shoots a negative of each of the four color printouts. When the page is ready to print, those negatives are transformed into plates for the printing press — one for each color of ink — which will produce the images shown here.

Printed art

STEP FOUR: As the presses roll, the newsprint passes across cylinders that, one after another, print each of the four color plates using the four process color inks. If the inks are correctly balanced — and if the newsprint is properly aligned as it passes through the press — then the colors will be accurate and the image will be sharply focused, or "registered." And only examination under a microscope will show how the differently colored ink dots produce the illusion of full color.

There are other ways to create art in color — cutting overlays, for instance. That's why it's vital, as you try new techniques, to develop good rapport with your printer and production crew.

ADDING COLOR TO A PAGE

This feature page from The Washington Times demonstrates that color doesn't need to be excessive to be effective. The designer, working with a limited color palette, has carefully balanced the color elements on this page.

Note the pastel orange screen used in the background at right. It's called a *graduated* screen because it gently fades from one tint to another. Graduated screens offer a bit more texture than standard color screens, but work best when their colors stay subtle.

"We've got spot purple on this page if we want it." Ohhhh, what a dangerous temptation that is . . . what a sure-fire way to turn a respectable newspaper into junk mail.

Yes, color can be a blessing — or a curse. It can delight your readers — or destroy your design. Using color successfully requires tight deadlines. Quality control. Extra money. Extra planning.

So *plan* for color. Don't just treat it like a surprise gift. And above all:

■ **Go easy.** Resist your initial urge to go overboard. Don't splash color around the page just to get your money's worth. Remember, black and white are colors, too. And black and white newspapers have managed to look handsome for centuries.

■ **Don't use color for color's sake.** Remember, it's a *news*paper. Not the Sunday funnies. If you're deciding between a color photo of circus balloons and a black-and-white photo of a bank holdup, choose the shot that's meaningful — not just pretty.

■ **Beware of colorizing false relationships.** Color creates connections, even where none actually exist. Put a *red* headline, a *red* chart and a *red* ad on the same page, and that tint will join them together in the reader's mind. That's dangerous.

Colors speak to each other. So if you don't want to connect elements, don't colorize them with the same hue.

■ **Use consistency.** Don't run a purple flag one day, a green flag the next; blue subheads here, red ones there. Give your paper a consistent identity by using consistent colors for consistent functions. Use this chart to plan ahead:

WHERE TO USE COLOR

THESE WILL *USUALLY* WORK IN COLOR:*

- ■ Illustrations
- ■ Charts, maps and info-graphics
- ■ Photos (full-color only)
- ■ Nameplates
- ■ Ads
- ■ Rules, headers and art in classified ads

THESE WILL *SOMETIMES* WORK IN COLOR:*

- ■ **Display headlines** (for big feature stories)
- ■ **Photo duotones** (for feature stories)
- ■ **Boxed stories/sidebars** (pastel screen tints only)
- ■ **Lift quotes, initial caps** (best if used in conjunction with color headlines or color illustrations)
- ■ **Decorative rules/bars**
- ■ **Signposts:** teasers,
- headers, indexes, etc. (but avoid competing with other color on page)
- ■ **Boxed subheads within a feature story**
- ■ **Borders around photos**

THESE WILL *RARELY* WORK IN COLOR:*

- ■ **Photographs** (printed with one spot color only)
- ■ **News headlines**
- ■ **Text type/cutlines**
- ■ **Boxed or screened hard news stories**

*Depending upon:
(1) Your choice of tint, and (2) Whether the color creates misleading relationships between unrelated elements on the page.

ADDING COLOR TO A PAGE

Adding color to a black-and-white page is a tricky thing. Where does it go? How much is too much?

For best results, remember that *a little goes a long way.* It's dangerous to dictate where color can or cannot be used — but as these examples show, some choices work better than others:

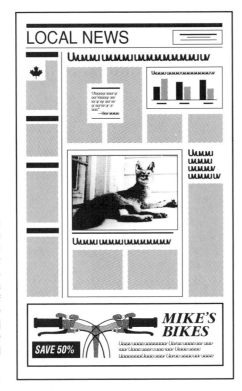

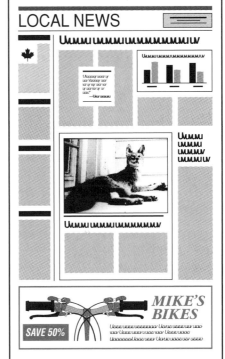

Here's a typical page in basic black. It may be gray, but it's not dull: By combining a variety of rules, bars and graphic elements, it presents an attractive mix of contrasts. In other words, it doesn't need extra decoration; any color we add should probably be *functional,* not *decorative.*

In the race to add color to this page, the advertiser got there first. And since that red ad is so distinctive and *loud,* any red we add to the news design will seem related, or connected, to that ad. That's a problem. To maintain a distinction between news and advertising, you can choose to use a minimum of editorial color. Here, we've applied red only to the header — and we've added 20% black to it, to give it a hue that's different from the ad below.

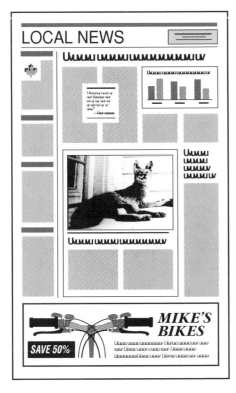

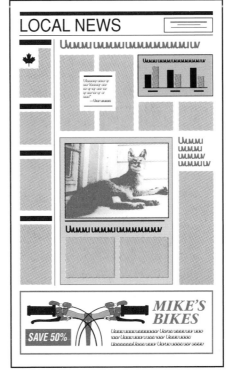

Without color in that ad, we're free to colorize our editorial layout. Still, we've used restraint — and we've used spot color for organization, not just decoration. Adding red to the bars in the header and news briefs helps anchor the layout; adding color to the bars in the bar graph gives them sharper identity. The drawing in the news briefs has been colorized for fun, not function — but that's OK.

We've made some bad choices here — and as a result, the page looks silly. Pink screens taint the credibility of the news. Red headlines and liftout quotes lose their integrity. Red rules and boxes distract the reader's eye, calling attention to unimportant design elements. And the red photo? It might work for special feature layouts, but this is *news.* The page is now weak — and worse, those colorized news elements all seem related, somehow, to Mike's Bikes.

COLOR GUIDELINES

This Fourth of July trivia page was done on the run: the designer had no art, no budget and no time to play. But this clever solution uses only type and spot color to turn a functional layout into a patriotic pattern. The red, white and blue colors instantly symbolize the theme of the story.

This page suffers from poor color choices. Green and purple — *not* a very popular color combo — are run as solid tones, and the complete lack of contrast makes the headline tough to read. The color green was probably meant to suggest money (see the dollar bill sign in the headline?), but the overall effect is dismal.

■ **Use appropriate colors.** Decorate a page the way you'd decorate your living room. And unless you live in a circus, that means playing up comfortable hues (blue and tan, for instance) and playing down harsh ones (pinks and greens). The integrity of a news story can be damaged if wild colors surround it, and the impact of a page can be negative if readers are turned off by your color choices.

Colors convey moods. "Hot" colors (red, yellow) are aggressive. "Cool" colors (blue, gray) are more restrained. So make sure your colors produce the effect you want. And remember, too, that certain color combinations have unshakeable associations. For example:

❏ *Red* = blood, Valentine's Day.
❏ *Green* = money, St. Patrick's Day.
❏ *Red + green* = Christmas.

Like it or not, these color cliches are lodged in your readers' brains. So make these colors work *for* you — not *against* you.

■ **Keep background screens as pastel as possible.** When we discussed background tints back on page 137, we saw how difficult it is to read text that's buried beneath a dark screen. Well, it's a problem whether the background is black, blue, brown, or *any* dark color. Whenever you run text in a sidebar, chart or map, keep all underlying screens as light as you can. (These will usually be below 20%, but actual numbers vary from press to press. Check with your printer to see what the lightest printable percentages are).

If you *must* add type to a dark screen, reverse it in a font that's big or bold enough to remain readable even if the printing registration is off.

This is 9-point type over a 100% cyan screen. Because the background tint is so intense, the words are hard to read.	This is 9-point type over a 10% cyan screen. Because the background tint is pale, the words are easy to read.	This is 9-point type over a 15% yellow/ 10% magenta screen. Because the colors are pale, the words are easy to read.	This is 10-point type over a 50% cyan/ 100% magenta screen. Because the type is reversed and bold, it's easy to read.

COLOR GUIDELINES

■ **Don't overreach your technology.** Color production is difficult to do well. It's costly. It's time-consuming. And in the hands of a sloppy printer, it's extremely disappointing. So it pays to learn your limits.

Drawings that look gorgeous on a computer screen often look like mud on newsprint. Color photos look *worse* than black-and-whites when the inking is poor or the registration is off (i.e., the color plates print out of alignment):

This color photo printed correctly. The color inks are properly balanced, so the colors are rich and true. The four color plates are properly aligned, so the image is crisp and well-focused.

This photo reveals the dangers of poor color production. The inks look washed out and badly balanced. And because the four plates are so far out of alignment, the image looks fuzzy — barely legible. If your color printing looks like this, you're better off using black and white.

So use color conservatively until you're *certain* of the results you'll get. And beware of small, detailed graphics or headlines that demand perfect color registration to succeed — or you'll face legibility problems like this:

THIS HEADLINE REGISTERS. . . . . THIS HEADLINE DOESN'T

■ **Watch the volume level of your colors.** Want your page to look like a Hawaiian shirt? That's what you'll get if you use *a)* too many solid tones, or *b)* too many different colors. So go easy. Use bold, vivid colors for *accent* only, in key locations (drawings, feature headlines, reverse bars). Elsewhere, for contrast, use lighter screens or pastel blends. And if you're designing with full color, try color schemes that accent one or two hues — not the whole rainbow.

Decorative colors are like decorative typefaces: In small doses, they attract; in large doses, they distract.

■ **Consult a color chart before you create new colors.** Some papers are afraid to mix colors, so they end up running all their color effects in basic blue, red and yellow. As a result, they look dull and unsophisticated.

But suppose you wanted to beef up your blue by adding a little black to it. How much black should you add? 10%? 30%? 50%? Or suppose you wanted to mix magenta and yellow to make orange: Should you simply guess at the right recipe — say, 20% magenta plus 50% yellow?

Don't guess. Instead, ask your printer to give you a color chart (right), which shows how every color combination looks when printed. You can even create your own chart — but be sure it's printed on the same paper your newspaper uses, so all your hues are true.

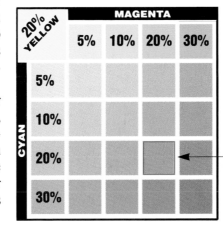

20% YELLOW	MAGENTA			
	5%	10%	20%	30%
5%				
10%				
CYAN **20%**				
30%				

A *color chart* shows how process inks look when they're combined. This portion of a chart, for instance, shows the tints you get when you add magenta and cyan to 20% yellow. The box highlighted at left shows the tint that results from mixing 20% yellow, 20% magenta and 20% cyan.

147

RISKY BUSINESS

*In your search for
The Ultimate Page Design,
you may be tempted to try
some of these effects.
But before you do, read on.*

BOXES & BOXES & BOXES

A box is a nice graphic effect. So does that mean that *many* boxes are a *real nice* graphic effect? Unfortunately, no. Some designers have a tendency to show off by piling boxes atop screens atop shadows, in hopes of creating cool 3-D skyscrapers. Other designers box news headlines, photos or cutlines to add pizazz. Cool it; don't overdo it.

The Mona Lisa
is one famous
painting by
Leonardo
da Vinci

DRUG PROBLEM

FESTIVAL

LEADERSHIP

THE OLD DAYS

High Fashion

NOVELTY TYPE

We've all seen amazing typography on movie posters, beer bottles and record jackets. But those are designed by highly paid professionals. *Your* daring headlines may well look clumsy — or illegible — if you choose goofy type or try artsy hand-lettering. So beware, beware of gimmicky type. Do you really want your readers to think you're a flake?

OVERPRINTING TEXT & ART

Wraparounds are a good way to let art and text interact. But what would happen, you ask, if you printed text *right over* art? It would look like this: disruptive and illegible. Sure, it works occasionally — on restaurant menus and birth certificates, for instance. But unless you find the perfect piece of art, position it precisely and print it crisply, you'll probably regret it.

**HEADLINES
SHOULD NOT POKE
OUT OF BOX TOPS**

And any time
you put text in
a box, you
should actually
box the box
with a rule —
don't just let it
float like this.

RAGGED SCREEN EFFECTS

When you print a screen on newsprint, it's going to look ragged around the edges. That's why most screens should be bordered and boxed, especially if they contain type. It's the only way to keep edges neat and clean. And avoid jutting type out of screens, too, like the headline at left. Your smartest choice: Find a different headline effect.

HEADLINE OVERKILL

This stacked headline may be clever, but it's quite a stack. It seems to go on and on and on: bar, headline, bar, headline, bar. . . When headlines get excessive, they get distracting. Keep them short and punchy. (This headline is really two separate heads joined together). In general, you should use rules and bars sparingly. A little decoration goes a long way.

.THE 1990
BEARS
ARE THEY
BETTER
OR JUST
BADDER?

GOOFY GIMMICKS

There's a time and a place for all of this stuff: type running sideways. Widgets in headlines. Super-expanded or condensed type. But most of the time, it's just clutter. The minute you get too fancy, an editor will ask you about "integrity" and "being taken seriously as a journalist." How will you respond?

HURRAY FOR HOLLYWOOD

Getting the JUMP
on SPRING

The lo♥e habit

■D·I·N·I·N·G
I·N S·T·Y·L·E

W e live in a visual age. We're bombarded with movies, videos, ads, photographs, maps, charts, diagrams. We're spoiled. And we've gotten lazy. When we want information, we say *show me* — don't *tell* me.

Yes, images are strong and seductive. Words take work. So most of us prefer images over words. Most of us would rather scan the pictures on that page at right than read this column of text. So what does that mean for newspapers? It means the dawning of the Age of Informational Graphics (or "infographics" for short). With infographics, newspapers can combine illustration and information into colorful, seductive packages. Infographics can be maps. Charts. Diagrams. Lists. They can work as tiny insets. Or as entire pages.

Do infographics junk up journalism? Some critics of USA Today think so; those cartoony charts and goofy graphs just trivialize the news, they say.

But remember: True journalism is *teaching.* You have information; your readers need it; therefore, you must teach it to them as quickly and clearly as you can. Simple as that.

Sometimes words work best. But other times, information transmits best *visually,* not verbally. Your job, as a newspaper designer, is to choose the best possible approach. This chapter will show you some of your options.

CHAPTER CONTENTS

■ **Current trends:** How the "information mosaic" has changed the way news is packaged..... **150**

■ **Computers & graphics:** Using computers to generate type, art and pages.............. **151**

■ **General guidelines:** Tips for compiling, editing and designing graphics and sidebars............ **152**

■ **Sidebars:** What they are, with a list of sidebar ideas............ **153**

■ **Fact boxes:** Compiling quick lists of key data to catch readers' eyes and add appeal.............. **154**

■ **Tables:** How to stack data into tabular rows so readers can make quick comparisons................ **155**

■ **Charts & graphs:** Guidelines for using line charts, bar charts and pie charts................ **156-157**

■ **Maps:** A look at the most common forms of newspaper maps,

with a few helpful tips and guidelines...................... **158-159**

■ **Diagrams:** Using more complex graphics to explain how something works............. **160-161**

■ **Graphics packages:** How to combine different infographics into a complex package................ **162**

CURRENT TRENDS

Years ago, when big stories broke, editors assigned reporters to cover every angle, to write miles and miles of text. And readers would read it.

Today, when big stories break, editors assign both reporters *and* graphic artists to cover every angle, to make stories understandable in both words *and* pictures. That's because today's readers are different. They absorb data in a variety of ways: through text, photos, charts, maps, diagrams. They want their news packaged in a sort of "information mosaic": a combination of words, images and statistics that simplify complex issues by approaching them from a variety of angles.

For instance, when the Hindenburg crashed in 1937, most newspapers ran a photo or two, but relied upon yards and yards of text to describe the tragedy. If the same disaster occurred today, you'd see pages like the one on the right below — full of locator maps, diagrams and dramatic sidebars.

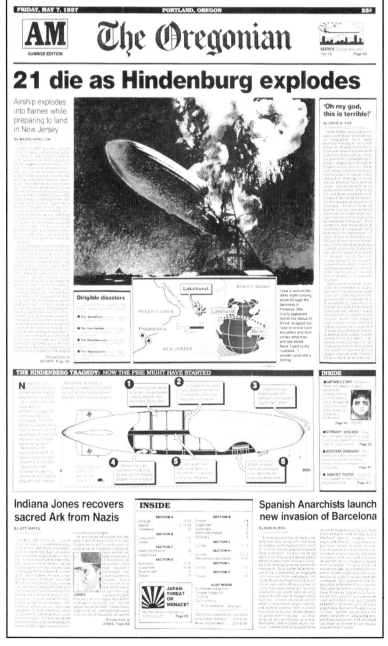

Above: The New York Times from May 7, 1937. Of the eight stories on Page One, five focus on the zeppelin disaster — but it's all narrative information. One dramatic photo is all that's shown (though it's played big). Inside the section, readers were given an extra page of disaster photos. At right: a fictionalized re-creation showing how a modern newspaper might have packaged the story using a locator map, a diagram, a list of previous accidents and a sidebar transcribing the live radio broadcast of the tragedy. These days, too, that lead photo would probably run in color.

COMPUTERS & GRAPHICS

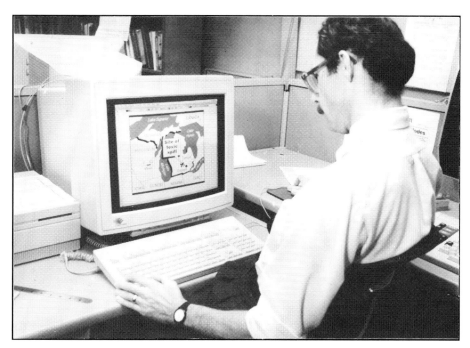

Infographic artist Clay Frost creates a Michigan map on a Macintosh computer in The Oregonian newsroom. This work station uses a 19-inch color monitor to help in the preparation of full-page color maps, charts and diagrams.

Computers and graphics go together like — well, like headphones and heavy metal. So if you're serious about newspaper design, get comfortable with computers. They're an indispensable tool, a graphic option that's fast becoming a necessity. And they're here to stay.

Newsrooms use computers in a variety of ways, including:

■ **Writing stories**. Most newsrooms tossed out their typewriters 10 years ago. Today, journalists are expected to type, edit, file stories, fit headlines and search through data bases using video terminals.

■ **Creating illustrations.** Today's drawing programs make it easy for artists to create full-color artwork in almost any style.

■ **Producing charts, graphs and maps.** Compare the two maps below. They look identical — but the computerized version was much easier to produce and could be modified quickly, if necessary.

■ **Pagination.** Some desktop publishing programs let you create entire pages electronically (this book, for instance, was designed using Quark Xpress). In the future, all newspaper type, photos and art will be paginated.

The most common computer in newsroom art departments is the Macintosh, produced by Apple Computer, Inc. (You'll often hear artists refer to graphics created on "the Mac.")

Several wire services produce computer graphics daily, transmitting them electronically to subscribers. For a low cost, this service allows small papers to package first-class graphics with each day's news — and helps papers create an ever-expanding library of maps, charts and diagrams.

This map was produced by tracing a Michigan map, typesetting the words, pasting them in place, cutting screens and sending everything to camera. Total time: 4 hours.

This map was drawn on a Macintosh using a MacDraw program. The artist called up a base map, typed in the names and output it to a printer. Total time: 20 minutes.

GENERAL GUIDELINES

"Graphical excellence is that which gives to the viewer the greatest number of ideas in the shortest time with the least ink in the smallest space."

— Edward R. Tufte

BEFORE YOU BEGIN . . .

Ask yourself:

❑ What's missing from this story? What would complete the picture for those who read it — or draw in readers who might otherwise turn the page?

❑ Is the text bogged down by a series of numbers? Details? Dates? Definitions? Comparisons? Can something be pulled out and played up?

❑ What data needs further clarification: Statistics? Geographical details? Trends? History? Does the story overestimate the readers' knowledge?

❑ How much time and space do we have for a graphic or sidebar? Can we squeeze in a quick list? A small map? A huge clip-'n'-save poster page?

❑ What's the point of this sidebar or graphic? Is there one clear idea we're trying to illustrate — or are we just compiling a lump of statistics?

COMPILING & EDITING GRAPHICS

■ **Collect data carefully.** Use reliable sources, as current as possible. Beware of missing data, estimates or projections. If information is uncertain or unverifiable, you must flag it for your readers.

■ **Edit carefully.** Every graphic — every chart, map or sidebar — *must* be edited. Check all math, then check it against the data in the text. Check all spelling. Check that the graphic matches all details mentioned in the text.

■ **Convert to understandable values.** Avoid kilometers, knots per hour, Celsius degrees. Convert foreign currency to U.S. dollars. Avoid any obscure terms, jargon or abbreviations that confuse or mislead.

■ **Simplify, simplify.** What's your point? Make it absolutely, instantly clear. Avoid clutter by eliminating the nonessentials and focusing only on key highlights. And don't assume the reader has read the story; your graphics and sidebars must stand on their own.

DESIGN & TYPOGRAPHY

■ **Develop graphics style guidelines.** You'll avoid confusion and create a consistent look if you adopt strict standards for all type styles and sizes, screen densities, source and credit lines, dingbats, etc. Find combinations that work, then print up sample graphics for every artist to consult.

■ **Make it readable.** Avoid type smaller than 8 point (except for source or credit lines). Use boldface to highlight key words. Keep all type horizontal (except for rivers or roads on maps). Use rules and careful spacing to keep elements from crowding each other and creating confusion.

■ **Give every sidebar or graphic a headline.** Even a short title ("What They Earn") clarifies your intent. Use consistent sizes, fonts and treatments.

■ **Box it.** Don't let graphics float amid the text. Just as you should border every photo, you should box every sidebar or graphic.

■ **Keep decoration to a minimum.** Use illustrations to tweak readers' attention (*This chart is about shipping — see the little boat? Get it?*), but don't junk up your data with cartoon clutter. Use reverses or color only to highlight key elements; otherwise, use pastel tint screens for backgrounds — especially behind type.

■ **Dummy graphics as you would a photo.** Graphics and sidebars are generally dummied like any other art element that's part of a story. Just make sure you avoid butting headlines or confusing placement.

SIDEBARS

A *sidebar* is any short story accompanying a bigger story. But a good sidebar is more than that — it's an entertaining alternative, a fresh perspective, a reader-friendly hook. Sidebars provide an opportunity to add extra reader appeal to any story, whether news or feature.

There are three things to remember about sidebars:

■ They should be tightly, brightly written.

■ They shouldn't be more than 10 inches long. (Longer than that, it's called a "related story.")

■ They often attract higher readership than the main story.

Sidebars, like charts, maps and diagrams, offer an informational alternative to narrative text. If done properly, they carve up complicated material into bite-size chunks — while providing graphic relief at the same time.

Take the page at right. When the Fourth of July rolled around, the question at The Oregonian was: What's left to say about flags and fireworks?

The answer: a fireworks info-page. There's a diagram near the top of the page showing how fireworks explode. There's a sidebar on the right listing where readers can watch local firework displays. The main story is full of trivia, history and fireworks lore. And along the bottom of the page, another sidebar takes a behind-the-scenes look at fireworks-launchers. (Note how their mug shots all look up toward the fireworks photos at the top of the page.)

Sidebars are usually specially packaged — boxed or screened — to make them stand out from the main story. To stand apart from this text block you're reading now, for instance, the sidebar below has been boxed; it uses a reversed header, a background screen and sans serif type for the text.

TEN TYPES OF SIDEBARS

1. Lists. Readers love lists, whether they're Top Ten countdowns, casts of characters (a brief who's who), chronologies (events leading up to today), or directories (where to go for help).

2. Quizzes/checklists. Ask readers: "Are you a . . . ?" Or write a trivia test about the topic in the main story.

3. Quotes. Collect a sampling of opinions by or about the character you're profiling.

4. For further information. . . Tell readers how to get involved: groups to contact, books to read, videos to rent, events to attend.

5. Step-by-step guides. Translate a complicated series of actions into an easy-to-follow "how-to" with photos or drawings.

6. Glossaries. Define key terms or jargon that readers should know.

7. Excerpts. Whenever you profile a creative artist (author, songwriter, comedian), include a brief, representative sample of his or her work.

8. Extended quotes/anecdotes. First-person reminiscences or oral histories lend flavor and authenticity to features.

9. Requests to readers. Let them write, phone, or vote on a mail-in ballot.

10. Fact boxes. Capsulized who-what-when-where-why boxes work for profiles, upcoming events (dates, times, ticket prices) or Disease-of-the-Week stories (symptoms, cures, side effects, etc.). See the next page for more details.

FACT BOXES

One of the most inviting types of sidebar is the "fast facts" box, which distills the who-what-when-where-why of a story into a concise package. By compiling fact boxes like those shown here, you can:
- Quickly catch the reader's attention.
- Introduce basic facts without slowing down the text of the story.
- Provide entertaining data for those who may not read the entire text.
- Add graphic variety to the story design.

A VANISHING SPECIES

The black rhinoceros has a prehensile upper lip, typical of a browsing animal, which distinguishes it from a white rhinoceros.

BLACK RHINOCEROS
Diceros bicornis

- **Population:** About 4,000, down from a population in 1970 of 65,000. About 150 black rhinos are in zoos worldwide.

- **Distribution:** small areas in southern and eastern Africa

- **Habitat:** rugged, hilly terrain and deep bush

- **Diet:** leaves and twigs, fruit, and herbs such as clover

- **Weight:** 2,195-3,000 pounds; a newborn calf weighs 55-88 pounds

- **Height:** 4½-6 feet

- **Length:** 10-12½ feet

- **Length of front horn:** 1½-4½ feet

- **Color:** gray

- **Longevity:** about 40-50 years

- **Description:** Rhinos generally are shy and retiring animals. They have poor eyesight, but have acute senses of smell and hearing. Although the three-toed animals are usually slow-moving, a black rhinoceros can charge at speeds up to 31 mph.

The two African species, the black and white, are both gray in color, with the black rhino slightly darker and smaller. The main difference is their ecological requirements: The black is a browser, feeding on leaves and twigs with its prehensile upper lip, while the white "square-lipped" rhino is a grazer, feeding mainly on grass.

A rhino horn has no bony central core, but consists of an aggregation of hollow keratin fibers, similar to hair.

Source: "RHINOS Endangered Species" by Malcolm Penny, Facts on File Publications

The Oregonian

Doers Profile

Ernest Postell Sr.

Vitae
President, Neighborhood Medical Training Inc.

Birthday
Aug. 5

Hometown
Sumter, S.C.

Maritial Status
Married to T. Postell

Self-Portrait Humanitarian

Motto If you're not getting better, you're bound to be worse, nothing stands still in this whole universe

Greatest Feat Established the first Emergency Medical Technician training program at Lorton Reformatory; trained community instructors in first-aid and organized Neighborhood Medical Training Inc., which offers medical self-help and emergency first-aid training

Walter Mitty Fantasy To have been an aide to Dr. Albert Schweitzer

Inspirations Dr. Cobb, Montague, Bishop H.C. Brooks, Dr. Martin Luther King Jr.

Hobbies Reading and hiking

Bad Habit Eating lying down

Restaurant Horn and Horn

Drink Lemonade

Car in Garage 1978 Cadillac

TV Programs WUSA-TV's J.C. Hayward

Books at Bedside Bible, medical books

Last Words I let my light shine so people could see my good works

Above: These brief bio boxes run twice-weekly on The Washington Times' social page.
At left: A large fact box from The Oregonian that accompanied a science page story.
At right: This short, simple fact box gives readers event highlights at a glance.

MUSIC PREVIEW

Toe Jam

What: Heavy-metal rock
Where: Reagan Memorial Amphitheater
When: 10 p.m. Friday
Tickets: $13.50-$22.50
Opening act: Ducks Deluxe

TABLES

How various taxpayers would fare under the conference bill

Comparison of taxes owed by various groups for 1988 under current law and under the bill proposed by the tax conference committee.

	Gross income	Current tax	Proposed tax	Percent change
Married couple				
with two children	$ 30,700	$ 2,197	$ 2,040	-7.1%
	61,050	4,651	4,839	+4.0%
	265,000	24,950	44,698	+79.2%
with no children	91,500	9,911	11,547	+16.5%
Single person	20,000	1,817	1,330	-26.8%
with one child	30,100	4,773	4,447	-6.8%
with no children	64,000	14,007	13,623	-2.7%
Retirees				
married, over 65	44,000	3,775	3,360	-11.0%
single, over 65	25,000	963	737	-23.5%

Source: Arthur Andersen & Co.

This table compares the effects two different tax plans would have on different types of taxpayers. Note the use of reverse headings along the top and boldface categories on the left; note, too, how rules and icons help organize listings.

The vocabulary of the South

Samples from the three principal Southern dialects.

General American	Hill	Plains	Coastal
Dragonfly	Snake feeder	Snake doctor	Mosquito hawk
Large porch	Veranda	Piazza	Gallery
Skin mite	Chigger	Chigger/red bug	Red bug
Andirons	Dog irons	Fire dogs	Fire dogs/andirons
Harmonica	French harp	Mouth harp	Mouth organ
Small tomatoes	Tommytoes	Salad tomatoes	Cherry tomatoes
Mantel	Fireboard	Mantelpiece	Mantelpiece/mantel
Pancakes	Flitters	Battercakes	Battercakes
Burrowing turtle	–	Gopher	Gopher
Closet	Closet	Closet	Locker
Paper bag/sack	Poke	Bag/sack	Bag/sack
Wishbone	Pulley bone	Pulley bone	Wishbone

Source: Emory University

This table uses words, not numbers, to let readers compare different terms from different Southern dialects. It's basically three vocabulary lists stacked side by side, with those screened areas on the map coded into the column headings.

A table is an age-old graphic device that's really half text, half chart. Unlike the charts on the next page, tables don't use lines, bars or pie slices to make their point; instead, they stack words and numbers in rows to let readers make side-by-side comparisons.

Tables are boxed rectangles that consist of: 1) headings running horizontally across the top of the chart; 2) categories running vertically down the left side; and 3) lists grouped in columns reading both *across* and *down*.

In effect, tables are neatly organized lists. To keep them as neat as possible, carefully space and align all rows and columns. Numbers align best flush right; words align best flush left (see above examples). In small tables, hairline rules between rows may help alignment; in bigger tables, too many lines can look dizzying, so screen effects or occasional rules (every 5 lines, for example) may work better. And remember: Keep all wording crisp and tight.

Tables can be used for a wide variety of statistical comparisons. Here, for instance, are three common formats easily adaptable to different sets of data:

	DATE 1	DATE 2	DATE 3
ITEM 1	$$$$	$$$	$$$$
ITEM 2	$$	$$$$	$$
ITEM 3	$$$$	$$$	$$$

In this table, you can compare different items (top to bottom) at different times (left to right). For instance, you could track the sales of different crops (corn, wheat, rice) in different years. Or you could compare school population totals (how many sophomores, juniors and seniors per year).

	TOPIC 1	TOPIC 2	TOPIC 3
NAME 1	Yes	Yes	No
NAME 2	No	Yes	Yes
NAME 3	Yes	Maybe	No

This table could compare the stances of three political candidates (top to bottom) on different issues (left to right); wider columns would allow longer responses. A similar table format could compare different laws in different cities, or show the features offered by different consumer goods.

	FEATURE 1	FEATURE 2	FEATURE 3
ITEM 1	Date	Number	Etc.
ITEM 2	Date	Number	Etc.
ITEM 3	Date	Number	Etc.

This table combines different types of data. To display track records, for instance, the events (high jump, shot put) could run top to bottom; the date, record and athlete's name could run left to right. This form of table could also be used to compare disasters (when, where, how many killed, etc).

CHARTS & GRAPHS

News is full of numbers: dollars, debts, crime statistics, budget percentages, election results. And the more complicated those numbers get, the more confused *readers* get. Take this text, for instance:

> **In 1968, 34,500 units were imported each year, comprising 16 percent of the annual total. By 1978, that number had risen to 77,400, and by 1988 more than 17,000 units were arriving monthly, representing an increase of 591 percent over 1967, the first full year of operation.**

Huh? You get the idea. When math gets heavy, charts and graphs come in handy. They present numerical data in a simple, visual way — and the simpler they are, the better they work. On the next two pages, we'll look at the three basic types of numerical graphics: line charts, bar charts and pie charts.

LINE CHARTS

The line chart (also called a fever chart) *measures changing quantities over time.* It uses three basic components: 1) a scale running vertically along one edge measuring amounts; 2) a scale running horizontally along the bottom measuring time; and 3) a jagged line connecting a series of points, thus illustrating a rising or falling trend.

Line charts are created by plotting different points, then connecting the dots to draw a curve. (Charts often include a background grid to help readers track the numbers.) Obviously, a line that rises or falls dramatically will impress readers more than one that barely shows a blip.

Line charts work best when tracing one simple statistic over time. But you can also plot additional lines to compare several different trends — as long as you clearly label *which* line represents *which* trend. (For instance, you could compare the sales of apples and oranges over the same period of time using a red line for apples, an orange line for oranges.)

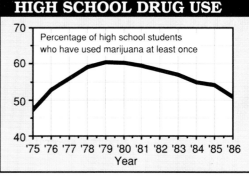

HIGH SCHOOL DRUG USE

Percentage of high school students who have used marijuana at least once

Note how this chart doesn't show the entire range of percentages from 0 to 100, but focuses on the relevant range.

BAR CHARTS

The bar chart *compares two or more items by sizing them as columns parked side by side.* It uses two basic components: 1) a scale running either horizontally or vertically along one edge showing data totals; 2) bars extending in the same direction representing the items being measured. Bars are usually stacked in a logical order: either alphabetically, chronologically or ranked by size.

In simple bar charts, each item may be labeled either inside the bar or at either end (as in the example at right). The bars may be screened or given 3-D shadow effects, as long as data isn't distorted.

In more complex bar charts — where the same items are compared to each other in different times or situations — each item is assigned its own color or screen pattern, which is then explained in a key or legend.

Background grids, though often helpful, aren't essential.

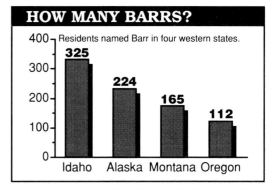

HOW MANY BARRS?

Residents named Barr in four western states.

325 — Idaho
224 — Alaska
165 — Montana
112 — Oregon

This data is not factual; rather, it is a clever pun devised for your amusement. Get it? A "Barr" chart?

CHARTS & GRAPHS

PIE CHARTS

The pie chart *compares the parts that make up a whole.* It usually consists of 1) a circle that represents 100% of something, and 2) several wedges (like slices of a pie) that divide the circle into smaller percentages. Each "slice" of the pie is an accurate proportion — which means that a segment representing 25% of the total would be one-quarter of the pie.

Figures for each slice are labeled either inside the slice (if there's room) or by scattering type, with pointers, around the outside of the pie. Slices are often shaded or color-coded for clearer distinction (or to emphasize one particular segment). As a rule of thumb, pies should be divided into no more than eight segments; otherwise, the slices get too thin.

To add impact, you can sometimes create pie charts from drawings or photos of the items being measured. For example, you can slice a dollar bill into sections to show where your tax dollar goes, or draw rings around a oil drum to break down the profits from a barrel of oil.

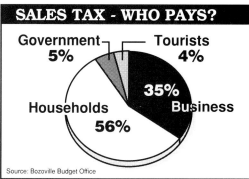

SALES TAX - WHO PAYS?

Government 5%
Tourists 4%
Business 35%
Households 56%

Source: Bozoville Budget Office

Note how this pie chart uses a tilted, 3-D pie, with each slice differently shaded.

GUIDELINES

■ **Keep it appealing.** Make it look easy to understand or you'll scare readers away. Depict one idea only — a concept readers can relate to, not something academic, insignificant or obscure.

■ **Keep it simple.** Use only what's relevant to the story (and understandable to readers.) Don't pile years and years onto a line chart if it's only recent trends that matter; don't slice pie charts into a dozen slivers if a few broad categories convey the same idea. Above all, don't overcrowd or overwork a chart. If you want to make several different points, you'll usually find that several charts are better than one.

■ **Keep it accurate.** Use trustworthy sources (and print their names in a source line at the bottom of the chart). Double-check their math — then have someone check *your* math when you're done.

Most of all, be sure all proportions are true. Slices in a pie chart should be mathematically precise; time units in a line chart should be evenly spaced; bars in bar charts should be equally proportioned. Computer programs can help you plot your figures accurately; if you're drawing graphs by hand, protractors and grid sheets are essential for accuracy.

■ **Dress it up.** Add screens, 3-D effects, illustrations and color — but add them to help organize and label the data, not just for decoration. Used poorly, these effects can distort your information and distract your readers. Used well, they can make dry statistics fresh and appealing (as the example at right shows). Proceed with caution.

■ **Label it clearly.** Make sure each element — every line, number and shading pattern — is explained. Add a legend, if necessary. Or write an introductory blurb at the top of the chart to tell readers what they're seeing.

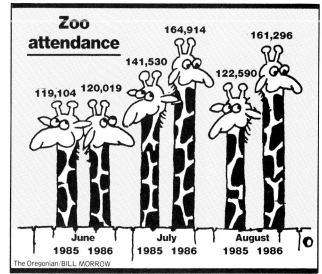

Zoo attendance

119,104 120,019 141,530 164,914 122,590 161,296

June 1985 1986   July 1985 1986   August 1985 1986

The Oregonian/BILL MORROW

How do you jazz up a bar chart that measures zoo attendance? By replacing plain, rectangular bars with cartoon giraffes. This informal treatment won't work on every chart, but succeeds here.

MAPS

The Oregonian

Two examples of locator maps: above, a simple, no-frills state map showing where to find the town of Promise, Oregon. Maps like this are usually run small, providing quick reference at a glance. At right is a locator map — actually, a 3-way state, city and street map — showing more complete details. To be readable, this map would need to run at least 2 columns wide.

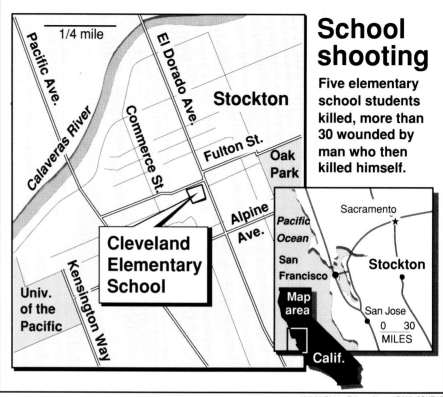

Knight-Ridder Tribune News / PAUL SOUTAR

Most Americans are poor geographers. They have a tough time remembering even the easy stuff, like where New York City is. (Hint: it's on the East Coast — that's the *right edge* of a U.S. map.) So how can we expect them to visualize volcanoes in Fiji? Riots in Lesotho? Train wrecks in Altoona?

With maps. Maps can enhance almost any news story, if you're ambitious enough, but they're especially important for:

❏ any story where a knowledge of geography is essential to the story's meaning (an oil spill, a border dispute, a plane crash), or

❏ any local story where readers may participate (a parade, a new gym).

Maps come in all sizes and styles — world maps, street maps, relief maps, weather maps, etc. But the maps most often produced in newsrooms are:

■ **Locator maps:** These show, as simply as possible, the location of a key place ("X" marks the spot), or tell the reader where something occurred.

■ **Explanatory maps:** These are used for storytelling, to show *how* an event progressed. Often using a step-by-step approach to label sequences, these maps are visually active (as opposed to passive locator maps).

■ **Data maps:** These show the geographical distribution of data, working like a chart to convey statistical information: population distributions, political trends, weather, etc. (See our examples of each map type above).

How are maps created? They're copied. Though you can't cut a map out of a road atlas and stick it in the paper (that's a copyright violation), you *can* trace a map's highlights, then fill in your own details as necessary.

Every paper should compile a library of maps in a variety of scales, from global to local. Buy a world atlas; collect state highway maps, city and county maps, even brochures from your local chamber of commerce (showing shopping areas, local parks, hiking trails, the layout of the airport).

Be prepared. You never know where news is going to break.

MAPS

FATAL CHICAGO SHOOTOUT

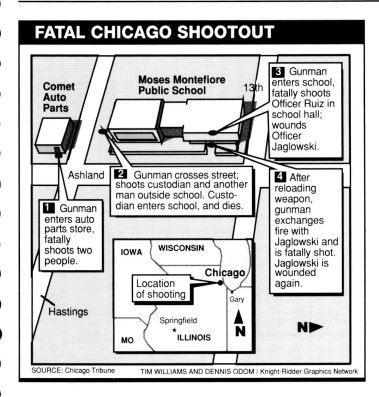

Comet Auto Parts

Moses Montefiore Public School 13th

3 Gunman enters school, fatally shoots Officer Ruiz in school hall; wounds Officer Jaglowski.

Ashland

2 Gunman crosses street; shoots custodian and another man outside school. Custodian enters school, and dies.

1 Gunman enters auto parts store, fatally shoots two people.

4 After reloading weapon, gunman exchanges fire with Jaglowski and is fatally shot. Jaglowski is wounded again.

Hastings

IOWA WISCONSIN

Chicago

Location of shooting

Gary

Springfield

MO ★ ILLINOIS

N

N▶

SOURCE: Chicago Tribune   TIM WILLIAMS AND DENNIS ODOM / Knight-Ridder Graphics Network

Getting out the vote in the United States

Low voter turnout on Election Day is a growing problem in the United States. Here is a state-by-state breakdown of the percent of eligible voters who voted in the 1984 presidential election.

Voter turnout

■ 40% - 50%   ▢ 50% - 60%   ▢ 60% - 70%

Knight-Ridder Chicago Tribune News/JUDY TREIBLE

At left, an explanatory map showing a step-by-step sequence of events. Note the 3-D building drawings; the inset locator map; the two "north" arrows. Above, a data map using tint screens to show state-by-state voting statistics.

GUIDELINES

■ **Create design guidelines for all maps.** You'll save time and give your maps a consistent look if you set clear standards for abbreviations, screens, line weights, symbols — and most important:

■ **Use type consistently.** Use designated fonts in designated sizes (sans serif will usually work best behind screens). Avoid type that's too big (over 12 point) or too small (under 8 point). Decide where you'll use all caps (countries? states?), where you'll use italics (bodies of water?), where you'll use boldface (key points of interest only?).

■ **Keep maps simple.** The whole planet can fit inside a one-column box, if necessary. Make your point obvious; trim away all unnecessary details. Anything that doesn't enhance the map's meaning will just distract attention.

■ **Keep maps dynamic.** Don't just re-create a dull road map; add shadow boxes, screens, 3-D effects, tilted perspectives — just be careful not to distort the map's accuracy or destroy its integrity.

■ **Keep north pointing "up."** If north isn't at the top of a map, include a "north" arrow to show where it is. Otherwise, the arrow isn't necessary.

■ **Add mileage scales whenever possible.** They give readers perspective.

■ **Match the map to the story.** Be sure that every significant place mentioned in the text is accounted for on the map.

■ **Use screens cautiously.** Remember, white areas "pop"; screened areas recede. Use light screen tints (10% is best), especially behind type.

■ **Center maps carefully.** Keep them as tightly focused as possible. If pockets of "dead" space occur, you can fill them with mileage scales, callout boxes, locator-map insets or illustrations.

■ **Assume your reader is lost.** To help him understand where he is, you may need to give your map a headline or an introductory paragraph. You may need to add a locator map to your *main* map if that makes it clearer. (For instance, if you draw a detailed street map, you should show what part of the city you're in.) Above all, include any familiar landmarks — cities, rivers, highways, shopping malls — that help your reader get his bearings.

DIAGRAMS

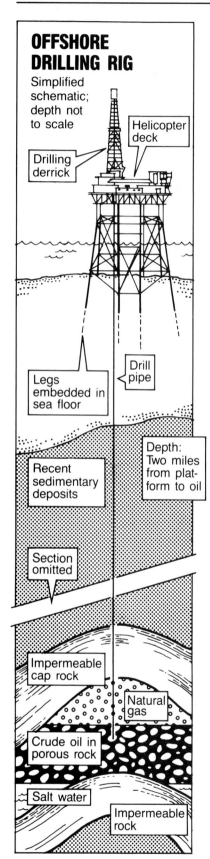

OFFSHORE DRILLING RIG

Simplified schematic; depth not to scale

Helicopter deck

Drilling derrick

Legs embedded in sea floor

Drill pipe

Depth: Two miles from platform to oil

Recent sedimentary deposits

Section omitted

Impermeable cap rock

Natural gas

Crude oil in porous rock

Salt water

Impermeable rock

This diagram provides a cutaway view of an offshore drilling rig, identifying both equipment and major geologic features.

Maps focus on the *where* of a story; diagrams focus on the *how*. Diagrams offer cutaway views, step-by-step analyses, itemized breakdowns of complex objects.

Whatever your topic, diagrams will work best if you:

■ **Focus tightly.** Pinpoint precisely what you need to explain before you begin. Should the diagram be passive? (Notice how the diagram at left simply points to each part.) Or should it be active? (Notice how the Theismann diagram below shows events in motion). Whatever the approach — whatever the topic — keep your diagram as simple as you can.

■ **Design logically.** Let your central image determine the diagram's shape (for instance, that oil rig is a deep vertical). If you're running a sequence, find a perspective that lets you show the steps in the most logical, easy-to-follow order.

■ **Label clearly.** Avoid clutter by using a consistent treatment for all *callouts* (sometimes called *factoids*), whether with pointer boxes, shadows, lines or arrows:

Callout   Callout   Callout   Callout   Callout

■ **Research carefully.** You're becoming an instant expert; readers will rely on your accuracy. Do your homework. Cross-check several references. Read the story. Study photos. Talk to outside experts or witnesses to the event. Visit the scene yourself, if you can. In short: Become a graphics reporter.

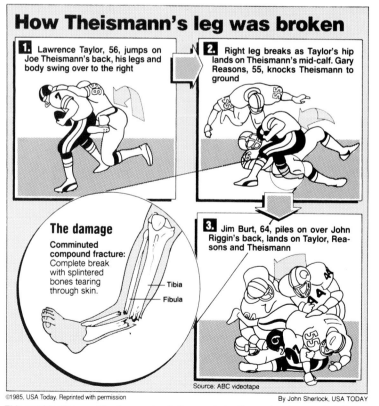

How Theismann's leg was broken

1. Lawrence Taylor, 56, jumps on Joe Theismann's back, his legs and body swing over to the right

2. Right leg breaks as Taylor's hip lands on Theismann's mid-calf. Gary Reasons, 55, knocks Theismann to ground

The damage

Comminuted compound fracture: Complete break with splintered bones tearing through skin.

Tibia

Fibula

3. Jim Burt, 64, piles on over John Riggin's back, lands on Taylor, Reasons and Theismann

Source: ABC videotape

©1985, USA Today. Reprinted with permission   By John Sherlock, USA TODAY

This combination graphic shows not only the events leading up to a key sports injury but also an anatomical diagram of the injured leg. The sequence works almost like a slow-motion replay — and the artist actually used a video playback to draw the frames.

DIAGRAMS

These two feature pages from the Rochester Times-Union show modern treatments of old holiday stories. Here, callouts contain interesting facts about the turkey's voice, brain, feathers, beak (turkeys are cannibalistic) and "snood."

A similar treatment anchors a story full of tips from department-store Santas. Callouts describe everything from Santa's ho-ho-ho to his basic black boots. Below, there's a touching sidebar about a local Santa who's slowly going blind.

Diagrams aren't limited to hard-news graphics. On occasion, a feature page can adapt basic diagram techniques to turn its lead art into something informational *and* entertaining.

The two pages shown above, for instance, use callouts to give readers an itemized breakdown of their lead images. This approach is a clever way to supplement the text (right) — or to eliminate text altogether (left). It can work with drawings or studio photos, anytime the subject (food, fashion, new products) lends itself to closer inspection.

In a similar way, a series of photos can be labeled in sequence to illustrate a step-by-step procedure (like our "How to build a mechanical" on page 140). That's a good way to make the photos more interactive with text.

These pages can be created by one photographer and reporter working together. You don't need a computerized art department to achieve professional results.

GRAPHICS PACKAGES

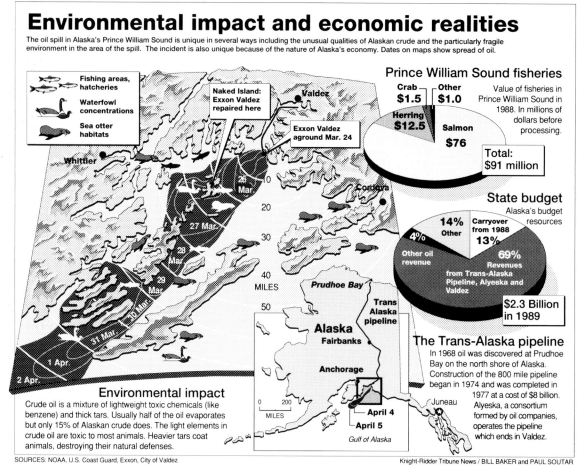

Environmental impact and economic realities

The oil spill in Alaska's Prince William Sound is unique in several ways including the unusual qualities of Alaskan crude and the particularly fragile environment in the area of the spill. The incident is also unique because of the nature of Alaska's economy. Dates on maps show spread of oil.

Fishing areas, hatcheries

Waterfowl concentrations

Sea otter habitats

Naked Island: Exxon Valdez repaired here

Valdez

Exxon Valdez aground Mar. 24

Whittier

Cordova

24 Mar
27 Mar
28 Mar
29 Mar
30 Mar
31 Mar
1 Apr
2 Apr

0
20
30
40 MILES
50

Prince William Sound fisheries

Crab $1.5 — Other $1.0

Herring $12.5

Salmon $76

Value of fisheries in Prince William Sound in 1988. In millions of dollars before processing.

Total: $91 million

State budget

Alaska's budget resources

14% Other

4%

Other oil revenue

Carryover from 1988 13%

69% Revenues from Trans-Alaska Pipeline, Alyeska and Valdez

$2.3 Billion in 1989

Prudhoe Bay

Trans Alaska pipeline

Alaska
Fairbanks

Anchorage

0   200
MILES

April 4
April 5

Gulf of Alaska

Juneau

The Trans-Alaska pipeline

In 1968 oil was discovered at Prudhoe Bay on the north shore of Alaska. Construction of the 800 mile pipeline began in 1974 and was completed in 1977 at a cost of $8 billion. Alyeska, a consortium formed by oil companies, operates the pipeline which ends in Valdez.

Environmental impact

Crude oil is a mixture of lightweight toxic chemicals (like benzene) and thick tars. Usually half of the oil evaporates but only 15% of Alaskan crude does. The light elements in crude oil are toxic to most animals. Heavier tars coat animals, destroying their natural defenses.

SOURCES: NOAA, U.S. Coast Guard, Exxon, City of Valdez

Knight-Ridder Tribune News / BILL BAKER and PAUL SOUTAR

At left, a graphic summary of a major Alaskan oil spill. Note how many different levels of information — geography, environmental impact, history, economics — are combined in one package. Without reading any additional text, you could familiarize yourself with the dynamics of this disaster just by studying this graphic. Below, one of several pages produced by The Chicago Tribune for the '88 Winter Olympics. Each page used the same format to analyze the techniques, equipment and course layout for the top Olympic events.

The bigger the news event, the more explanation it needs — and the more complex its graphics become. That's why you'll often see dazzling infographics, like the ones on this page, combining charts, maps and diagrams into one reader-friendly package.

Done well, these packages present as much (or more) information as any news story. But to do these graphics packages well, you'll need:

■ **Time.** Some, like the Olympics page at right, are parts of special series that take months to assemble. Most megagraphics need at least several days to prepare and can't be rushed without dismal results.

■ **Teamwork.** These aren't solo efforts. They demand cooperation and planning for the research, reporting, art and layout to come together smoothly.

■ **Expertise.** Sorry to say, these packages are terribly difficult to produce. Don't tackle anything this tricky until you've honed your graphics techniques.

■ **A firm commitment of space.** Don't let them reduce your full-page package down to 2 columns at the last minute. Get the space you need *guaranteed.*

Above all, don't overdo it. Both packages shown here, for instance, take readers right to the edge of "information overload." A slick graphics package lures us in; a sloppy one frightens us away.

CHAPTER CONTENTS

■ **Exercise answers:** From the chapter on story design.......... **164**

■ **Exercise answers:** From the chapter on page design......... **165**

■ **Exercise answers:** From the chapter on photos & art......... **169**

■ **Glossary:** A guide to newspaper design terms....................**173**

■ **Index**.............................. **178**

■ **Acknowledgments**........... **180**

EXERCISE ANSWERS: STORY DESIGN

Exercise questions are on page 53.

1 A 5-inch story should be dummied either in one leg 5 inches long or in two legs 2.5 inches long. You should generally avoid dummying legs shorter than 2 inches, which would rule out a 3-column layout for this story.

MORE ON:

■ **Headline sizes:** Typical ranges for tab and broadsheet pages.................. 16

■ **Headline codes:** What we mean by a 1-30-3 head........ 17

■ **Story designs** using only text.... 30

■ **Mug shots:** How to design them into stories 32

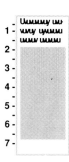

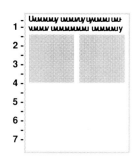

Though styles vary from paper to paper, this story might use a 1-30-3 or 1-30-2 headline on Page One, and a 1-18-2 or 1-24-2 at the bottom of an inside page.

On Page One, this 2-column layout might use a 2-30-2 or 2-24-2 headline. At the bottom of an inside page, it would become a 1-line headline: 2-18-1 or 2-24-1.

2 Your three best options are the 1-column format, the 2-column format and the 4-column format (in the 4-column format, the mug could be dummied at either the right or left side).

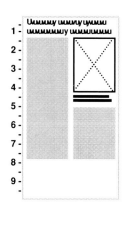

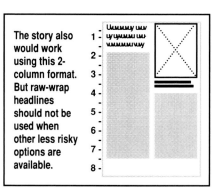

The story also would work using this 2-column format. But raw-wrap headlines should not be used when other less risky options are available.

In a 3-column layout, the headline would have to run over the photo, with roughly a half-inch of text below the photo. That's not enough; you *must* dummy at least 1 inch of text in any leg. For this layout to work, you need either more text or a smaller mug indented into any of the three legs.

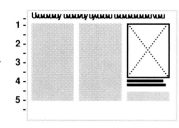

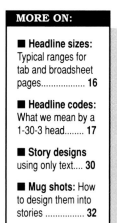

EXERCISE ANSWERS: STORY DESIGN

3 1. Avoid dummying photos between the headline and the start of the text. As a result, this story seems to begin in the second column.

2. The headline wraps clumsily around that left-hand mug. Ordinarily, all lines in a news headline should be even with each other (here, both lines should be 4 columns wide).

3. Mug shots shouldn't be scattered through the story, but grouped evenly whenever possible. The two middle legs might work best in this layout.

4. Mug shots should run at the top of each leg of text, not at the bottom.

---

4 Because this is the day's top story — and because that photo grows stronger and more dramatic the bigger it runs— you should run the photo *at least* 3 columns wide. (A 2-column treatment of that photo would weaken its impact and make the story seem relatively insignificant.)

But because it's a busy news day, you can't afford to devote too much real estate to this story — which is what would happen if you ran the photo 5 or 6 columns wide.

So the best approach is one that uses the photo either 3 or 4 columns wide. Here are the most common, dependable design options:

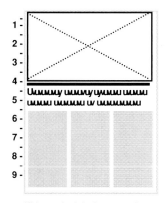

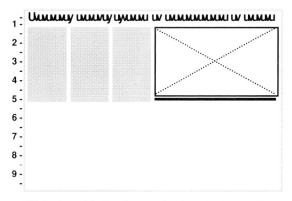

This vertical design uses the photo 3 columns wide, which means it's 23 picas deep — or just under 4 inches. This is a good, clean, reliable solution.

This horizontal design also uses the photo 3 columns wide. The text fits snugly alongside the photo, and everything squares off cleanly. But there's a problem with the banner headline: Half of it covers just the photo, not the text, and as a result the overall design looks long, thin and ungraceful.

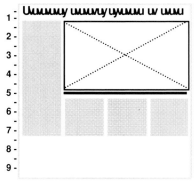

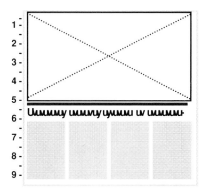

Another good solution using the photo 3 columns wide, with an L-shaped text block. (If the story were shorter, the legs under the photo might seem shallow.)

This design uses the photo 4 columns wide. From the photographer's point of view, it's the best solution, since the large photo gives the story drama and impact.

EXERCISE ANSWERS: STORY DESIGN

5 Most designers would choose the tighter, vertical shot of Springsteen as the lead photo. The horizontal photo is interesting, but less dynamic; Springsteen's face is obscured, and there's too much empty black space between Springsteen and the woman giving him that salute.

Your design options for this story are limited. Since the vertical photo is so strongly directional to the left, it must be dummied somewhere along the right side of the layout. With that in mind, these become the two most common solutions using a strong dominant photo:

Using the horizontal photo as lead, you'd need to play it 4 or 5 columns wide to give it impact. If you played it 4 columns wide, it might not be as strong, the layout might not be as clean, and the second photo might be too similar in size. This is the better solution — though the story would need to lose an inch, and the second photo would be cropped a bit thinner.

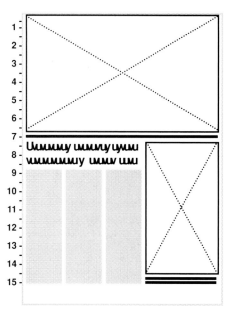

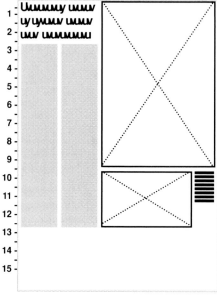

Using the vertical photo as lead, you'd need to play it 3 columns wide to give it impact (playing it 4 columns wide would make it way too huge). The only remaining question, then, is where to put the second photo. Here, we sized it a bit larger than 2 columns wide, so both photos could share a cutline. It's less blocky than running both photos the same width — and it fits.

6 **A** There's no need to use a raw-wrap headline in this layout. That last leg of text might collide with text from another story. Instead, the headline should be one line that's 4 columns wide across the top of the story.

B The photo is poorly placed. It should never be dummied between the headline and the start of the text. Instead, it should scoot over one or two columns to the right.

C This story design is not rectangular. Assuming the photo belongs to that top story, the text should square off along the bottom edge of the photo. To do that, either the text must be deeper or the photo must be shallower.

Note: If both stories related to that photo, you could argue that the two stories and one photo together form *one* package, shaped rectangularly. And that would be acceptable.

D Both photos are sized too similarly. One needs to be clearly dominant for this design to work best.

E The reader is forced to jump blindly across the photo in the middle two legs. That's occasionally permissible for some feature pages, but it's awkward and risky for news layouts.

F Headlines should generally cover only the text; this head is too wide. And photos should not be sized identically like this — one should dominate. *But* if this were a before/after sequence that needed to create visual impact, this treatment might be effective.

EXERCISE ANSWERS: PAGE DESIGN

❶ The box below is 40 picas wide. Using 1-pica margins and gutters, here are the text widths for 2-, 3- and 4-column layouts:

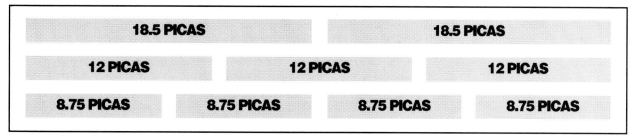

18.5 PICAS   **18.5 PICAS**

12 PICAS   **12 PICAS**   **12 PICAS**

8.75 PICAS   **8.75 PICAS**   **8.75 PICAS**   **8.75 PICAS**

❷ Here are three acceptable layouts — and one that just won't work:

Exercise questions are on page 78.

This layout allows you to run both stories at their full lengths. The smaller story uses a raw wrap, and its second leg of text keeps the headlines from butting. This layout works best when used, as it is here, at the top of an inside page.

This layout uses a raw wrap for the bigger story, and that third leg of text keeps both headlines from butting. The smaller story has been cut by an inch to fit. This layout looks a bit odd, but it satisfies the requirements for this page.

This layout forces you to trim the smaller story by an inch while boxing it beside the first story. This treatment works best if the smaller story is a special news feature; otherwise, avoid boxing stories just to keep headlines from butting.

NOTE: This common solution may have been your first response — but it won't work here. Those long horizontal headlines take up too much space and force you to cut the stories more than an inch apiece. They won't fit.

❸ **A** The page has no dominant element; all three stories have the same weight and impact, and all the headlines are the same size. In addition, everything is horizontal and static. The page needs more art, and that photo should not be dummied at the bottom of the page.

B The photo is ambiguous — which story does it go with? Are all those stories at the top of the page related? You can't be sure. The boxed story on the left butts awkwardly against that banner headline (this is sometimes called an "armpit"). The lead story is not a rectangular shape. And the right-hand leg of text seems to come up an inch short.

C The page is off-balance; all the art is on the left side, forcing four stories to stack up along the right edge. The page seems divided into two sections (for this reason, you should avoid deep gutters running the full depth of the page). And there's not enough text under the mug shot.

EXERCISE ANSWERS: PAGE DESIGN

4 The best solution is B; it's well balanced and properly organized. In example A, the entire midsection of the page is gray and type-heavy, while the top of the page uses two small, weak headlines that could mistakenly be related to that big photo. In example C, the photo is ambiguous (it could belong either to the story alongside or below) and headlines nearly collide. In example D, the lead photo is ambiguous again, and both photos are bunched together. ,

5 Many page designers park promo boxes and indexes in the bottom right corner of the page, as "page-turners" that send you off into the paper. Using that philosophy, our first solution (below left) would be preferable. But if you choose to use the promo box as a graphic element to break up those gray stories, you could slide it toward the middle instead (below right). In either case, it works best at the very bottom of the page.

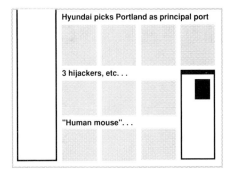
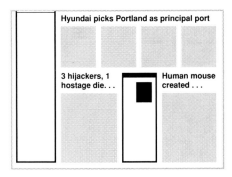

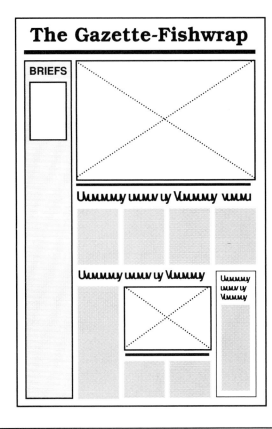

6 If the lead photo is strong, it should be played as large as possible — and in this case, there's room to run it 4 columns wide at the top of the page. Once that photo and its story have been anchored, your options are limited for those other two stories. This solution balances the art, mixing horizontal and vertical shapes. The small story is boxed to keep the headlines from butting — but that's OK, since it's a "bright" feature.

EXERCISE ANSWERS: PHOTOS & ART

Exercise questions are on page 107.

1 The two strongest images — the ones that say "woman jockey" in the most arresting way — are the race photo and the tight portrait. The other two should be supporting photos; they're informational, but not really interesting enough to dominate the page.

Here are three likely layouts using the race photo as the lead. If you've created a radically different page, congratulations — but check the guidelines on page 98 to be sure you haven't made some mistakes.

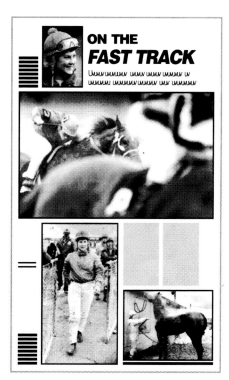

In this design, the race photo is used as the lead shot and runs across the top of the page, sharing a cutline with the photo below. (That's a photo credit floating below the cutline in the right margin.) The other two photos are stacked across the bottom of the page.

Note how the page is divided into three horizontal layers. In the second layer, the photo and the story could have swapped positions, with the photo running along the left side of the page — but then we'd have two similarly sized photos parked one atop the other. To avoid that, we could transpose the two bottom photos — but then the mug shot would be looking off the page. This layout, then, balances its elements well and avoids violating the directionality of the mug.

This layout isn't very different from the one at left. The race photo runs big across the top; together, the four photos form a "C" shape with the story tucked in the middle. (The page at left forms a backwards "C.") The sidesaddle headline treatment provides an alternative to the more standard approach used at left. The headline and deck form one wide column; the leg of text sits alongside it. (That leg is pretty wide and could run as two legs instead.)

One final note: All three of these layouts close with the shot of the jockey washing her horse. Does that seem like an appropriate "closer"? Or would we make a stronger exit by closing with the shot of the jockey walking off the track, splattered with mud?

This design, like the one at left, uses the small portrait to set up the headline; pairing those two elements shows instantly *who* is on the fast track. The cutline beside the mug also describes the action in the lead photo below. The other two photos stack along the bottom of the page, with the photo credit floating in the left margin.

Note how headline, text and two vertical photos are all given an extra indent.

If there's a drawback to this layout, it's that it uses a big headline, a big deck, big photos — and a small amount of text. At some papers, editors may prefer to downsize those photos and increase the amount of copy.

EXERCISE ANSWERS: PHOTOS & ART

These layouts represent three common design approaches using the portrait of the jockey as the dominant photo. That portrait is strongly directional. As a result, your options are more limited, since you must position the lead photo looking *into* rather than *off of* the page.

Getting all four photos to fit properly is tricky when you're working around a directional dominant photo. In this case, the race photo is used as a scene-setter at the top of the page. The lead portrait runs below it, sharing a cutline. The other two photos fit in the space below the lead.

Some would say this is a very clean design, with the art aligning on one side of the page, the text running in one leg alongside. Others might find it too off-balance, with a preponderance of weight on the left side.

That leg of text is a bit too long, and could be relieved if a liftout quote were indented halfway down.

Here, the lead photo runs at the top of the page, and the other photos arrange themselves in the rectangular module below. Note how the shapes and sizes of the photos vary. This helps to avoid static, blocky configurations.

If there are drawbacks to this design, they would be:

1) The excessive white space along the left edge of the page, around the cutline and photo credit. That's hard to avoid, however. It's hard to size that horse-washing photo much wider. The cutline, too, is about as big as it should be.

2) The small amount of text. Playing these photos as big as they are doesn't leave much room for the story. This is a very photo-heavy layout.

Here's a page that gets a bit crowded at the top but seems to work anyway. Three photos are grouped together in a tight unit; the race photo, however, is set apart from the rest to gain extra emphasis (and give the page more of a "racing" feel).

The racing photo also could have been dummied in the right-hand three columns instead of the center three; in that case, a 2-line, 2-column deck would have been preferable.

EXERCISE ANSWERS: PHOTOS & ART

2 There are several options that could be added to this selection of photos. Among them:

1) A stronger racing shot — one with clearer details and a greater sense of motion, perhaps shot from a more dramatic angle.

2) More emotion — the thrill of victory, the agony of defeat. These four photos fail to capture any athletic dramatics.

3) An interaction shot, showing how this woman jockey relates to her colleagues in a male-dominated sport.

4) Detail shots — whips, boots, saddles, even trophies — especially some racing apparel or artifact that is unique to this jockey.

3 Here are some of the major problems on these pages. Remember: When it comes to page design, tastes can be very subjective. You don't have to agree with every nitpick — but you should understand the principles that underlie our design guidelines.

The text snakes around the photos in a clumsy, unattractive way— and that first leg of text is way too deep. There's no white space designed in to this page, which results in a layout that feels dense and crowded, more like a typical news page than a photo spread. And that feeling is reinforced by the sizes of the photos — the lead photo isn't quite dominant enough, and there's no sense of interplay among the rest of the pictures.

The lead photo faces off the page. If this page design were flopped, that problem could have been avoided. But there's still a problem with that big cutline blob in the center of the page. It's unclear which photo or photos it belongs to. (Does the bottom photo have a cutline?) There's too much trapped white space in the middle of the page. There's also too much white space above the headline. Finally, there's not much variety in the sizes of those secondary photos.

Overall, this page looks handsome, but there are some subtle problems. It's divided into three very separate chunks: 1) big photo, 2) gray text, and 3) small photos. There's no interplay between elements; in fact, this seems like a standard page design that you could plug *any* photos into. It's too formulaic. In addition, there's no white space, and the shapes are too blocky and static. It's also difficult to determine which cutline describes the center photo in the bottom row.

EXERCISE ANSWERS: PHOTOS & ART

4 **A.** The photographer's crop for this photo comes in tightly on both police officers but leaves a bit of air between them and the sides of the frame. The top crop almost reaches that officer's head; the bottom crop leaves a bit of foreground pavement below the suspect's shoes.

B. After you properly crop the photo on page 108, it should measure roughly 16 picas wide by 12.8 picas deep. Using a proportion wheel, there are two ways to find the photo's depth if its width were enlarged to 45 picas:

1. Find the original cropped width (16) on the inner wheel. Line that number up with the new width you need (45) on the outer wheel.

2. Find the original cropped depth (12.8) on the inner wheel. The number it lines up with — 36 — will be the new depth of the photo.

***Or* you could try it this way:**

1. After proper cropping, your original photo measures 16 by 12.8. On the proportion wheel, line up 16 on one wheel, 12.8 on the other.

2. As you look around the wheel, all the figures will be paired in the ratio of 12.8:16. So if you check 45, it's lined up with 36. This method will show you all possible proportions for a photo once it's been properly cropped.

GLOSSARY

Agate. Small type (usually 5 and a half-point) used for sports statistics, stock tables, classifieds, etc.

Air. White space used in a story design.

All caps. Type using only capital letters.

Armpit. An awkward-looking page layout where one story's banner headline sits on top of a different headline.

Ascender. The part of a letter extending above the x-height (as in b, d, f, h, k, l, t).

Attribution. A line identifying the source of a quote.

Banner. A wide headline extending across the entire page.

Bar. A thick rule. Often used for decoration, or to contain type for subheads or standing heads.

Bar chart. A chart comparing statistical values by depicting them as bars.

Base line. An imaginary line that type rests on.

Bastard measure. Any non-standard width for a column of text.

Blow up. To enlarge a photo or illustration for reproduction.

Body type. Type used for text (in newspapers, it usually ranges from 8 to 11 points).

Boldface. A heavier, darker weight of a typeface; used to add emphasis (the word "boldface" here is in boldface).

Border. A rule used to form a box or to edge a photograph.

Box. A ruled border around a story or art.

Broadsheet. A full-size newspaper, measuring roughly 14 by 23 inches.

Bug. Another term for a sig or logo used to label a story; often indented into the text.

Bullet. A type of dingbat, usually a big dot (•), used to highlight items listed in the text.

Bumping/butting heads. Headlines from adjacent stories that collide with each other. Should be avoided whenever possible.

Byline. The reporter's name, usually at the beginning of a story.

Callouts. Words, phrases or text blocks used to label parts of a map or diagram (also called *factoids*).

Caps. Capital or uppercase letters.

Caption. A line or block of type providing descriptive information about a photo; used interchangeably with *cutline*.

Centered. Art or type that's aligned symmetrically, sharing a common midpoint.

Character. A typeset letter, numeral or punctuation mark.

Column. A stack of text; also called a *leg*.

Column inch. A way to measure the depth of text or ads; it's an area one column wide and one inch deep.

Column logo. A graphic device that labels regularly appearing material by packaging the writer's name, the column's name, and a small mug or drawing of the writer.

Column rule. A vertical line separating stories or running between legs within a story.

Compressed/condensed type. Characters that are electronically narrowed; i.e., turning this M into M.

Continuation line. Type telling the reader that a story continues on another page.

Continuous tone. A photo or drawing using shades of gray. To be reproduced in a newspaper, the image must be converted into a *halftone*.

Copy. The text of a story.

Copy block. A small chunk of text accompanying a photo spread or introducing a special package.

Copyright. Legal protection for stories, photos or artwork, to discourage unauthorized reproduction.

Crop. To indicate where a photo should be trimmed before it runs in the paper; usually done by making crop marks in the margins of the photo.

Cutline. A line or block of type providing descriptive information about a photo.

Cutoff rule. A horizontal line running under a story, photo or cutline to separate it from another element below.

Cutout. A photo where the background has been removed, leaving only the main subject; also called a *silhouette*.

Deck. A small headline stacked below the main headline; also called a *drop head*.

GLOSSARY

Descender. The part of a letter extending below the baseline (as in g, j, p, q, y).

Dingbats. Decorative type characters (such as bullets, stars, boxes, etc.) used for emphasis or effect.

Display headline. A non-standard headline (often with decorative type, rules, all caps, etc.) used to enhance the design of a feature story, photo spread or special news package.

Doglegs. L-shaped columns of text that wrap around art, ads or other stories.

Dot screen. A special screen used to produce tiny rows of dots, thus allowing newspapers to print shades of gray.

Double burn. The process by which two different elements are overlapped when printed (for instance, printing type on top of a photo); also called *overprinting*.

Double truck. Two facing pages on the same sheet of newsprint that are treated as one unit.

Downstyle. A headline style where only the first word and proper nouns are capitalized.

Drop head. A small headline running below the main headline; also called a *deck*.

Drop shadow. A thin shadow effect added to characters in a headline.

Dummy. A small, detailed page diagram showing where all elements go; also, the process of drawing up a layout.

Dutch wrap. Text that extends into a column alongside its headline; also called a *raw wrap*.

Duotone. A halftone that uses two colors, usually black and a spot color.

Ear. Text or graphic elements on either side of a newspaper's flag.

Em. An old printing term for a square-shaped blank space that's as wide as the type is high; in other words, a 10-point em space will be 10 points wide.

En. Half an em space; a 10-point en space will be 5 points wide.

Enlarge. To increase the size of photos or artwork.

Expanded/extended type. Characters that are electronically widened: i.e., turning this M into M.

Fake duotone. A halftone effect created by printing a black halftone over a background tint in a second color, or by aligning a spot-color line shot over a black halftone.

Family. All the different weights and forms (italic, boldface, condensed, etc.) of one typeface.

Feature. A non-hard-news story (a profile, preview, quiz, etc.) often given special design treatment.

Fever chart. A chart connecting points on a graph to show changing quantities over time; also called a *line chart*.

Filler. A small story or graphic element used to fill space on a page.

Flag. The name of a newspaper as it's displayed on Page One; also called a *nameplate*.

Flat color. An extra color ink added to a page; also called *spot color*.

Float. To dummy a photo or headline in an empty space so that it looks good to the designer, but looks awkward and unaligned to everyone else.

Flop. To create a backwards, mirror image of a photo or illustration by turning the negative over during printing.

Flush left. Elements aligned so they're all even along their left margin.

Flush right. Elements aligned so they're all even along their right margin.

Folio line. Type at the top of an inside page giving the newspaper's name, date and page number.

Font. All the characters in one size and weight of a typeface (this font is 10-point Times).

Four-color. The printing process that combines cyan (blue), magenta (red), yellow and black to produce full-color photos and artwork.

Full frame. The entire image area of a photograph.

Graf. Newsroom slang for "paragraph."

Graph. Statistical information presented visually, using lines or bars to represent values.

Grid. The underlying pattern of lines forming the framework of a page; also, to align elements on a page.

Gutter. The space running vertically between columns.

H and J. Hyphenation and justification;

GLOSSARY

the process of sending a story through a computer to see how the text will stack when printed.

Hairline. The thinnest rule used in newspapers.

Halftone. A photograph or drawing that has been converted into a pattern of tiny dots. By screening images this way, printing presses are able to reproduce shades of gray.

Hammer head. A headline that uses a big, bold word or phrase for impact and runs a small, wide deck below.

Hanging indent. Type set with the first line flush left and all other lines in that paragraph indented (this text is set with a 10-point hanging indent).

Header. A special label for any regularly appearing section, page or story; also called a *standing head.*

Headline. Large type running above or beside a story to summarize its content; also called a *head,* for short.

House ad. An advertisement promoting the newspaper or a newspaper feature; small house ads are often used as fillers.

Hyphenation. Breaking a word with a hy-phen at the end of a line (as in the previous two lines).

Indent. A portion of a column set in a narrower width. The first line of a paragraph is usually indented; columns are often indented to accommodate art, logos or initial caps.

Index. An alphabetized list of contents and their page numbers.

Infographic. Newsroom slang for "informational graphic"; any complex map, chart or diagram used to analyze an event, object or place.

Initial cap. A large capital letter set at the beginning of a paragraph for decoration or emphasis.

Inset. Art or text set inside *other* art or text.

Italic. Type that slants to the right, *like this.*

Justification. Mechanically spacing out lines of text so they're all even along both right and left margins.

Jump. To continue a story on another page; text that's been continued on another page is called the *jump.*

Jump headline. A special headline treatment reserved for stories continued from another page.

Jump line. Type telling the reader that a story is continued from another page.

Kerning. Tightening the spacing between letters.

Kicker. A small, short, one-line headline, often underscored, placed above a larger headline.

Layout. The placement of art and text on a page; to *lay out* a page is to design it.

Lead-in. A word or phrase in contrasting type that precedes a cutline, headline or text.

Leading. Vertical spacing between lines of type, measured in points.

Leg. A column of text.

Legibility. The ease with which type characters can be read.

Letter spacing. The amount of air between characters in a word.

Liftout quote. A graphic treatment of a quotation taken from a story, often using bold or italic type, rules or screens.

Line chart. A chart connecting points on a graph to show changing quantities over time; also called a *fever chart.*

Line shot. Reproduction of a photo or artwork resulting in only two tones: black and white (no screened shades of gray), as opposed to a *halftone.*

Logo. A word or name that's stylized in a graphic way; used to refer to standing heads in a newspaper.

Lowercase. Small characters of type (no capital letters).

Margins. The space between elements on a page.

Masthead. A block of information, including staff names and publication data, often printed on the editorial page.

Measure. The width of a headline or column of text.

Modular layout. A design system that views a page as a stack of rectangles.

Mortise. Placing one element (text, photo, artwork) so that it partially overlaps another.

Mug shot. A small photo showing a person's face.

Nameplate. The name of a newspaper as it's displayed on Page One; also called a *flag*.

Offset. A printing process, used by most newspapers, where the image is transferred from a plate to a rubber blanket, then printed on paper.

Orphan. A short word or phrase that's carried over to a new column or page; also called a *widow*.

Overlay. A clear plastic sheet placed over a pasted-up page, containing elements to be screened, overprinted, or printed in another color.

Overline A small headline that runs above a photo; usually used with stand-alone photos.

Pagination. The process of generating a page on a computer.

Paste-up. A page assembled for printing where all type, artwork and ads have been placed into position (usually with hot wax). To *paste up* a page is to place those elements on it.

Photo credit. A line that tells who shot a photograph.

Pica. A standard unit of measure in newspapers. There are 6 picas in one inch, 12 points in one pica.

PMT. A photographic paper used for shooting halftones. Short for photomechanical transfer; also called a *velox*.

Point. A standard unit of measure in newspapers. There are 12 points in one pica, 72 points in one inch.

Porkchop. A half-column mug shot.

Process color. One of the four standard colors used to produce full-color photos and artwork: cyan (blue), magenta (red), yellow or black.

Proof. A copy of a pasted-up page used to check for errors. To check a page is to *proofread* it.

Pyramid ads. Advertisements stacked up one side of a page, wide at the base but progressively smaller near the top.

Quotes. Words spoken by someone in a story. In page-design jargon, a *liftout quote* is a graphic treatment of a quotation, often using bold or italic type, rules or screens.

Ragged right. Type that is not *justified;* the left edge of all the lines is even, but the right edge is uneven.

Raw wrap. Text that extends into a column alongside its headline; also called a *Dutch wrap*.

Refer (or reefer). A line or paragraph, often given graphic treatment, referring to a related story elsewhere in the paper.

Register. To align different color plates or overlays so they're perfectly positioned when they print.

Reverse. A printing technique that creates white type on a dark background; also called a *drop out*.

Roman. Upright type, as opposed to slanted (italic) type; also called *normal* or *regular*.

Rule. A printing term for a straight line; usually produced with a roll of border tape.

Runaround. Text that wraps around a photo or artwork; also called a *wraparound* or *skew*.

Sans serif. Type without serifs: This is sans serif type.

Scale. To reduce or enlarge artwork or photographs.

Screen. A pattern of tiny dots used to create gray areas; to *screen* a photo is to turn it into a *halftone*.

Serif. The finishing stroke at the end of a letter; type without these decorative strokes is called *sans serif*.

Sidebar. A small story accompanying a bigger story on the same topic.

Sidesaddle head. A headline placed to the left of a story, instead of above it; also called a *side head*.

Sig. A small standing head that labels a regularly appearing column or feature.

Silhouette. A photo where the background has been removed, leaving only the main subject; also called a *cutout*.

Skew. Text that wraps around a photo or artwork; also called a *wraparound or runaround*.

Skyboxes, skylines. Teasers that run above the flag on Page One. If they're boxed (with art), they're called *skyboxes* or *boxcars;* if they use only a line of type, they're called *skylines*.

Solid. A color (or black) printed at 100% density.

Spot color. An extra color ink added to a page; also called *flat color*.

Spread. Another term for a page layout;

usually refers to a photo page.

Stand-alone photo. A photo that doesn't accompany a story; usually boxed or labeled to show it stands alone; also called *wild art.*

Standing head. A special label for any regularly appearing section, page or story; also called a *header.*

Style. A newspaper's standardized set of rules and guidelines. Newspapers have styles for grammar, punctuation, headline codes, design principles, etc.

Subhead. Lines of type, often bold, used to divide text into smaller sections.

Summary deck. A special form of deck, smaller and wordier than most decks, that capsulizes the main points of a story.

Table. A graphic or sidebar that stacks words or numbers in rows so readers can compare data.

Tabloid. A newspaper format that's roughly half the size of a regular broadsheet newspaper.

Teaser. An eye-catching graphic element, on Page One or section fronts, that promotes an item inside; also called a *promo.*

Tint. A light color, often used as a background tone, made from a *dot screen.*

Tombstoning. Stacking two headlines side by side so that they collide with each other; also called *bumping* or *butting heads.*

Trapped white space. An empty area, inside a story design or photo spread, that looks awkward or clumsy.

Tripod. A headline that uses a big, bold word or phrase and two smaller lines of deck squaring off alongside.

Underscore. To run a rule below a line of type.

Uppercase. Type using capital letters.

Velox. A photographic paper used for shooting halftones. Short for photomechanical transfer; also called a *PMT.*

Weight. The boldness of type, based on the thickness of its characters.

Well. Ads stacked along both edges of the page, forming a deep trough for stories in the middle.

White space. Areas of a page free of any type or artwork.

Widow. A short word or phrase that makes up the last line of text in a paragraph. (See *orphan.*)

Wraparound. Text that's indented around a photo or artwork; also called a *runaround* or *skew.*

X-height. The height of a typical lowercase letter.

INDEX

A

ads, 72, 145

B

bad juxtapositions, 76
bad photos, 88-89
bar charts, 156
bastard measures, 11, 19, 61
bastard type, 11
Bernstein, Lois, 36
boxes, 121
boxing stories, 49, 60, 121, 148
broadsheet, 56
bugs, 112-113
butting headlines, 59, 65
bylines, 10, 118

C

calculator, 12
callouts, 160-161
caricatures, 102
charts, 156-157
Chicago Tribune, 162
Christian Science Monitor, 57, 75
Cincinnati Enquirer, 74
color, 141-147
Colorado Springs Gazette Telegraph, 68
column logos, 112
computers, 151
Cosby variations, 127-131
credit lines, 99, 119
cropping photos, 90-91
current design trends, 6-8
cutlines, 10, 22-23, 99
cutoff rules, 11, 121

D

Daily Oklahoman, 56
decks, 4, 10, 116
Detroit Free Press, 111
diagrams, 160-161
dingbats, 117
display headlines, 10, 138-139, 148
dominant photo, 42-43, 65
dot screens, 93, 136-137
double trucks, 74-75
dummy, 24-28

E

editorial pages, 8
exercise answers, 164-172
exercises, 53-54, 78-79, 107-108

F

facing pages, 75
fact boxes, 154
feature art checklist, 104-105
feature design options, 127-131
feature pages, 7
fitting stories, 70-71
flag, 10, 110
flopping, 106
flow chart, Page One design, 69

folio, 11, 120

fonts, 17
framing, 106

G

glossary, 173-178
good photos, 83-87
graphics (see infographics)
graphics packages, 162
gutter, 11

H

halftones, 93
hammers, 15, 62
headers, 10, 111-112
headlines, 10, 14-17, 98, 120
headline sizes, 16
Hindenburg, 150
history of design, 4-5

I

icons, 113
illustrations, 102-103
indents, 132-133
index, 10
infographics, 10, 103, 150-162
initial cap, 10, 117
insets, 135
inside page design, 72-73

J

jump heads, 11, 123
jump lines, 10, 11, 123
jumps, 71, 123

K

kickers, 15

L

Lauper, Cyndi, 39
leading, 18
liftout quotes, 11, 114-115, 132
line charts, 156
line shots, 93
locator maps, 158-159
logos, 10, 111-113

M

Macintosh computers, 151
maps, 158-159
mechanical, how to build, 140
Minnesota Daily, 57, 68
modular design, 66-67
mortises, 135
mug shots, 10, 32-34, 52

N

New York Journal, 5
New York Times, 30, 150

O

opinion pages, 8
Orange County Register, 25, 55, 56, 66-67
Oregon Journal, 5
Oregonian, 5, 6, 8, 28, 56, 95, 101, 102, 103, 111, 126, 150, 153

P

page design: with art, 64-65; without art, 58-63
Page One design, 68-69
Philadelphia Inquirer, 4
photographs, 20-21
photo credits, 11, 99, 119
photo cutouts, 11, 106, 134
photo guidelines, 82
photo illustrations, 101
photo spreads, 95-99
pica pole, 12
picas, 12
pie charts, 151
point sizes, 16
points, 12
process color, 142-143
proportion wheel, 12, 92
Publick Occurrences, 4

Q

quotations (*see* liftout quotes)

R

ragged right/left, 18, 23
raw wraps, 15, 62
refers, 10, 122
rescaling photos, 92
reverse heads, 10, 136-137
reverses, 136-137
Risky Business, 106, 142
Rochester Democrat and Chronicle, 122
Rochester Times-Union, 74, 102, 111, 122, 161
rules, 121
rules of thumb, 77

S

Sacramento Bee, 101
San Francisco Examiner, 68
screens, 136-137, 142, 144-147
series logos, 113
serifs, 16-17
sidebars, 11, 147
sidesaddle heads, 15
sigs, 11, 112-113
skews, 132-133
slammers, 15
spacing, 120
special sections, 8
sports sections, 7
spot color, 142, 144-145
stand-alone photos, 94
standing heads, 111
stealing art, 106
story design: without art, 30-31; with mug shots, 32-34; with one horizontal photo, 36-38; with one vertical photo, 39-41; with big vertical and small horizontal photo, 44-45; with big horizontal and small vertical photo, 46-47; with two

verticals, 48-49; with two horizontals, 50-51
studio shots, 100
subheads, 11, 117
Sun News, 110

T

tables, 155
tabloids, 6, 57
Tall Ships, 74
Tall Stacks, 74
teasers, 10, 122
text, 11, 18-19
text shapes, 35
tilting photos, 106
Times (Beaverton, Ore.), 75, 126
tripods, 15
Twain, Mark, 4
typefaces, 17, 148

U

U., The National College Newspaper, 68, 121
USA Today, 7, 30, 56

V

Virginian-Pilot and The Ledger Star, 36, 95

W

Washington Times, 7, 8, 103, 111, 126
wraparounds, 132-133

ACKNOWLEDGMENTS

Writing a book is like winning an Oscar — you *can't* leave the stage until you've thoroughly thanked everyone who labored behind the scenes.

The author is very grateful to the following friends and colleagues:

■ **Support and encouragement:** Patty Kellogg, without whose insight, meticulous editing and relentless enthusiasm this book would never have been finished; John Hamlin, friend and true believer; Bill Hilliard, Peter Thompson and Sue Hobart, for their trust and patience through it all.

■ **Production:** Clay Frost, for being such a sporting graphics ace; Reed Darmon; Steve Cooper; The Oregonian camera crew.

■ **Editing:** Dan Gustafson; Rob Melton; Ray Stanczak; Jack Hart; Peggy McMullen; J. Ford Huffman; Nancy Fullwiler; Bob Kraft; Ian Harrower.

■ **Art and photography:** Fred Ingram; Steve Dipaola; Randy Rasmussen; Michael Lloyd; Tim Jewett; Ross Hamilton; Steve Nehl; Kraig Scattarella; Dana Olsen; Doug Beghtel; John Sherlock; Lois Bernstein; Joe Spooner.

■ **Printing and promotion:** Stephanie Oliver; Kathryn Botsford; Bill Meyer.

■ **Other contributors:** Kristine Snipes; Michal Thompson; Vergil S. Fogdall; Alex Burroughs; Marc Bona; Joe Gagne.

■ And, of course, my sweet Robin. Again.

CREDITS

The following photographers, artists and publications were not previously identified in the text or cutlines:

Front cover: Fred Ingram
1, 4 (bottom), 5 (top): From the professional library of Vergil S. Fogdall.
7: (top) Copyright 1988, USA TODAY. Reprinted with permission; (bottom) reprinted with permission of The Washington Times
9: Kraig Scattarella
13: Copyrighted, Chicago Tribune Company, all rights reserved, used with permission.
14: Weekly World News
20: All photos copyright Associated Press and Wide World Photo, Inc., except Oswald photo, copyright 1963 by Bob Jackson, and Truman photo, The Bettman Archive.
21: (top and left) Kraig Scattarella; (right) Tim Jewett
22: Kraig Scattarella
25: The Orange County Register
28: The Oregonian
30: (left) Copyright ©1988 by The New York Times Company. Reprinted by permission; (right) copyright 1988, USA TODAY. Reprinted with permission.
36: Copyright 1985 Lois Bernstein/The Virginian-Pilot
39: Randy Wood
43: (top left) Max Gutierrez; (bottom left and top right) Robert E. Shotwell; (bottom

right) Holley Gilbert
53: Michael Lloyd
54: (left): Claudia J. Howell; (right) Ross Hamilton
55: The Orange County Register
59: The Morning Oregonian
66: The Orange County Register
68: (top left) Reprinted with permission from The San Francisco Examiner. © 1988 San Francisco Examiner.
74: Reprinted with permission of the Gannett Rochester Newspapers, Rochester New York, 1990.
76: Both copyright Associated Press and Wide World Photo, Inc.
82: Randy L. Rasmussen
83: (top) Randy L. Rasmussen; (center and bottom) Tim Jewett
90: Randy L. Rasmussen
91: Dana Olsen
93: Tim Jewett
94: Michael Lloyd
96: Tim Jewett
100: (left) Dana Olsen; (center) Doug Beghtel; (right) Randy L. Rasmussen
107: Randy L. Rasmussen
108: (bottom) Steve Nehl
109: The Sun News (Myrtle Beach, S.C.)
110: The Sun News
111: Times-Union (Rochester, N.Y.)
112: (bottom) Reed Darmon
114: (bottom left) Copyright Associated Press and Wide

World Photo, Inc.
127-131: Photo courtesy of The National Broadcasting Company, Inc.
132: (top right) Joe Spooner; (bottom) photo by Jesse Gerstein for Oscar de la Renta, spring 1989
134: William Duke
135: Randy L. Rasmussen
136: (bottom) Tim Jewett
137: Michael Lloyd
140: Steve Dipaola
141: Copyright ©1990 Oregonian Publishing Co.
142: (top) Michael Lloyd; (bottom) Tim Jewett
146: Copyright ©1990 Oregonian Publishing Co.
147: Paul Peterson
148: train by Joe Spooner
149: Copyrighted, Chicago Tribune Company, all rights reserved, used with permission.
150: Copyright ©1937 by The New York Times Company. Reprinted by permission.
151: (top) Steve Dipaola; (bottom) Clay Frost
156: Clay Frost
158-159, 160: Copyright Knight-Ridder Tribune Network
162: Copyrighted, Chicago Tribune Company, all rights reserved, used with permission.
Back cover photo: Robin Harrower